30 Toy Vehicles of Wood

30 Toy Vehicles of Wood

Ronald D. Tarjany

Tarjany Publications
PO Box 8846 Calabasas CA 91302

Printed in United States of America

10 9 8 7 6 5 4 3 2 1
First Edition

ISBN 0-9674668-2-2

This Book was Produced by
TARJANY PUBLICATIONS
PO Box 8846, Calabasas, CA 91302

Editorial: Cyndee Duffy

Copy Editor: Inge Kriegler

Design: Les Ventura

Illustrations: David R. Shea

Photography: T. R. Douglass

Front cover photo: Frank G. Farkas

Contents

Acknowledgments

I would like to extend my appreciation to the many people who have helped in the preparation of this book.
I want to thank my friend, T.R. Douglas for taking all the black and white photographs. He did an excellent job with the short deadline he was given.
Thanks to Inge Kriegler, whose persistent encouragement helped me to complete this book; and for her help in correcting the manuscript.
Thanks to all my woodworking friends who have been helpful over the many years. With a special thanks to Fred Little who first got me interested in building wood toy vehicles.
Thanks to the following people who helped in their own way: Mike Andrews, Judy Coats, Jon Melborn, Jane and Jammie Smith, Ann Smoths, Pete Thore and Bill Zernon.
Without the help of these people this book would never have made it to press.

Dedication

This book is dedicated to my late father, Alex D. Tarjany for encouraging me to work with my hands, and providing me with a shop in our home where I learned the many skills of woodworking. I am grateful to him for his help and guidance while I was growing up and for showing me not only the proper use of tools, but also the proper care of tools.

Introduction

Over the years I have tried my hand at various aspects of woodworking and find toy making the most enjoyable and most relaxing. Vehicles of all types are what I have focused on most. Some woodworking disciplines such as furniture making takes up so much room in the wood shop, that only one project can be worked on at one time. The size of most wood toys is small so several toys can be in work at the same time. I find it more enjoyable to work on a project I like rather than working one project from start to finish.

Since my woodworking experience goes back to the early 1950's when I was a teenager, I have accumulated quite a number of power and hand tools. Every wood toy maker may have a different idea on how to build that toy and what are the best tools to use. My idea of the perfect, minimum wood toy shop, would include a band saw, a bench drill press and a bench disc sander. These are the power tools I used the most when I built the toy vehicles for this book.

All you need to do to build a wood toy is lay out the pieces for the toy on the thickness of material needed. Drill all the holes in each piece. A bench drill press will drill a more accurate hole than a hand held drill motor. Cut the pieces on the band saw and sand the rough edges on the disc sander to get an even, smooth surface. I always cut away from the line and then sand the edge to the line. This gives the accurate size that is needed to have everything fit just right. With a sanding block, sand the pieces and test fit the pieces. Glue the pieces together and admire your work.

To make the work a bit easier other power tools can be added to the shop. Some of these tools would be a hand held orbiting sander, circular saw, scroll saw, belt sander and router. No matter what tools you may have, start building that first wood toy vehicle. You will enjoy it immensely.

Happy toy making.

BLOCK'Y Tank Truck

The block'y tank truck makes a nice looking toy with its large, short tank at the rear. The tank is not difficult to build and a wood lathe is not needed to build the tank for this toy. To build this toy, use hardwood or pine.

The body (**A**) is cut to a size of 1 1/2" wide by 5 1/4" long from 3/4" stock. Mark the two axle holes 1/4" from the bottom and 1 1/8" from the front edge and 7/8" from the rear edge for the other hole. Drill the two 9/32" dia holes. Chamfer the lower front and rear edges of the base as shown in the drawing.

Cut the roof (**B**) to size. Chamfer the front top edge 1/4" by 45 degrees on a disc sander. Sand the two top side edges 1/8" by 45 degrees as shown in the drawing.

The tank is built up of three 3/4" thick disks (**C**) with a hole in the center and a small flat on each piece. Mark center points 4 1/2" apart and 1 1/2" from one edge of a pine board. Set a compass 1 3/4" apart and draw three 3 1/2" dia circles. Clamp a scrap of 3/4" x 1 1/2" pine along the edge where the circle fell off the first board. This piece of scrap allows the cutter to be always cutting and will eliminate chipping at the flat. Set a circle cutter to cut the circles, chuck to your drill press and cut slowly. Open the hole in the center of each piece to 3/8" dia

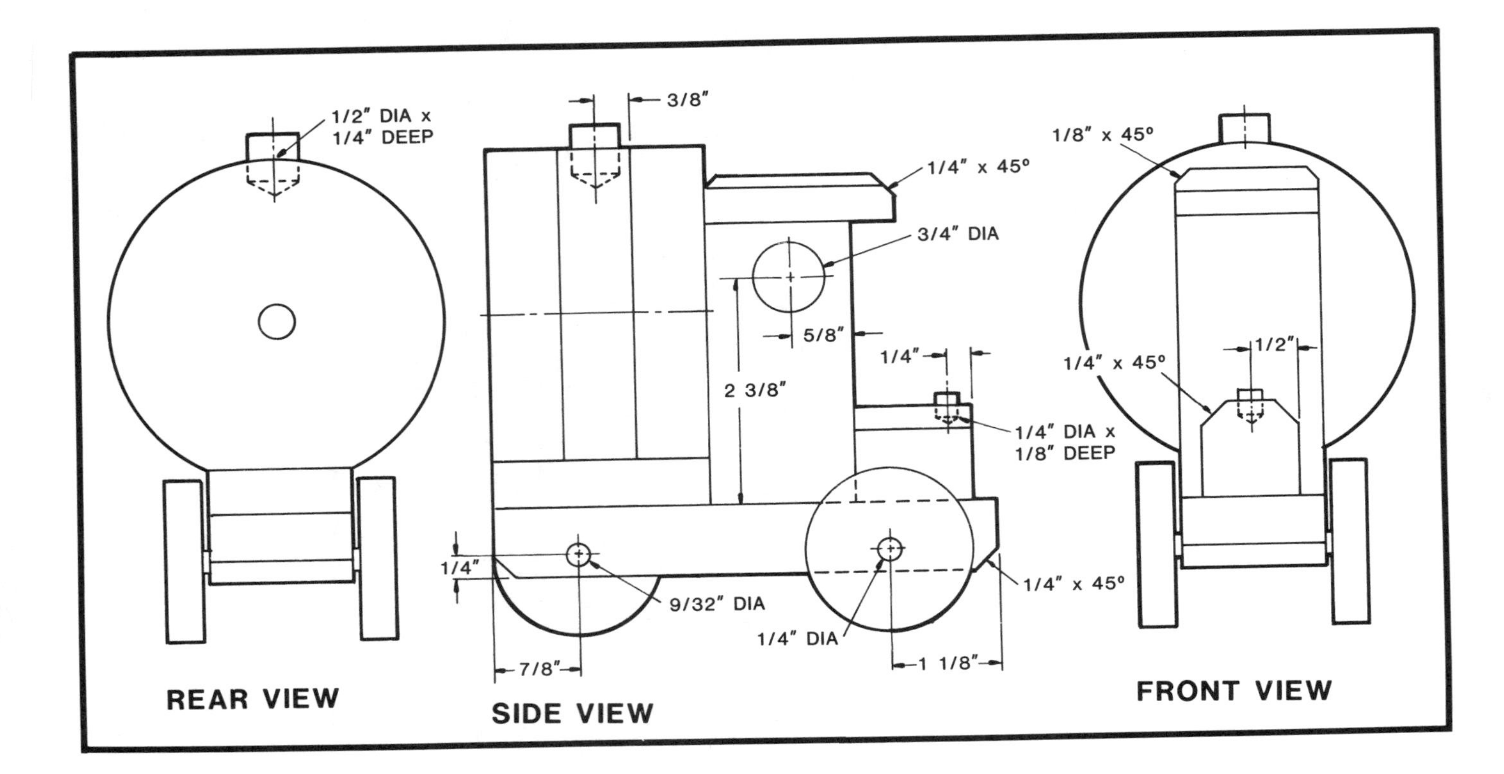

unless your circle cutter uses a 3/8" dia drill.

Next the tank bed (**H**) is cut to a size of 1 1/2" wide by 2 1/4" long from 1/2" stock. Make sure the length is equal to three thicknesses of the material that will be used for the tank.

Cut the cab (**D**) to size. Use a band saw and cut away from the line and then sand to the line. Locate the side window on the cab using the dimensions on the drawing. Drill through using a 3/4" dia drill or a Forstner bit if you have one.

Cut the hood (**E**) to a size of 1" wide by 1" tall by 1 1/4" long. Use a disc sander to add the 1/4" by 45 degree chamfer along both side top edges. Mark and drill a 1/4" dia hole 1/8" deep for the radiator cap.

Cut out four wheels (**G**) with a 1 7/8" dia hole saw, from 3/8" stock. Sand the cut surface smooth and round over the edges. Cut the two axles (**I**) to length from 1/4" dia dowel. Cut the radiator cap (**F**) from the same size dowel. Cut the tank dowel (**K**) that runs through the center hole of the tank disks from 3/8" dia stock. Cut the tank hatch (**J**) from 1/2" dia dowel.

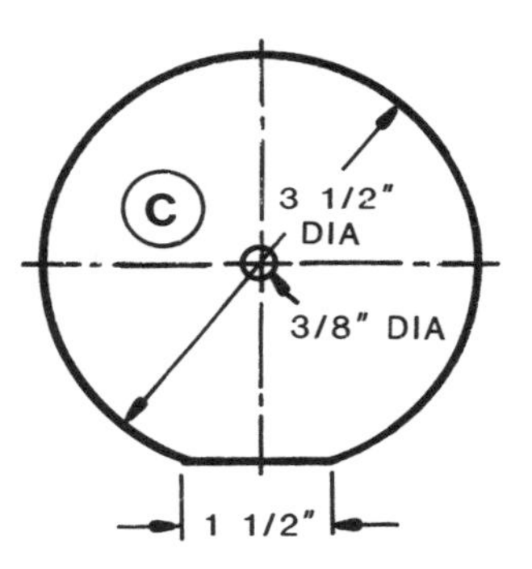

TANK DISK DETAIL

Sand all surfaces with 80-grit sandpaper, do not round over the edges yet. Then sand with 100-grit followed with 150-grit sandpaper. Use a tack cloth to dust all the wood parts.

Glue the tank bed to the body flush with the back edge. Allow to dry, then glue the cab to the body and the hood to the body and the cab. Glue the roof to the cab. Glue the three tank segments together aligning with the dowel through

LIST OF MATERIALS

FINISHED DIMENSIONS IN INCHES

A	BODY	3/4 x 1 1/2 x 5 1/4
B	ROOF	1/2 x 1 1/2 x 2
C	TANK DISK (3)	3/4 x 3 1/2 DIA
D	CAB	1 1/2 x 1 1/2 x 3
E	HOOD	1 x 1 x 1 1/4
F	RADIATOR CAP	1/4 DIA x 1/4
G	WHEEL (4)	3/8 x 1 3/4 DIA
H	TANK BED	1/2 x 1 1/2 x 2 1/4
I	AXLE (2)	1/4 DIA x 2 3/8
J	HATCH	1/2 DIA x 1/2
K	TANK DOWEL	3/8 DIA x 2 1/4

the center hole. Make sure the flats are all in line to insure it will set flat on the base. When dry, drill a 1/2" dia hole 1/4" deep in the center of the tank at the top. The flat on the bottom will help to make this hole straight and true. Glue the cap in place. Glue the tank assembly to the bed. Glue a wheel on one end of each axle. Allow to dry overnight.

Finally, round over all exposed edges with sandpaper and remove the dust with a tack cloth. Apply a child-safe finish, and allow to dry. Slip the axle into the holes in the body and glue the other wheels to the axles. Leave a slight space between the base and the wheels.

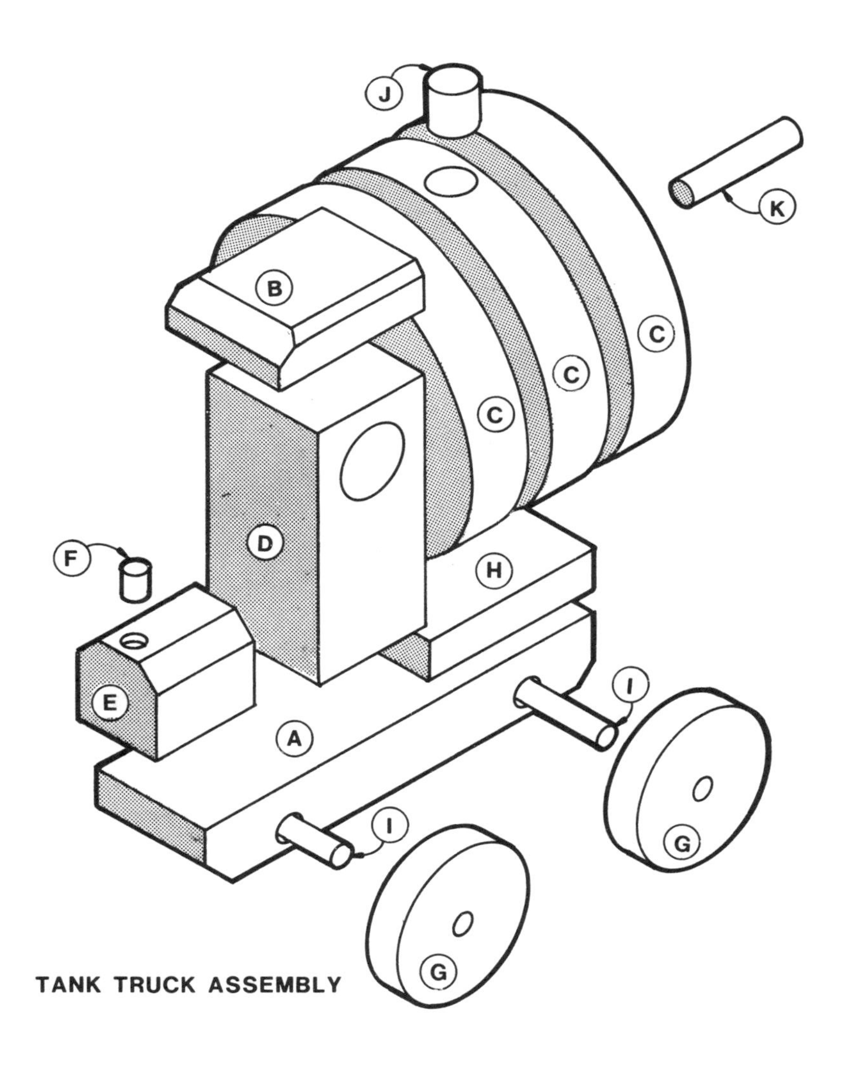

TANK TRUCK ASSEMBLY

TOY

Jeep

The toy jeep is a good facsimile of the WWII military jeep and will surely be a favorite of that youngster who receives this toy. Our toy was built of pine and maple dowels.

Cut the base (**A**) to size as indicated in the list of materials. Mark and drill the two 9/32" dia axle holes as shown in the side view drawing. Locate and drill the gear shift hole as shown in the top view drawing.

Cut the two sides (**B**) to size from 1/2" stock. Mark the center of the cutouts to clear the wheels and cut the openings with a 2 1/4" dia hole saw. Lay out the notch and cut with a band saw.

Cut the hood (**F**) to size. Round-over the two top edges with a 1/4" router bit. Mark and drill the two 1/2" dia headlight holes 3/8" deep. Glue the hood to the base.

Cut the windshield (**L**) to size. Lay out the opening as indicated on the drawing.

Drill a hole in each corner of the opening. Insert the blade of a scroll saw or coping saw into one of the holes and saw to the next hole. When the cutting is complete, remove the wood scrap and the blade. Finish the inside edges with a file and sanding block. Drill the hole for the steering wheel column at the location and angle indicated on the drawing. Glue the windshield to the hood and base. Glue the sides in place and clamp overnight. Put a scrap of wood between the side and the clamp to eliminate marks by the clamp.

Cut the seat back (**H**) and seat bottom (**I**) to size. Add the chamfer to both pieces to get the eight degree tilt-back for the seat. Sand the other edge to a radius. Glue the seats between the sides and to the base.

Cut the back (**G**) and two rear sides (**J**). Drill the spare tire peg hole in the back. Glue the rear sides to the inside of the sides to cover up the opening to clear the wheels. Glue the back to the base and between both sides.

Cut the front bumper (**K**) and rear bumper (**M**) to size. Glue both pieces in place flush with the bottom of the base and with an equal overhang on each side.

Cut the steering wheel (**E**) and steer-

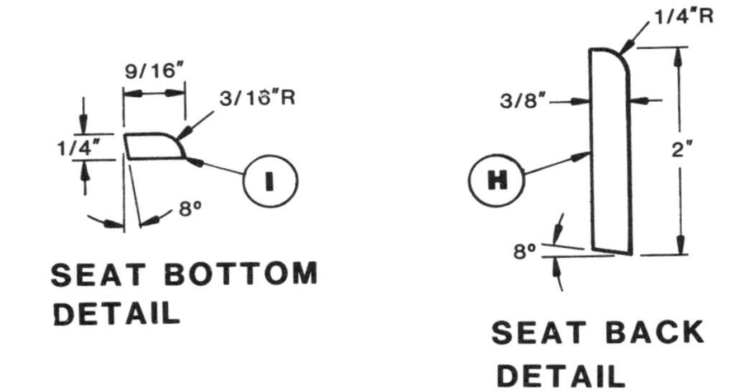

SEAT BOTTOM DETAIL

SEAT BACK DETAIL

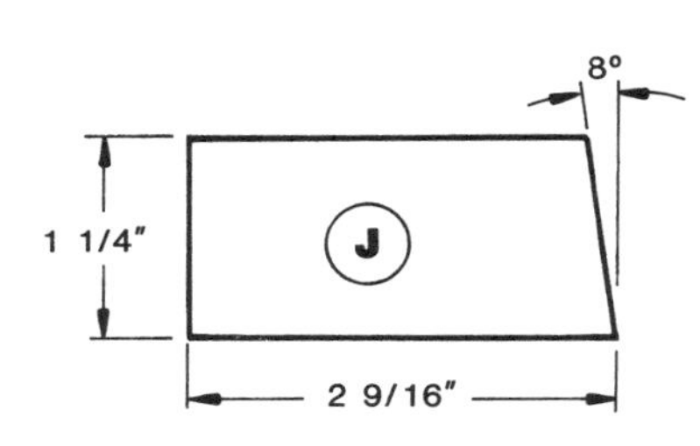

REAR SIDE DETAIL

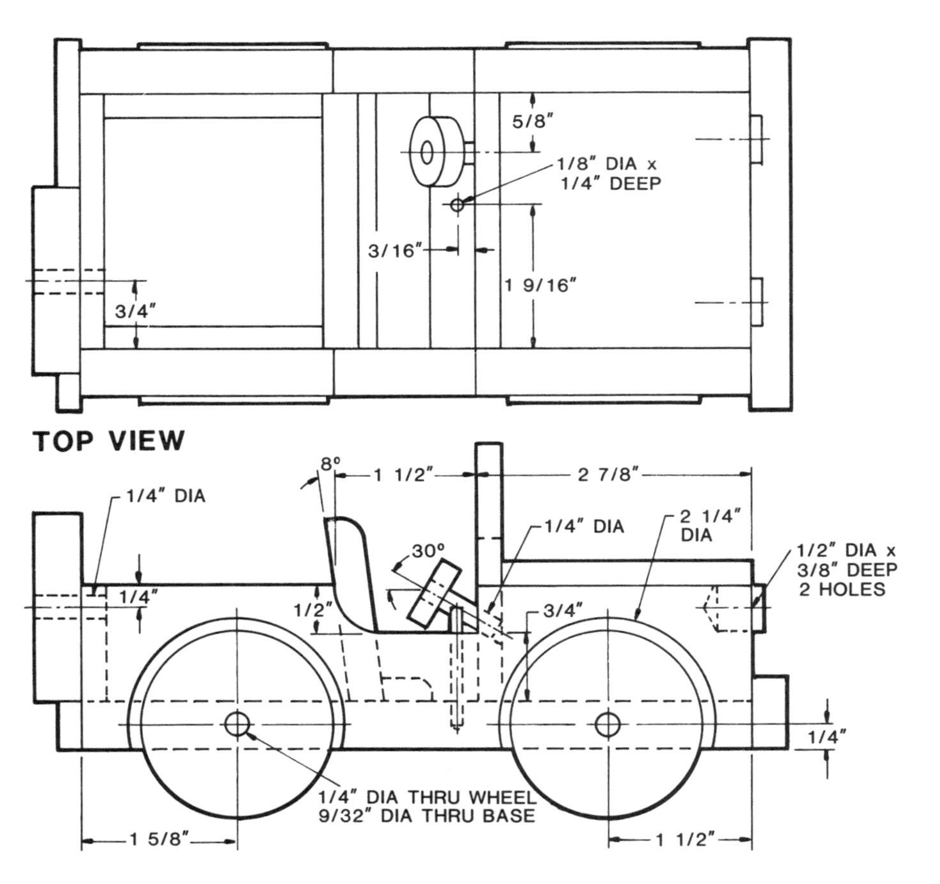

TOP VIEW

SIDE VIEW

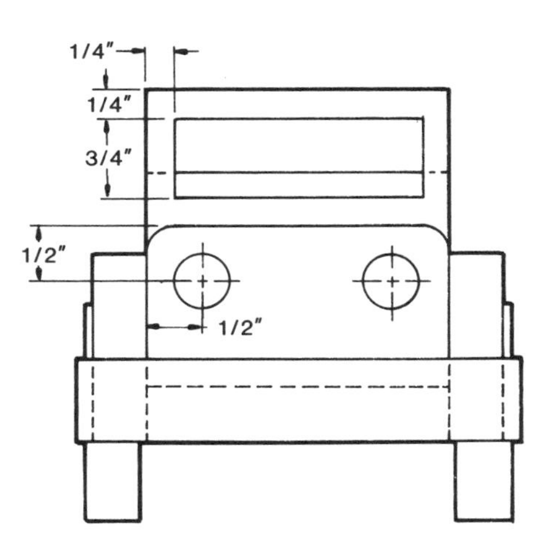

FRONT VIEW

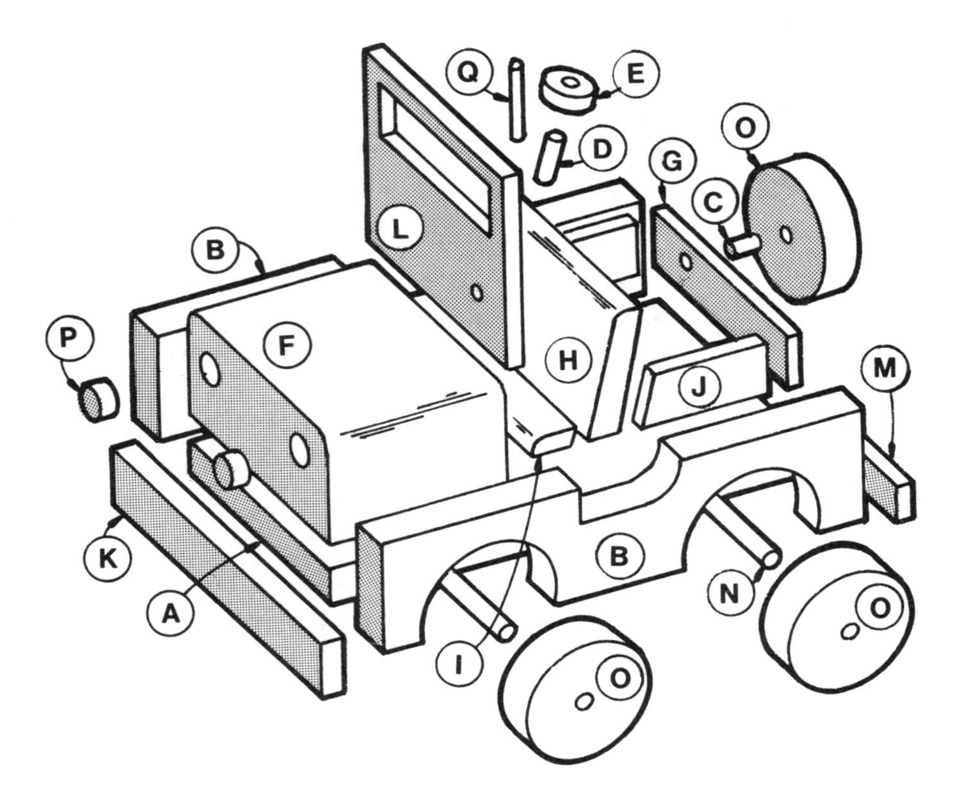

TOY JEEP ASSEMBLY

ing column (**D**) to size. Glue together and then glue the other end of the column into the hole in the windshield.

Cut the gear shift (**Q**) from 1/8" dia dowel. Glue into the hole in the base.

Wheels (**O**) are cut from 1/2" stock with a circle cutter in a drill press. Sand the cut surface smooth and round over the edges. Cut two axles (**N**) and a spare wheel dowel (**C**) to length from 1/4" dia dowel. Cut two headlights (**P**) from 1/2" dia dowel. Glue one wheel onto each axle and the spare wheel dowel. Glue the headlights into place in the holes in the hood.

Allow the glue to dry overnight and then sand to remove all sharp edges and remove the dust with a tack cloth. Apply a child-safe finish, and allow to dry overnight. Slip the axles into the holes in the base and glue the other wheels to the axles.

LIST OF MATERIALS

FINISHED DIMENSIONS IN INCHES

A	BASE	1/2 x 2 3/4 x7
B	SIDE (2)	1/2 x 1 3/4 x 7
C	SPARE WHEEL DOWEL	1/4 DIA x 3/4
D	STEERING COLUMN	1/4 DIA x 7/8
E	STEERING WHEEL	3/4 DIA x 1/4
F	HOOD	1 1/2 x 2 3/4 x 2 5/8
G	BACK	1/4 x 1 1/4 x 2 3/4
H	SEAT BACK	3/8 x 2 x 2 3/4
I	SEAT BOTTOM	1/4 x 9/16 x 2 3/4
J	REAR SIDE (2)	1/4 x 1 1/4 x 2 9/16
K	FRONT BUMBER	3/8 x 3/4 x 4
L	WINDSHIELD	1/4 x 2 3/4 x 2 3/4
M	REAR BUMPER	1/4 x 1/2 x 4
N	AXLE (2)	1/4 DIA x 3 7/8
O	WHEEL (5)	1/2 x 2 DIA
P	HEADLIGHT (2)	1/2 DIA x 1/2
Q	GEAR SHIFT	1/8 DIA x 1 1/4

MAC
Delivery Truck

We built our mac delivery truck with material from the scrap box. Lacking a well supplied scrap box, purchase the material from any lumber yard. A piece of 1 1/2", 1/2", 3/8" and 1/4" thick stock will be needed. Use either softwood or hardwood, however, with all the curved cuts we recommend pine.

Start by laying out the body parts and fenders on a 1/2 inch grid square to make a full size pattern. Mark the point on each grid line where the outline crosses the grid line. Join the marks with straight and curved lines.

Transfer the outline and the hole centers of the body (**A**) onto a piece of 1 1/2" stock using carbon paper between the pattern and the wood. Cut the parts out using either a band saw or a scroll saw. Cut only the cab area for now and leave about 1/4" stock at the rear. Drill the two axle holes with a 1/4" bit.

Next transfer the outline and the hole centers of the side (**B**) and fender (**C**) onto a piece of 1/2" stock. Lay out two of each piece. Cut the parts out with a band saw. Use a hole saw to cut the hole in the sides and fenders to clear the wheel. Use a drum sander in a drill press to smooth the inside cuts of the sides and fenders. Drill a 1/4" dia hole 1/8" deep in the front of each fender for the headlights. Sand only the remaining edges of the fenders and the front edge of the sides, but do not round over the body edges yet.

Before gluing the sides to the body make sure there is equal distance in the opening around the rear wheel. Take one circular scrap from the wheel opening in the side and slip it onto a 1/4" dia dowel

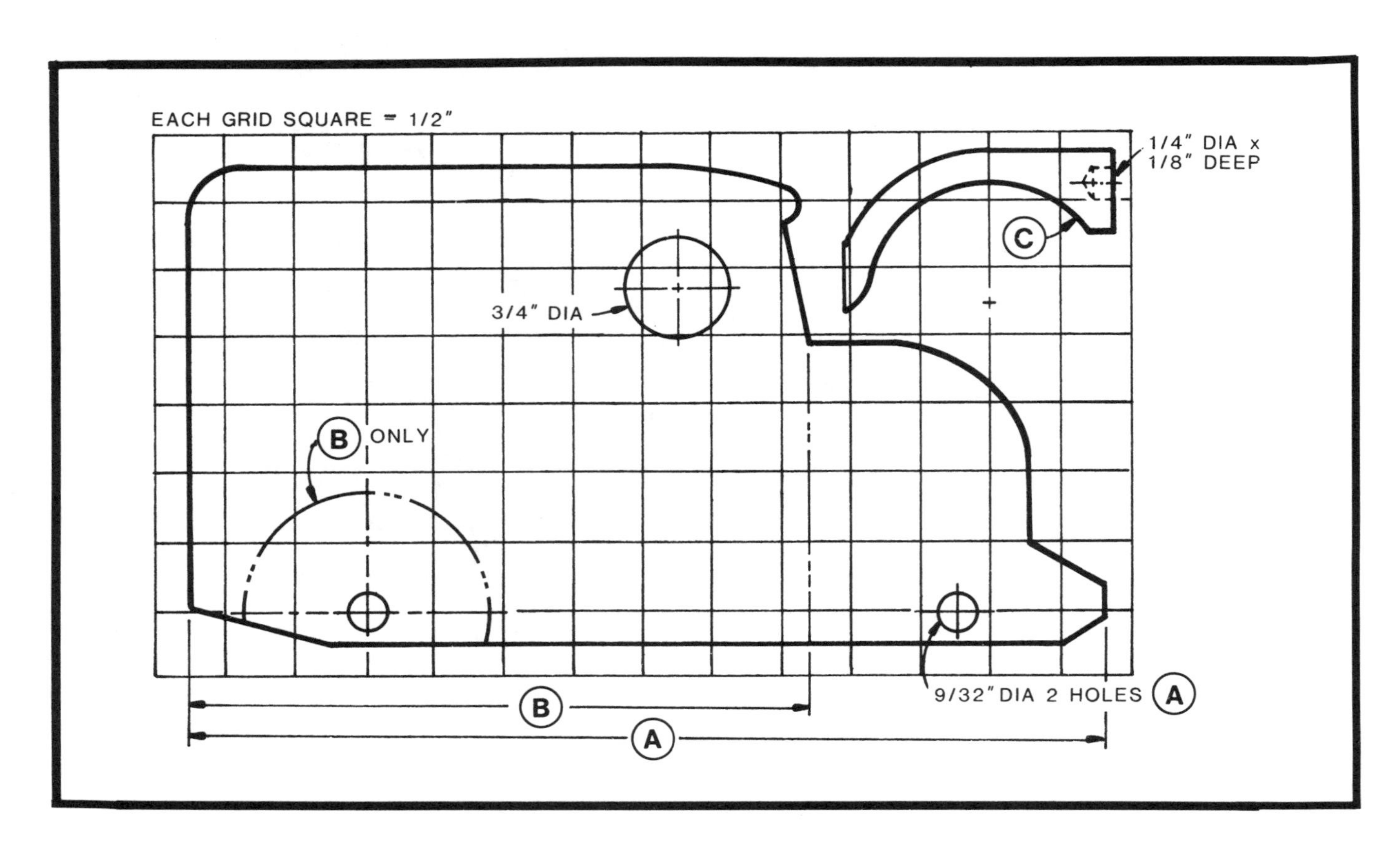

and then slide the dowel into the 1/4" dia axle hole in the rear of the body. This will make checking the clearance easier. Adjust the side if needed, glue and then clamp it. Allow the glue to set and repeat the procedure for the other side. Clamp the pieces together using scrap wood between

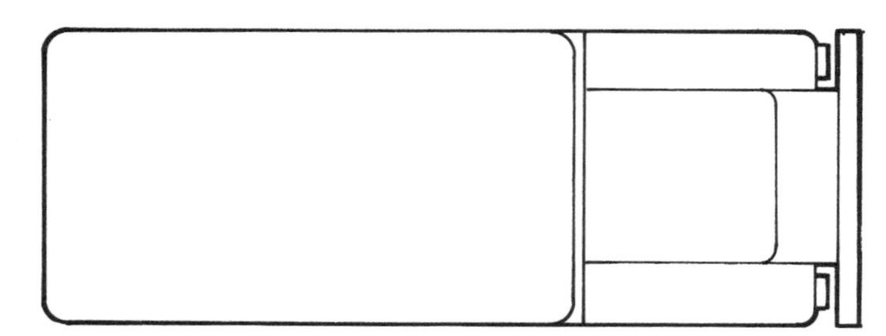

TOP VIEW

SIDE VIEW

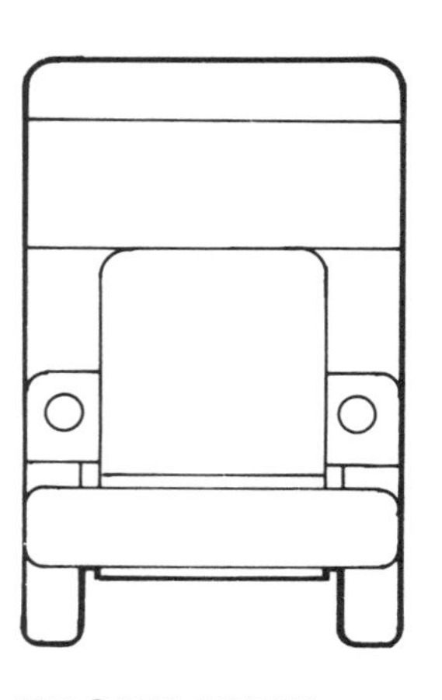

FRONT VIEW

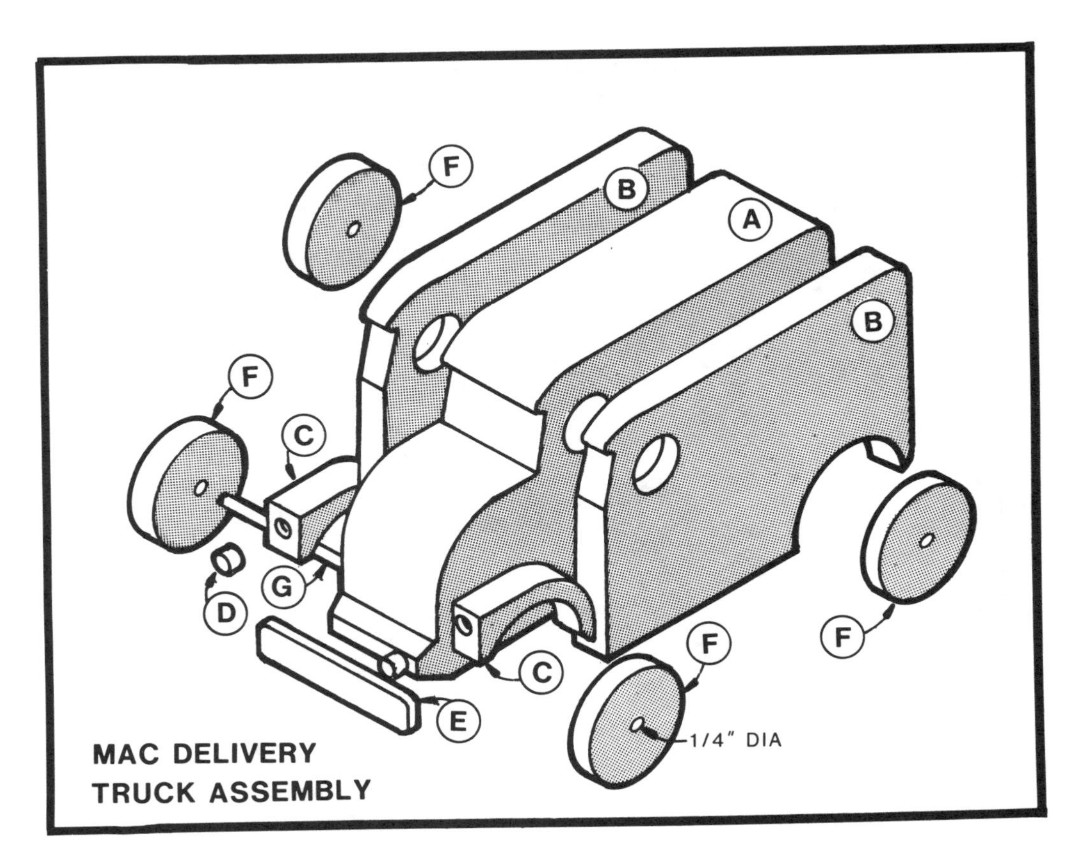

MAC DELIVERY TRUCK ASSEMBLY

LIST OF MATERIALS

FINISHED DIMENSIONS IN INCHES

A	BODY	1 1/2 x 3 1/2 x 6 5/8
B	SIDE (2)	1/2 x 3 1/2 x 4 1/2
C	FENDER (2)	1/2 x 1 1/4 x 2
D	HEADLIGHT (2)	1/4 DIA x 1/4
E	BUMPER	1/4 x 1/2 x 2 1/2
F	WHEEL (4)	1 1/2 DIA x 3/8
G	AXLE (2)	1/4 DIA x 2 1/2

the sides and the clamp. When dry drill the 3/4" dia side window hole and enlarge the axle holes with a 9/32" dia drill.

Next the fenders can be glued and clamped to the body. After the glue has dried cut the rear of the body to the required length. File and sand flush any mismatch between the layers of the built-up body. Sand the sides smooth and round all sharp edges.

Cut the bumper (**E**) from 1/4" stock. Sand a 1/8" radius on the four corners. Glue the bumper to the front of the body.

Cut two each of the headlights (**D**) and axles (**G**) from 1/4" dia dowel. Glue the headlights into the holes in the fenders.

Wheels (**F**) are cut from 3/8" stock with a hole saw in a portable electric drill. Take the four wheels and slip a 1/4" dia bolt with a washer under the head through the center hole. Add another washer and snug down with a nut. Chuck up in a drill press and sand all the wheels with a wide sanding block while the drill press is running. This will insure that all the wheels will be the same size. Chuck up each wheel separately on the bolt and round the edges with sandpaper as the wheel turns. Glue one wheel to each axle.

Dust all parts with a tack cloth and finish with a child-safe, nontoxic finish. When dry slip the axles through the holes in the body and glue the other wheels to the axles leaving about 1/16" gap between the inside of each wheel and the body.

SLAB'Y

Station Wagon

The slab'y station wagon is very easy to build and it could be the ideal first project for any novice woodworker. Basic hand tools are all that is necessary: a coping saw, hand drill and 1/4, 9/32, 3/4 inch drill bits. If you have power tools, you can use them. A router and a router bit will make rounding over the edges easier.

Begin by laying out a 1 inch grid pattern on a piece of card stock. Mark the point on each grid line where the outline crosses the grid line. Join the straight lines with the aid of a straightedge and freehand the curved lines. Mark the center of the holes.

Lay the pattern on the piece of 3/4" thick pine with a piece of carbon paper underneath and trace the outline. With a sharp pointed tool prick the centers thru the card stock into the wood.

Saw out the body (**A**), then drill the ten 3/4" dia holes for the window corners. Insert the coping saw blade thru one hole and cut out the window. Repeat the procedure for the rest of the windows. Drill the two 9/32" dia holes for the axles. Sand the sides smooth and round over all edges. Don't forget to round over all the window opening edges.

Cut the four wheels (**B**) from 3/4" thick pine stock and drill a 1/4" dia hole in the centers for the axles. The wheels must be sanded together to ensure that they are all the same diameter. Take a 1/4" bolt with a washer under the head and slide the four wheels onto the bolt. Add another washer followed by a nut. Add a scrap of wood smaller in diameter than the wheel with a hole in the center under each washer to protect the wheel surface. Chuck the bolt into drill press and while the wheels are turning, sand the wheels with a sanding block. Bolt up each wheel separately, and sand a radius to both edges. The two axles (**C**) are cut 2 3/8" long from 1/4" dia wood dowel.

Sand all surfaces with medium, then fine followed by extra fine sand paper. The grade of paper used does not have to be exact, but an 80, 100 and 150 grit is good.

Wipe all parts with a tack cloth to remove all the dust left from sanding. Glue one wheel to each axle and when dry finish the body and wheels with a good grade of child-safe finish. Don't forget to finish the other end of the axle. It's best not to finish the axle surface, since the finish build-up may cause the axle not to rotate freely in the axle hole in the body. Allow to dry overnight and then slip the axle through the body and glue the other wheel to the axle.

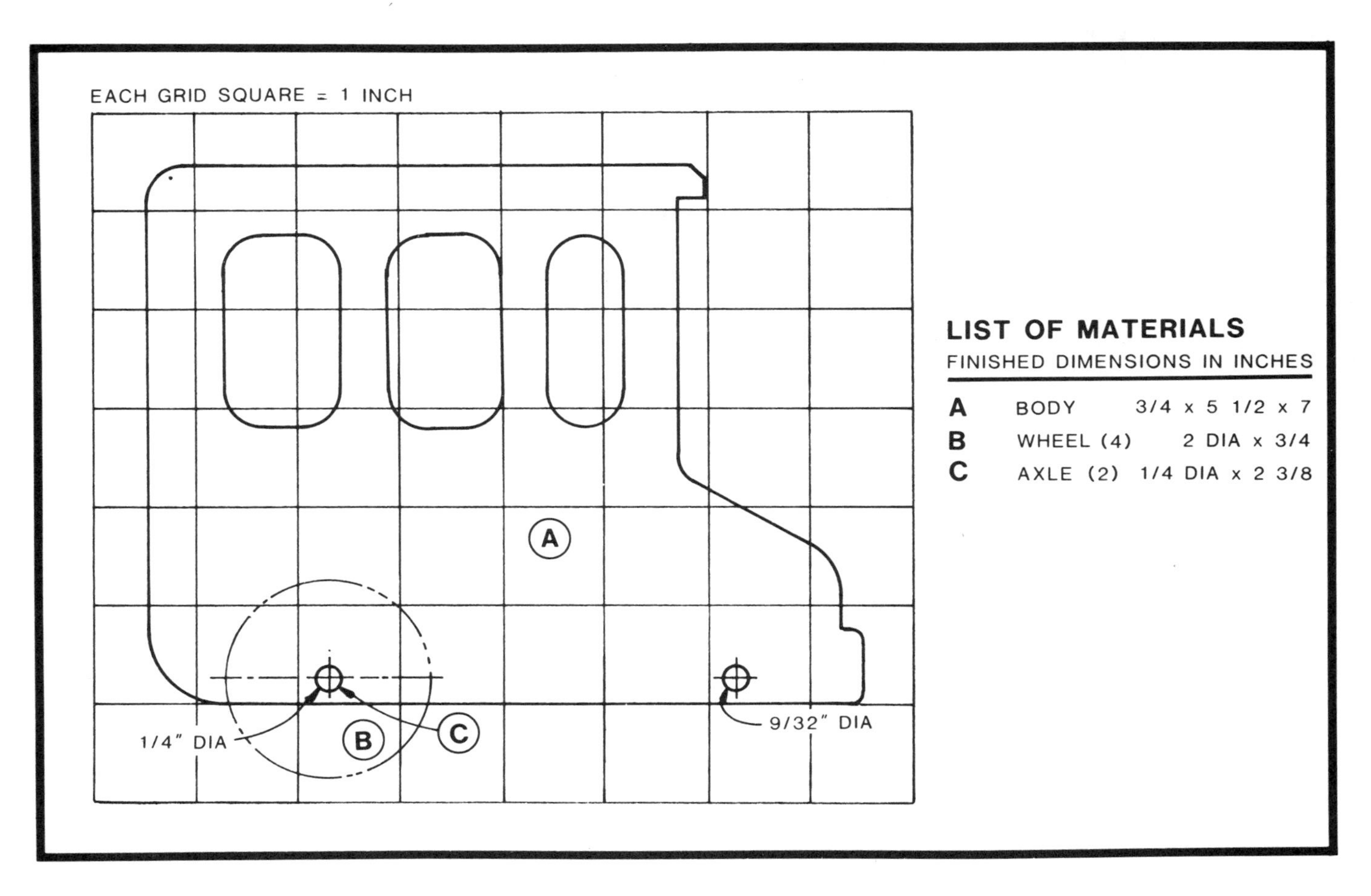

LIST OF MATERIALS

FINISHED DIMENSIONS IN INCHES

A	BODY	3/4 x 5 1/2 x 7
B	WHEEL (4)	2 DIA x 3/4
C	AXLE (2)	1/4 DIA x 2 3/8

MAC

Coupe

Just a few simple hand tools are all that is necessary for this wooden vehicle. A coping saw will make fast work of the curved cuts. Softwood will make the cuts even easier. We used a scrap of 2x4 hem fir left over from a room addition for the body and clear pine door molding trim for the rest of the parts.

Lay out the body and fender on a 1/2 inch grid square to make a full size pattern. Mark the point on each grid line where the outline crosses the grid line. Join the straight lines with the aid of a straightedge and freehand the curved lines. Mark the center of the holes and fender radius.

Transfer the outline and the hole centers of the body (**A**) onto a piece of 1 1/2" stock using carbon paper between the pattern and the wood. Cut the part out using either a band saw, scroll saw or coping saw. Drill the two 1/4" dia axle holes, the 14"dia by 5/8"deep hole and the 3/4" dia window hole.

Next transfer the outline and the hole centers of the fenders (**C**) onto a piece of 1/2" stock; two fenders are required. Cut the parts out with a band saw. Use a hole saw to cut the hole in the fender to clear the wheel. Use a drum sander in a drill press to smooth the inside cuts of the fenders. Drill a 1/4" dia hole 1/8" deep in

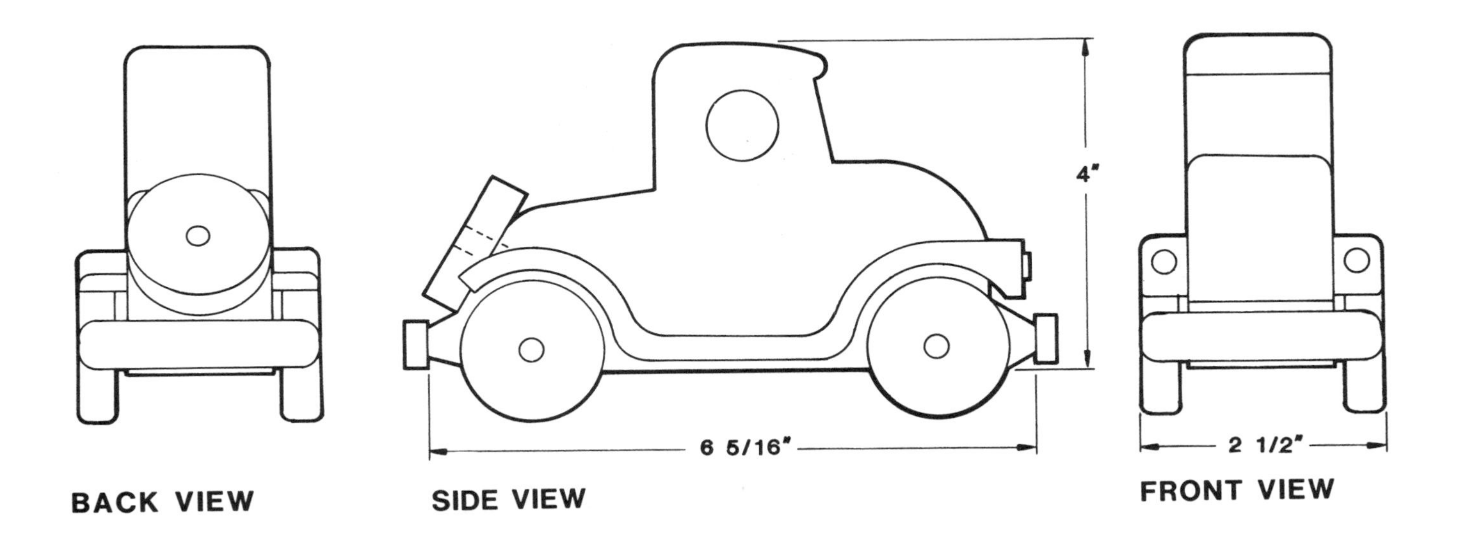

the front of each fender for the headlights. Sand the remaining edges of the fenders, but do not round over the edges yet.

Wheels (**F**) are cut from 3/8" stock with a hole saw in a portable electric drill. Take the five wheels and slip a 1/4" bolt with a washer under the head through the center hole. Add another washer and snug down the nut. Chuck up in a drill press and sand all the wheels with a wide sanding block while the drill press is run-

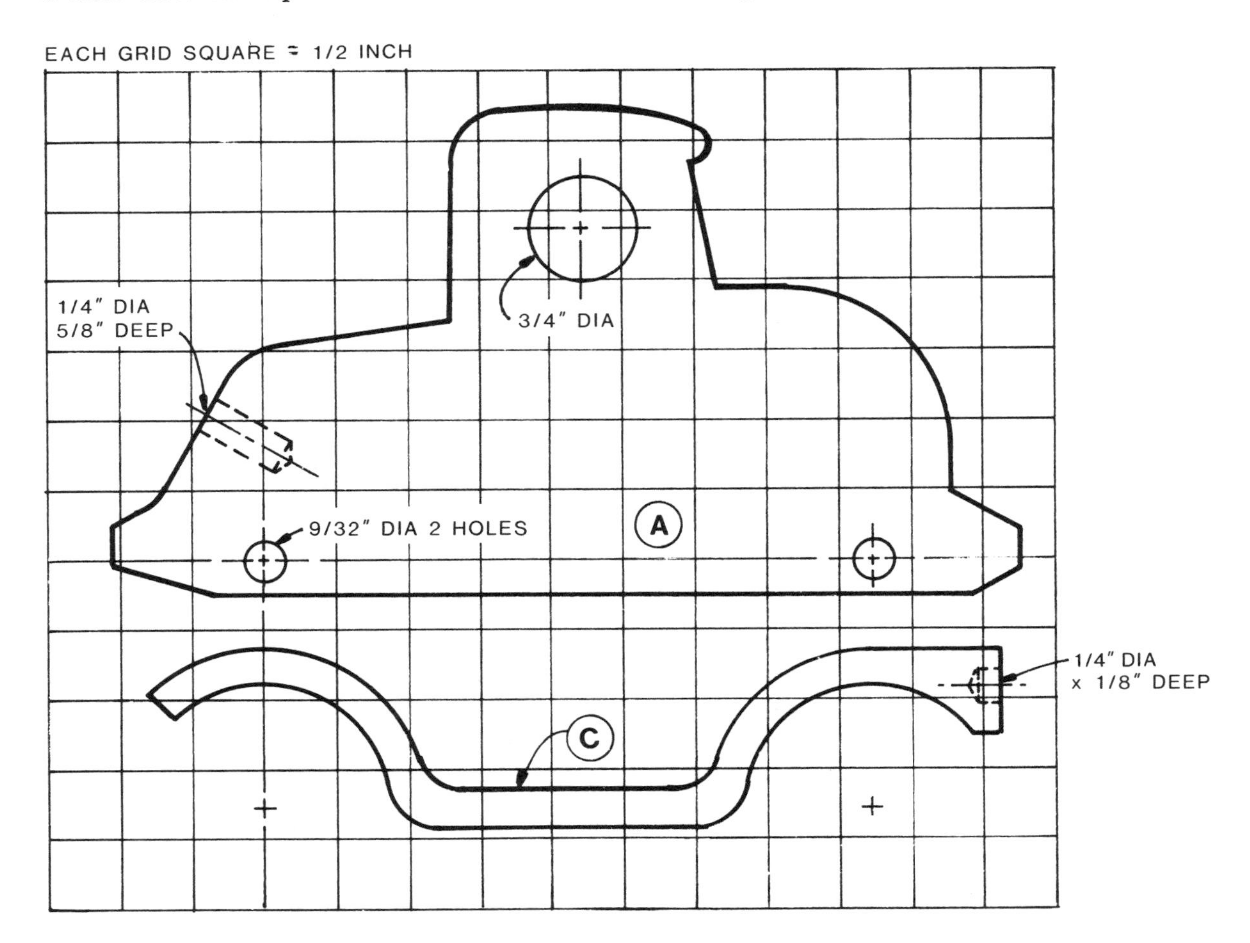

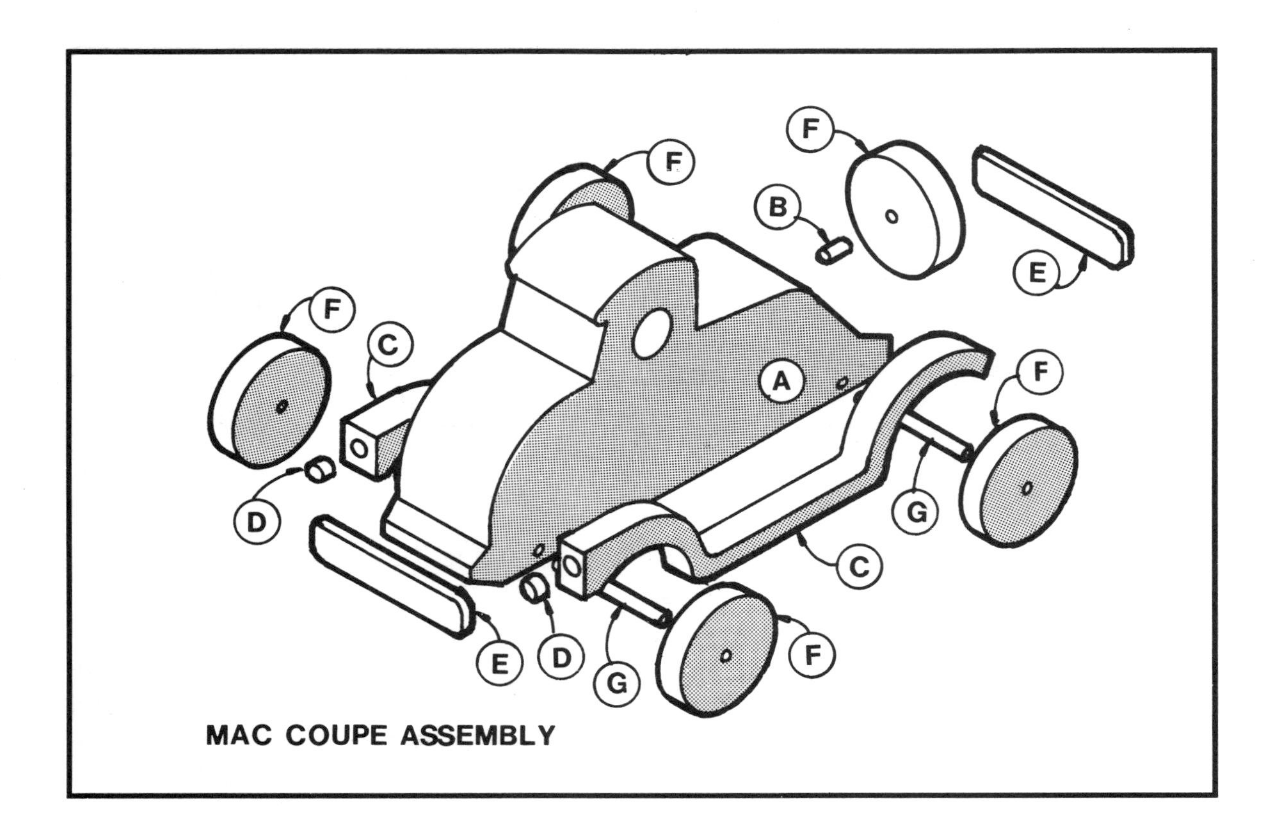

MAC COUPE ASSEMBLY

ning. This will make sure that all the wheels will be the same size. Chuck up each wheel separately on the bolt and round the edges with sandpaper as the wheel turns. Glue one wheel to each axle.

Glue the fenders to the body making sure there is equal distance in the opening around the wheels. Take the wheel axle assemblies and slide the axles into the 1/4" dia axle holes in the body. This will make checking the clearance between the wheel and fender opening easier. Adjust the fender if needed and then clamp. Allow the glue to set and repeat the procedure for the other side. Clamp the pieces together using scrap wood between the fenders and the clamp. When dry enlarge the axle holes with a 9/32" dia drill.

After the glue has dried, sand and round all sharp edges. Cut two bumpers (**E**) from 1/4" stock. Sand a 1/8" radius on the four corners. Glue one bumper to the front of the body and the other to the rear. Center the bumpers on the body.

Cut two headlights (**D**), a spare wheel peg (**B**) and two axles (**G**) from 1/4" dia dowel. Glue the headlights into the holes in the fenders. Glue one wheel to each axle and the spare wheel peg.

Dust all parts with a tack cloth and finish with a child-safe, nontoxic finish. When dry slip the axle through the holes in the body and glue the other wheel to the axle leaving about 1/16" gap between the inside of each wheel and the body.

LIST OF MATERIALS

FINISHED DIMENSIONS IN INCHES

A	BODY	1 1/2 x 3 1/2 x 6 3/8
B	SPARE WHEEL PEG	1/4 DIA x3/4
C	FENDER (2)	1/2 x 1 1/4 x 6
D	HEADLIGHT (2)	1/4 DIA x 1/4
E	BUMPER (2)	1/4 x 1/2 x 2 1/2
F	WHEEL (5)	3/8 x 1 1/2 DIA
G	AXLE (2)	1/4 DIA x 2 1/2

SMALL STEAM Freight Train

Of all the wood toys, probably the steam train is the most fascinating for small children. Some designs are quite elaborate with a lot of small detail, while others are simple. This design is compact and has just enough detail to make it "cute". We built our toy of pine and hardwood dowels.

Most of the wheels are a plain flat design, except for the drivers, which have four holes to show an easy to make spoke design. Any commercial wheels can be substituted to give the train a different look.

THE LOCOMOTIVE

First cut all the pieces as indicated in the list of materials. The 1 5/8" dia dowel can be purchased from any full service lumber center; it is used for banisters.

Lay out the radius at the rear of the base (**A**) and the chamfer at the front. Cut the radius and chamfer away from the line and sand to the line. Locate the center of the pin and axle holes and drill 9/32" dia.

Build up the cab (**B**) by gluing up the three pieces and allowing to dry overnight. Locate the center of the window and drill the 3/4" dia hole. Cut the cab roof (**J**) from 3/4" stock and sand the chamfer on both sides.

Drill the 3/8" dia hole 1/4" deep in the center of the boiler (**C**) face. Cut the large diameter firebox (**F**) with a hole saw. When using a standard length hole saw the 1 1/4" thick piece will have to be cut part way through and then turned over and cut the rest of the way. Sand the cut surface smooth.

Glue the boiler to the base, centered on the base and flush with the top of the sloping surface. Glue the firebox to the base and boiler and allow to dry. When the glue dries, lay out the three holes on the boiler base assembly. Drill the two 1/2" and the 5/8" dia holes 1/2" deep followed by a 1/4" dia hole through the base (see the drawing). Cut three dowels to length and glue into the holes flush with the base bottom.

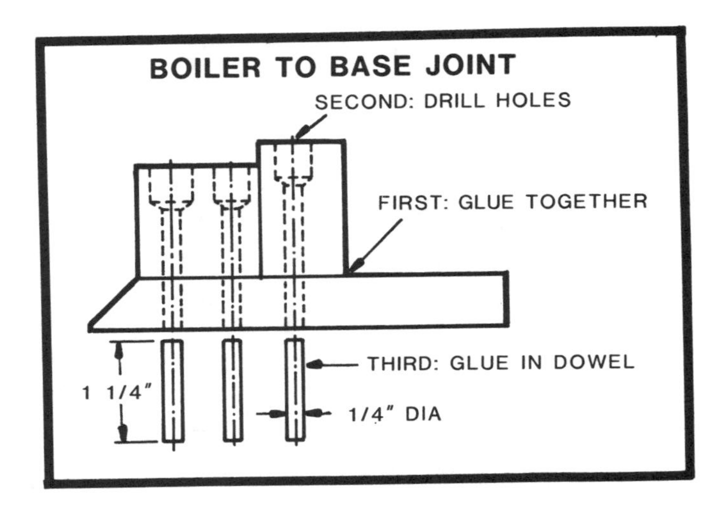

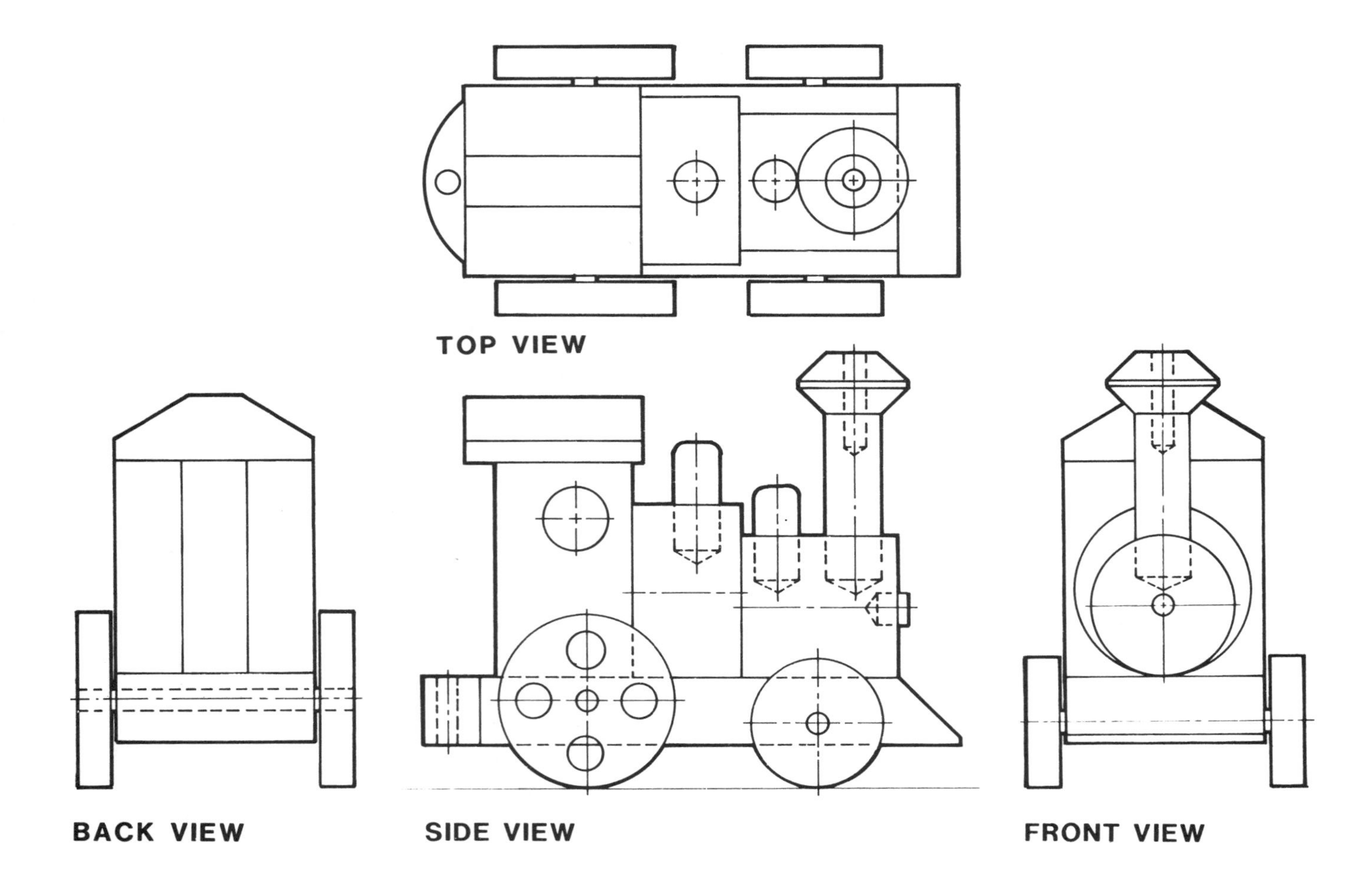

Take a length of 1/2" dia dowel and sand a radius all around the end by rotating it against a disc sander. Cut to length for the dome (**D**) and sand another end and cut to length for the dome (**E**). Apply a small amount of glue into the two dome holes and insert the domes.

Cut the smokestack (**G**) to length and drill a 1/4" dia hole 3/8" deep in the center of one end. Cut dowel (**H**) to length from 1/4" dia stock. Lay out a 1 1/4" dia circle on a 3/4" thick stock for the stack (**I**) and drill a 1/4" dia hole through the center. Cut away from the line. Slip a 1/4" dia bolt thru a washer and the stack hole, followed by another washer and a nut. Chuck into a drill press and file the diameter smooth. Then, file the taper on each side. Remove the bolt and glue the stack to the dowel and then to the smokestack. Apply a small amount of glue into the smokestack hole in the boiler and insert the smokestack assembly into the hole.

Lay out the two 2" dia drivers (**K**) on 3/8" thick stock. On a 1 3/16" dia circle lay out the four equally spaced holes. Drill the four 7/16" dia holes and the 1/4" dia

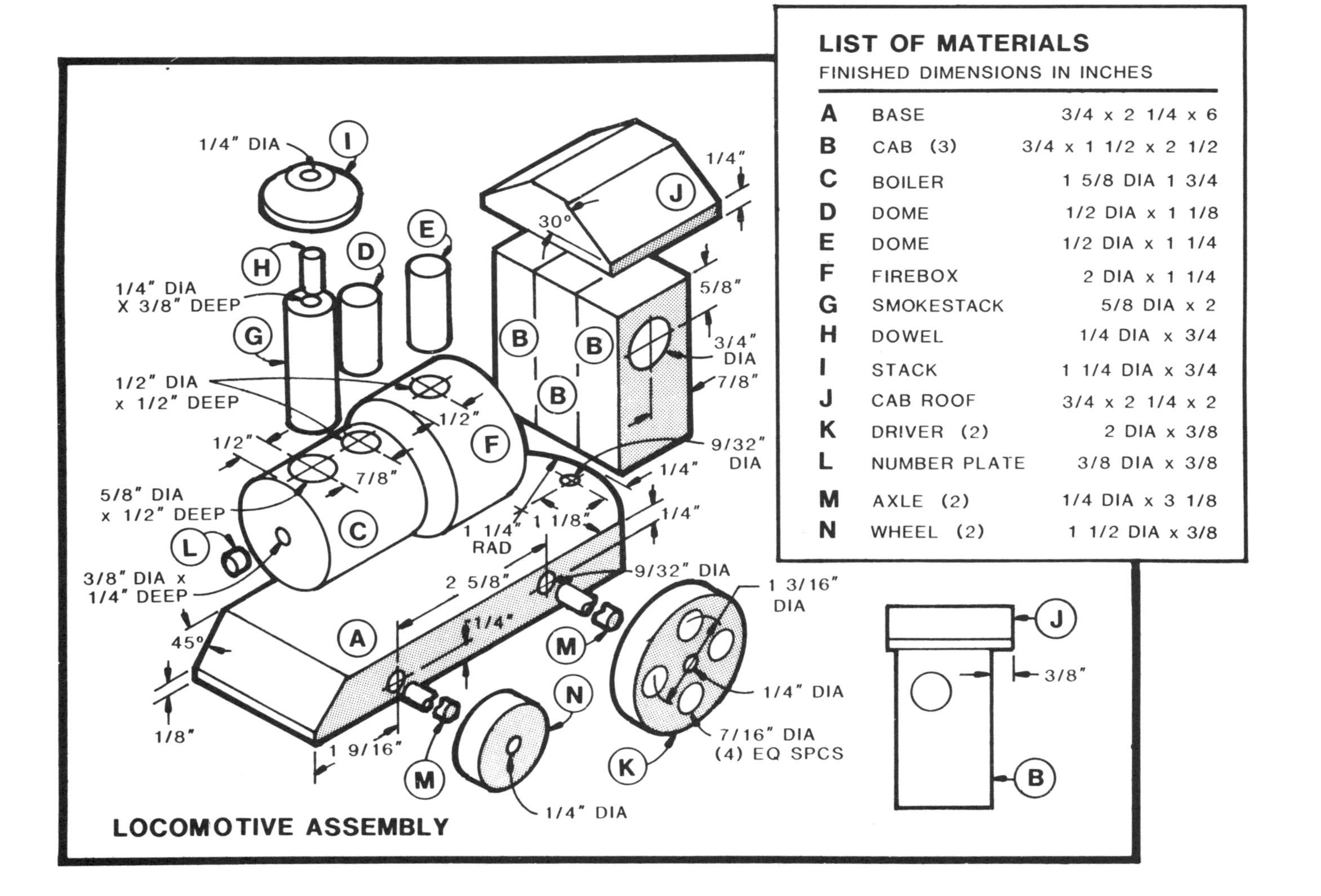

LIST OF MATERIALS

FINISHED DIMENSIONS IN INCHES

A	BASE	3/4 x 2 1/4 x 6
B	CAB (3)	3/4 x 1 1/2 x 2 1/2
C	BOILER	1 5/8 DIA 1 3/4
D	DOME	1/2 DIA x 1 1/8
E	DOME	1/2 DIA x 1 1/4
F	FIREBOX	2 DIA x 1 1/4
G	SMOKESTACK	5/8 DIA x 2
H	DOWEL	1/4 DIA x 3/4
I	STACK	1 1/4 DIA x 3/4
J	CAB ROOF	3/4 x 2 1/4 x 2
K	DRIVER (2)	2 DIA x 3/8
L	NUMBER PLATE	3/8 DIA x 3/8
M	AXLE (2)	1/4 DIA x 3 1/8
N	WHEEL (2)	1 1/2 DIA x 3/8

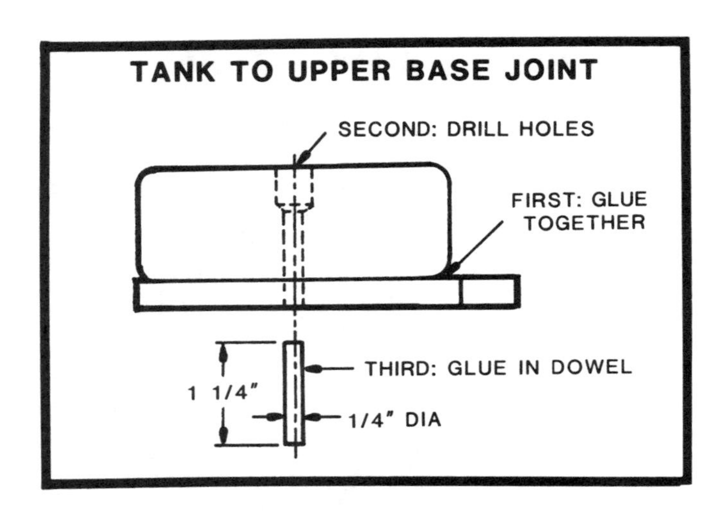

hole in the center of each wheel. Cut and sand to the finished diameter. Make the two wheels (**N**) from 3/8" thick stock. Sand the cut surface of the wheels and radius the edges. Cut the two axles (**M**) to length from 1/4" dia dowel and the number plate (**L**) from 3/8" dia dowel. Glue one wheel to each axle. Apply a small amount of glue into the number plate hole and insert the number plate.

Glue the cab to the base and firebox. Glue the roof to the top of the cab with a 3/8" overhang at the rear of the cab.

Set the steam locomotive aside to allow the glue to dry and start work on the tank car.

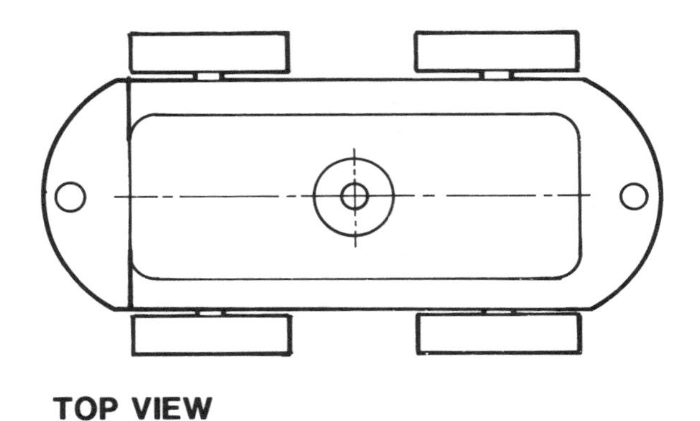

TOP VIEW

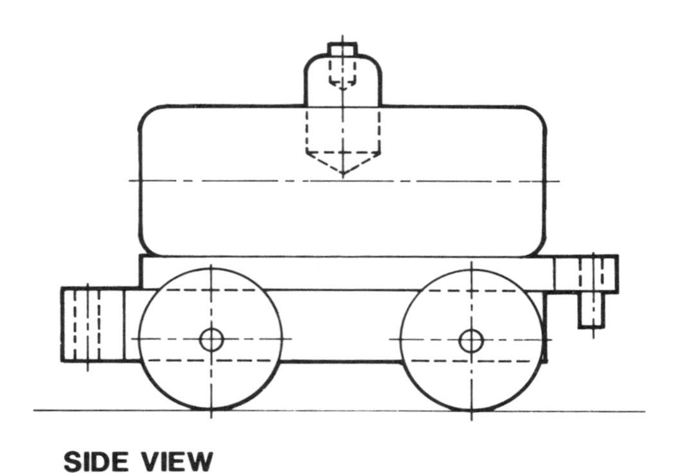

SIDE VIEW

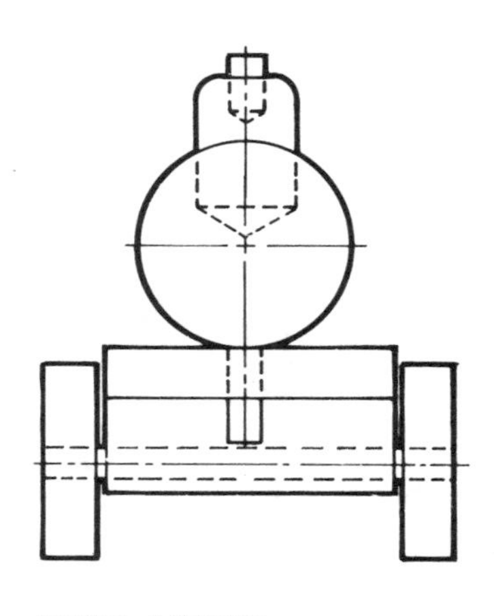

END VIEW

THE TANK CAR

The tank car has a base and upper base with a pin that will slip into another car to join them together. The other end has a hole to accept the pin from another car. Cut the upper base (**P**) and base (**Q**) to size as indicated in the list of materials. Lay out the radius and pin locations on both pieces. Mark the center of both axle holes using the dimensions in the tank car assembly drawing. Drill the 9/32" dia axle holes and pin clearance holes. Drill the 1/4" dia hole in the upper base for the pin. Cut and sand the radius at the ends. Glue the upper base to the base 3/4" in front of the radius.

Cut the tank (**R**) 4 1/4" long from 1 5/8" dia dowel. Sand the radius at both ends by holding the dowel at an angle against a sanding belt while rotating it slowly. Remove only a small amount of material and change the angle several times for the radius. Glue the tank flush with the straight end of the upper base and in the center. Clamp and allow to dry overnight. When the glue dries, lay out the hole on the tank base assembly. Drill the 3/4" dia hole 1/2" deep followed by a 1/4" dia hole through the base. Cut the dowel to length and glue into the hole flush with the base bottom.

Take a length of 3/4" dia dowel and sand a radius around one end for the dome (**T**). Drill a 1/4" dia hole 1/4" deep in the center and cut to length. Cut the cap (**S**) to length from 1/4" dia dowel. Glue the dome into the tank and the cap into the hole in the dome.

Make the four wheels (**N**) from 3/8" thick stock. Sand the cut surface of the

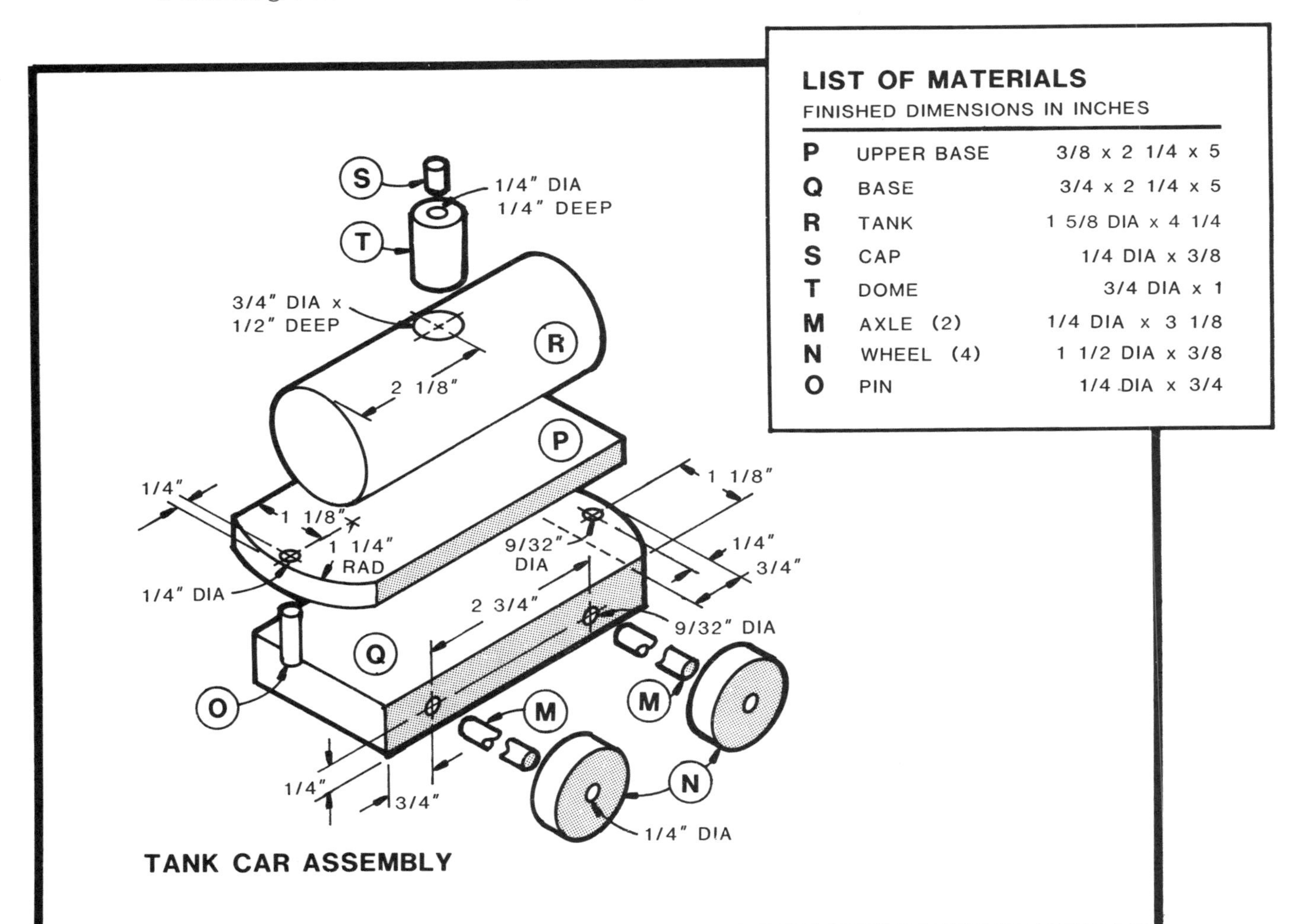

LIST OF MATERIALS

FINISHED DIMENSIONS IN INCHES

P	UPPER BASE	3/8 x 2 1/4 x 5
Q	BASE	3/4 x 2 1/4 x 5
R	TANK	1 5/8 DIA x 4 1/4
S	CAP	1/4 DIA x 3/8
T	DOME	3/4 DIA x 1
M	AXLE (2)	1/4 DIA x 3 1/8
N	WHEEL (4)	1 1/2 DIA x 3/8
O	PIN	1/4 DIA x 3/4

TANK CAR ASSEMBLY

wheels and radius the edges. Cut the two axles (**M**) to length from 1/4" dia dowel. Glue one wheel to each axle. Cut the pin (**O**) 3/4" long from 1/4" dia dowel and glue into the hole in the upper base.

Set the tank car aside to allow the glue to dry and start work on the caboose.

THE CABOOSE

Bringing up the end of the small steam freight train is a caboose. Cut the upper base (**U**) and base (**V**) to size as indicated in the list of materials. Lay out the radius and pin locations on both pieces. Mark the center of both axle holes using the dimensions in the caboose assembly drawing. Drill the 9/32" dia axle holes and pin clearance hole. Drill the 1/4" dia hole in the upper base for the pin. Cut and sand the radius at the ends. Glue the upper base to the base 3/4" in front of the radius.

Cut the three body (**W**) pieces from 3/4" stock and glue together to form the 2 1/4" wide body. When the glue dries drill the 3/4" dia hole for the window. Glue the body 1/2" from the back edge of the upper base.

Next cut the roof (**Y**) from 3/8" stock. Cut the cupola (**X**) from a piece of 3/4" by

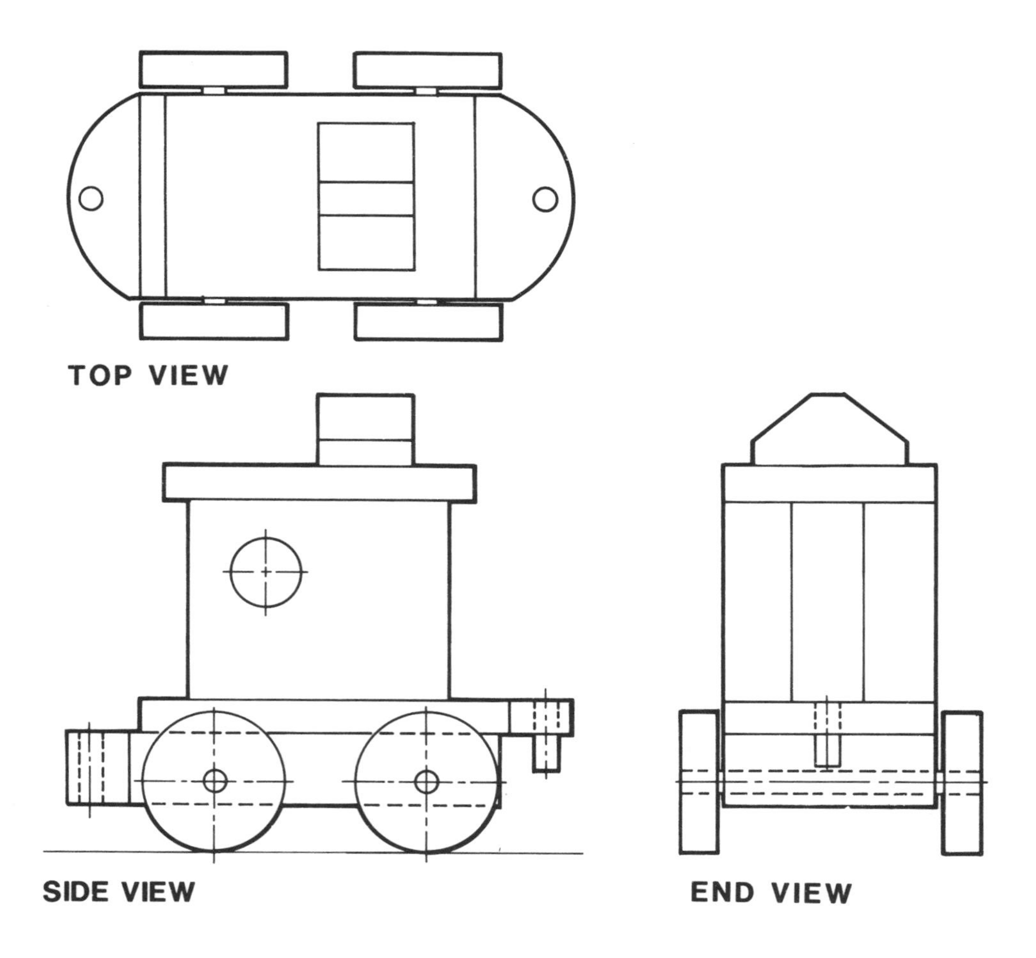

1 5/8" stock. Sand the two bevels and then cut to 1" long.

Glue the roof to the body with a 1/4" overhang at the front and rear. Glue the cupola to the roof 5/16" from each side and 5/8" back from the front edge of the roof.

Make the four wheels (**N**) from 3/8" thick stock. Sand the cut surface of the wheels and radius the edges. Cut the two axles (**M**) to length from 1/4" dia dowel. Glue one wheel to each axle. Cut the pin (**O**) 3/4" long from 1/4" dia dowel and glue into the hole in the upper base.

FINAL ASSEMBLY

Finally, round over all exposed edges with sandpaper and remove the dust with a tack cloth. Apply a child-safe finish.

Slip the axles into the holes in the base and glue the other wheels to the axles. Leave a small space between the base and the wheel.

Hook the tank car up to the locomotive and the caboose to the tank car and you're ready to highball with your small steam freight train.

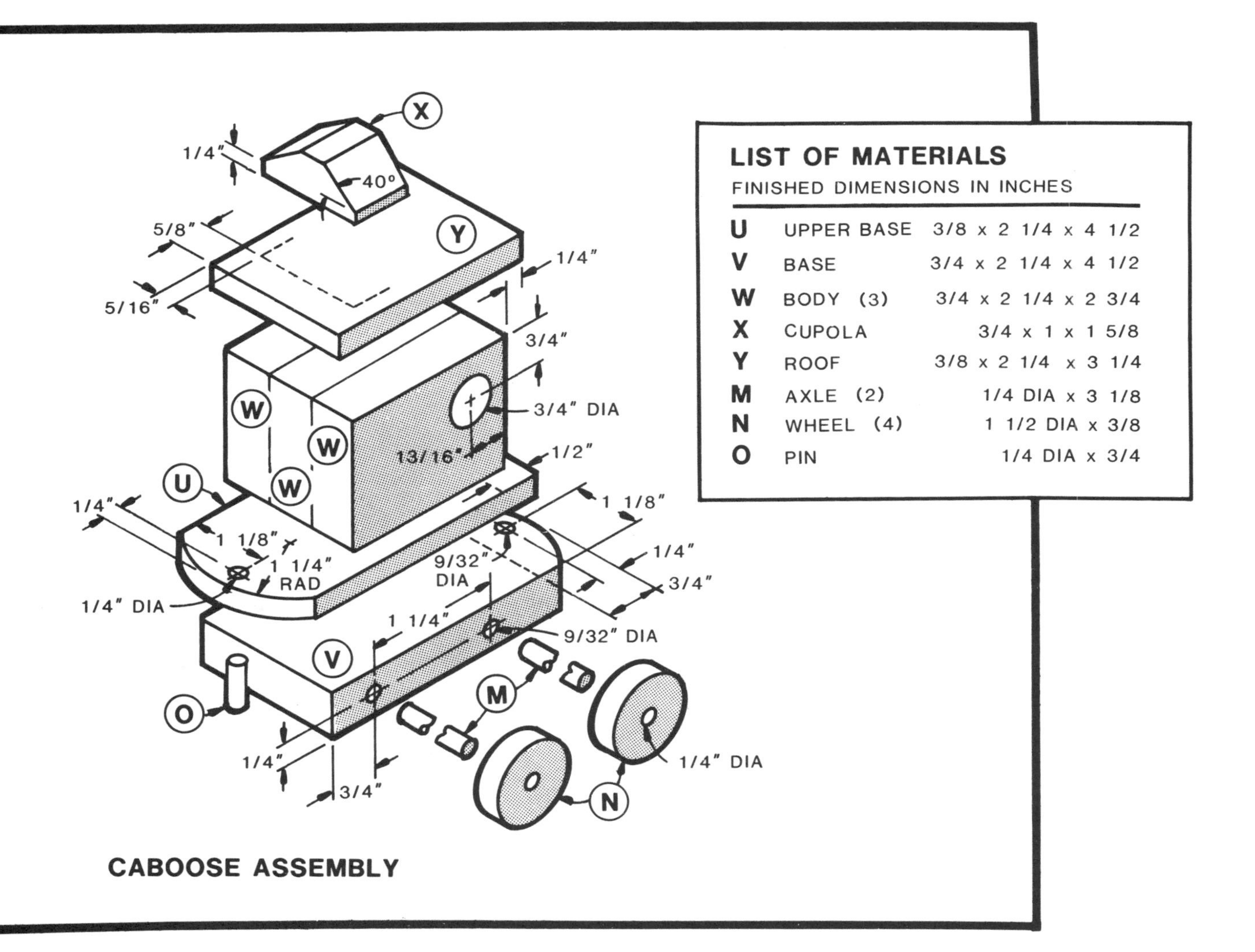

LIST OF MATERIALS

FINISHED DIMENSIONS IN INCHES

U	UPPER BASE	3/8 x 2 1/4 x 4 1/2
V	BASE	3/4 x 2 1/4 x 4 1/2
W	BODY (3)	3/4 x 2 1/4 x 2 3/4
X	CUPOLA	3/4 x 1 x 1 5/8
Y	ROOF	3/8 x 2 1/4 x 3 1/4
M	AXLE (2)	1/4 DIA x 3 1/8
N	WHEEL (4)	1 1/2 DIA x 3/8
O	PIN	1/4 DIA x 3/4

CABOOSE ASSEMBLY

TOY

Pickup

The toy pickup is a natural wood toy to build since the full size pickup trucks are very popular with adults. It will be a favorite of that youngster who receives this toy. Our toy was built of pine and maple dowels.

Cut the base (**A**) to size as indicated in the list of materials. Mark and drill the two 9/32" dia axle holes.

Lay out the two sides (**B**) on 1/2" stock. Mark the center of the cutouts to clear the wheels. Make the cuts with a band saw and cut the wheel openings with a 2 1/4" dia hole saw. Sand a 1/4" radius on the front of both sides. Mark the headlight and two taillight holes on each side as shown in the side detail drawing. Drill the 1/4" dia holes 1/4" deep for the headlights and two 3/16" dia holes 1/4" deep for the taillights in each side.

The hood (**D**) is cut to size. Round over the front edges with a 1/2" router bit. Glue the hood to the base. Keep the front edge of the hood flush with the base. Glue

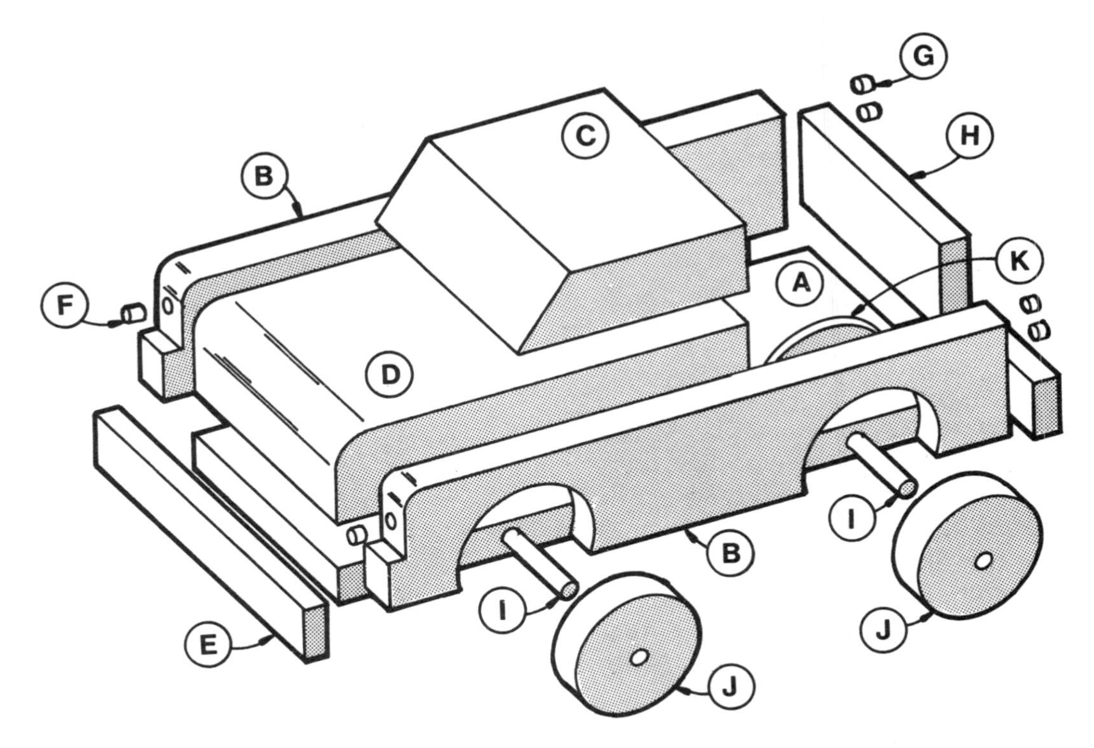

TOY PICKUP ASSEMBLY

the sides in place and clamp overnight. Put a scrap of wood between the side and the clamp to avoid marks by the clamp.

Cut the cab (**C**) to the size as listed in the list of materials. Cut the 50 degree miter for the windshield. Glue the cab to the top of the hood with the back edges flush.

The tailgate (**H**) is cut to size. Glue the tailgate between the sides and to the base. Cut the two covers (**K**) from 1/8" stock. Glue the covers to the inside of the sides to cover up the opening that clears the wheel.

Cut the two bumpers (**E**) to size. Glue one bumper to the front of the sides and base flush with the bottom of the base and with an equal overhang on each side. Glue the other to the back.

Wheels (**J**) are cut from 1/2" stock with a circle cutter in a drill press. Sand the cut surface smooth and round over the edges. Cut two axles (**I**) to length from 1/4" dia dowel. Cut two headlights (**F**)

LIST OF MATERIALS

FINISHED DIMENSIONS IN INCHES

A	BASE	1/2 x 2 3/4 x 9
B	SIDE (2)	1/2 x 1 3/4 x 9
C	CAB	1 x 2 3/4 x 2 3/8
D	HOOD	1 1/2 x 2 3/4 x 5
E	BUMPER (2)	3/8 x 3/4 x 4
F	HEADLIGHT (2)	1/4 DIA x 3/8
G	TAILLIGHT (4)	3/16 DIA x 3/8
H	TAILGATE	3/8 x 1 1/4 x 2 3/4
I	AXLE (2)	1/4 DIA x 3 7/8
J	WHEEL (4)	1/2 x 2 DIA
K	COVER (2)	1/8 x 1 x 2 1/2

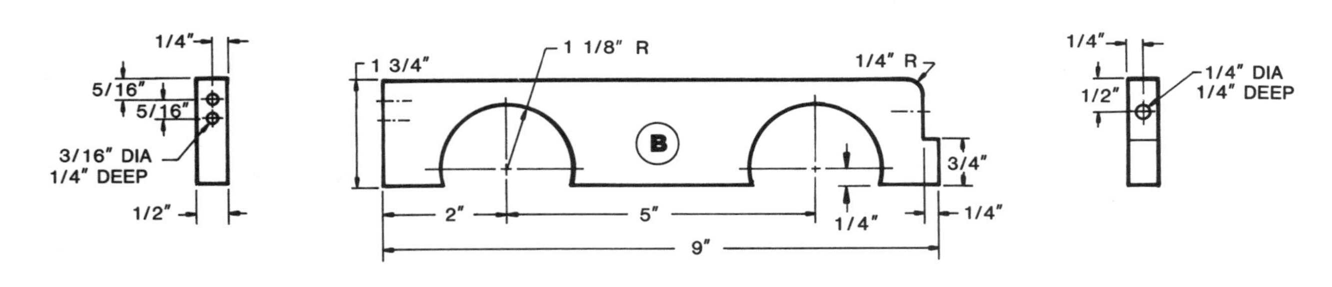

SIDE DETAIL

from 1/4" dia dowel and four taillights (**G**) from 3/16" dia dowel. Glue one wheel onto each axle. Glue the headlights and taillights into the holes in the sides.

Allow the glue to dry overnight and then sand to remove all sharp edges. Remove the dust with a tack cloth. Apply a child-safe finish, and allow to dry. Slide the axles into the holes in the base and glue the other wheels to the axles.

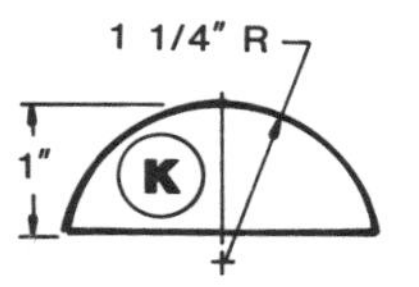

COVER DETAIL

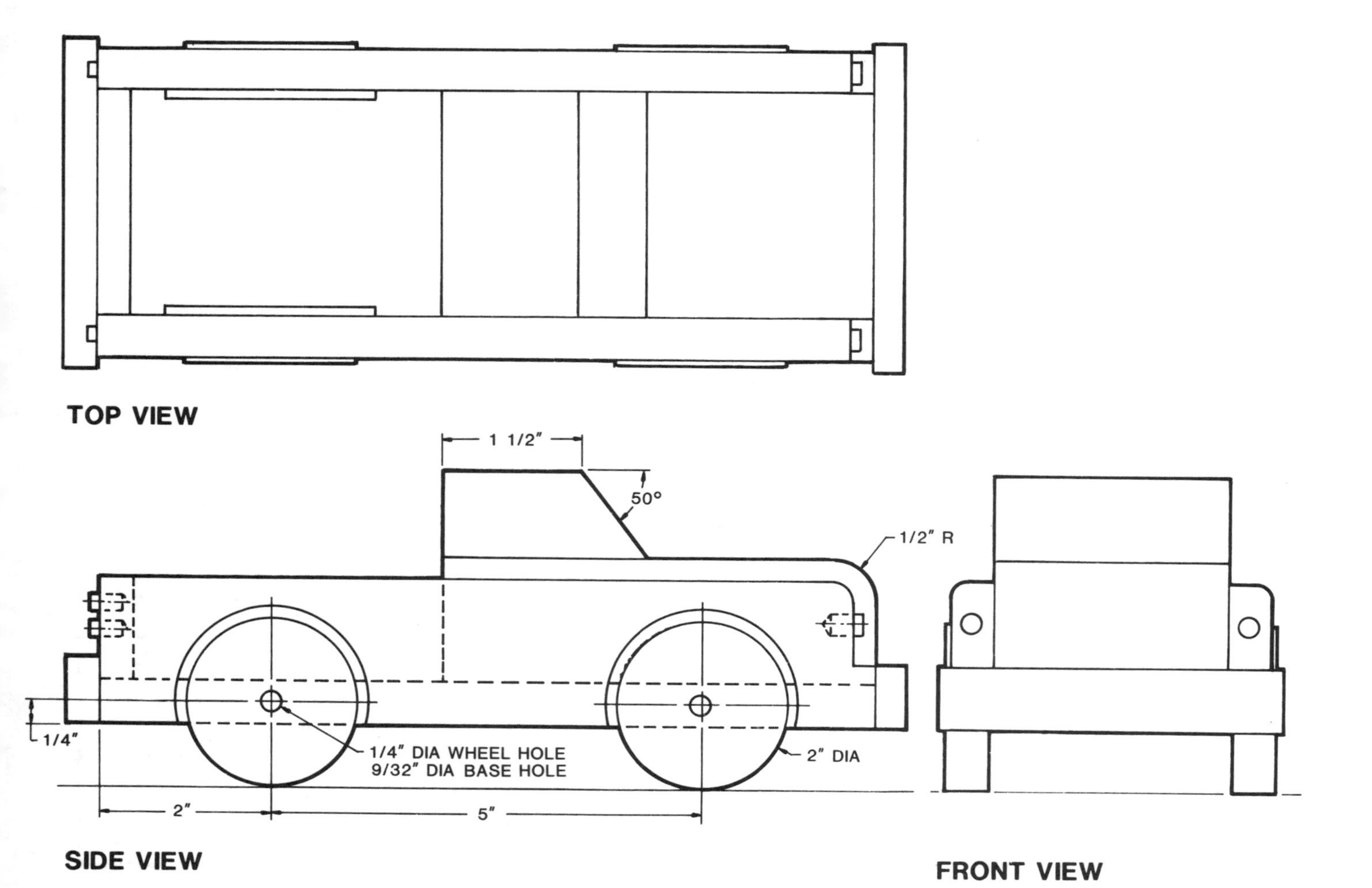

TOP VIEW

SIDE VIEW

FRONT VIEW

BIG RIGS

Pair of Doubles

The big rigs pair of doubles is an impressive small toy. The amount of detail is minimal so the average woodworker can build this toy. Fuel tanks, exhaust stacks and cab lights can be added for a little more detail.

TRACTOR

Cut the base (**A**) from 1/2" stock to 2" wide by 4 1/4" long. Lay out the two long notches and cut with a band saw. When we drill the front wheel wells later, we will get the front notches in the base. Locate and drill the rear 9/32" dia hole.

The cab (**C**) is cut from 1 1/2" stock 2" wide by 2" long. The windshield is cut 1" up from the bottom and back 15 degrees. Locate and drill the two 1/4" dia 1/8" deep headlight holes.

Glue the cab to the base 1/8" back from the front. This should make the cab flush with the notch in the base. When dry use a 1 3/8" Forstner bit to drill the front wheel well 9/16" deep in both sides of the cab base assembly. Drill the 9/32" dia hole.

Cut the 3/4" wide by 3/4" long trailer hitch plate (**M**) from 1/2" stock. Drill the 9/32" dia hole in the center of the block. Glue to the base 3/8" from the back and centered on the base.

Cut two headlights (**D**) 1/4" long from 1/4" dia dowel. Glue the headlights into the holes in the cab.

FRONT TRAILER

Cut three van blocks (**K**) from 3/4" stock to 2 1/2" wide by 6" long. Glue the blocks together and clamp until dry.

The tandem block (**J**) is cut from 1/2" stock 1 1/8" wide by 2 3/8" long. Then cut the tandem axle block (**N**) from 1/2" stock 1 1/8" wide by 3 1/16" long. Lay out and drill the two 9/32" dia axle holes and the 3/16" dia hitch pin clearance hole. Chamfer the lower back edge 1/4" down from the top surface and 30 degrees back.

Glue the tandem block to the underside of the van blocks 3/8" from the back edge and 9/16" from the side. Then, glue the tandem axle block flush to the front edge of the tandem block. Lay out and drill the 1/4" dia hitch pin hole 1/2" deep 1" back from the front edge and 1 1/8" from the side.

Cut the hitch pin (**B**) to length from 1/4" dia dowel. Glue the hitch pin into the hole in the van body.

TRAILER HITCH

Cut the hitch plate (**E**) from 1/4" stock to 3/4" wide by 3/4" long. Lay out and drill the 9/32" dia hole.

Lay out the hitch (**F**) on 1/4" stock and locate the two holes. Cut the hitch out and sand the edges. Drill the 9/32" dia hole and the 3/16" dia hole.

Cut the hitch block (**G**) from 1/2" stock to 1 1/8" wide by 1 1/2" long. Lay out the center of the axle hole and drill with a 9/32" dia bit.

Glue the hitch plate to the hitch. Slip the shank of a 9/32" drill through both holes to insure they line up. When dry remove the drill and glue the assembly to the hitch block 1/8" from the rear edge.

Cut the front hitch pin (**H**) to length from 3/16" dia dowel. Glue the hitch pin into the hole in the hitch.

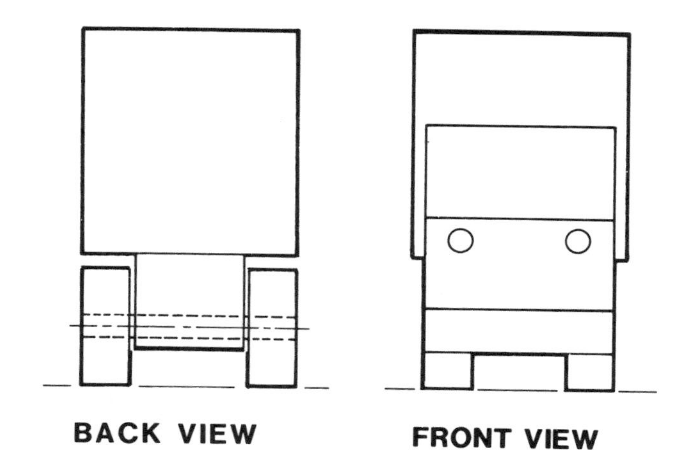

BACK VIEW FRONT VIEW

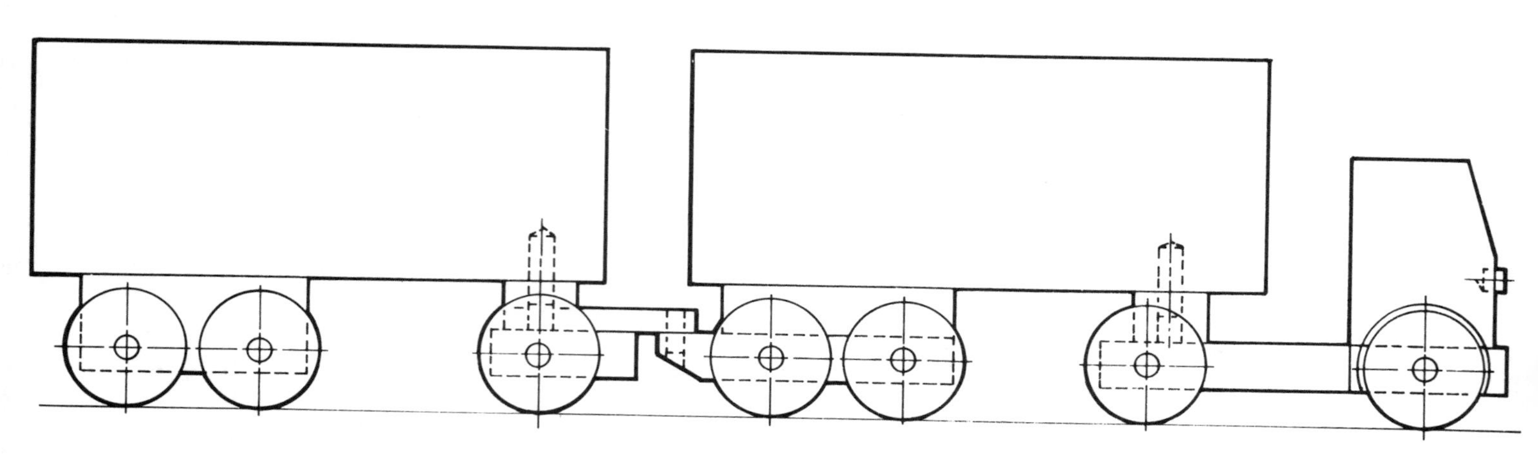

SIDE VIEW

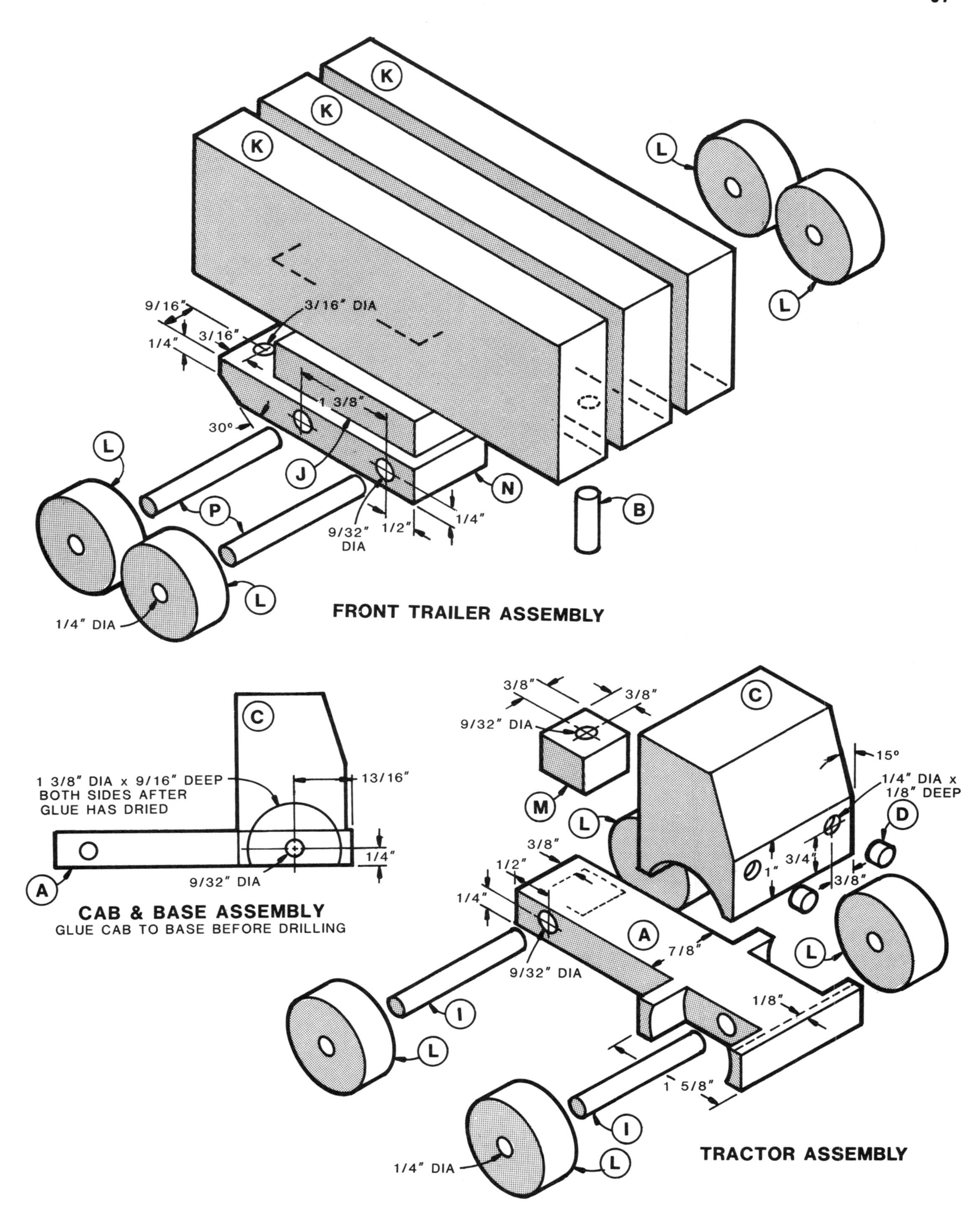

K
K
K
L
L
9/16″
3/16″ DIA
3/16″
1/4″
1 3/8″
30°
L
J
N
P
B
9/32″
DIA
1/2″
1/4″
L
1/4″ DIA
FRONT TRAILER ASSEMBLY
C
1 3/8″ DIA x 9/16″ DEEP
BOTH SIDES AFTER
GLUE HAS DRIED
13/16″
1/4″
A
9/32″ DIA
CAB & BASE ASSEMBLY
GLUE CAB TO BASE BEFORE DRILLING
3/8″
3/8″
9/32″ DIA
C
15°
1/4″ DIA x
1/8″ DEEP
M
L
D
3/8″
1/2″
3/4″
1″
3/8″
1/4″
A
7/8″
9/32″ DIA
L
1/8″
I
L
1 5/8″
I
1/4″ DIA
L
TRACTOR ASSEMBLY

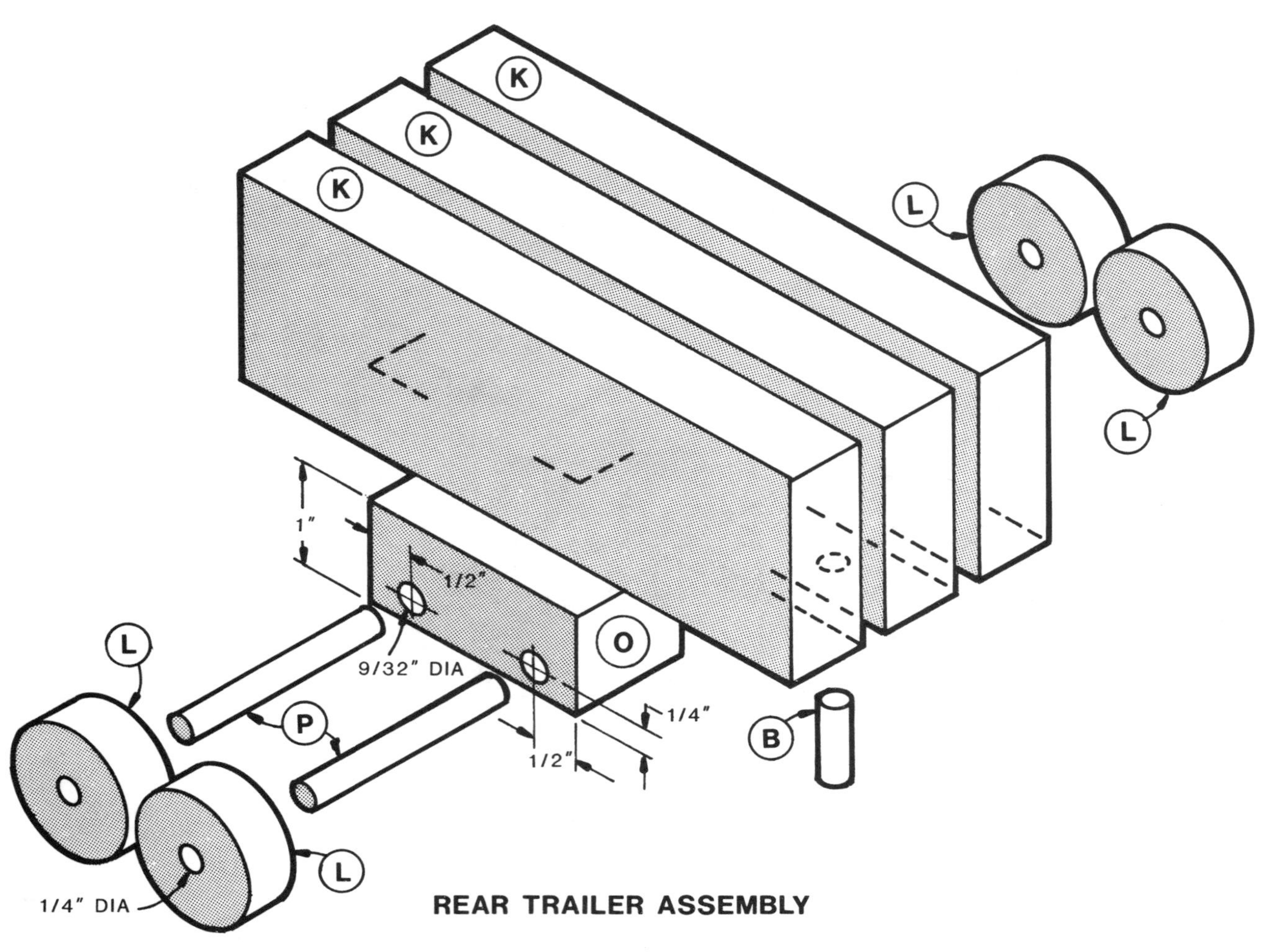

REAR TRAILER ASSEMBLY

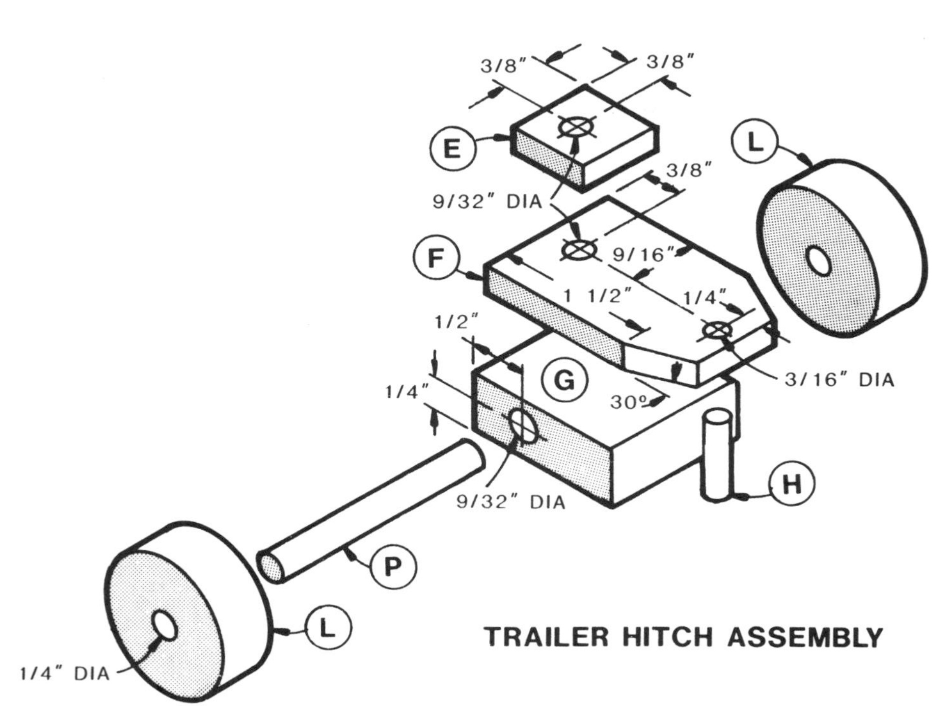

TRAILER HITCH ASSEMBLY

REAR TRAILER

The rear trailer body is again built up of three van blocks (**K**) 3/4" by 2 1/2" by 6". Glue the blocks together and clamp until dry.

The axle block (**O**) is cut to a finished size of 1" thick by 1 1/8" wide by 2 3/8" long. Locate the two axle centers and drill the two 9/32" dia holes.

Glue the axle block to the underside of the trailer body 1/2" from the back edge and 9/16" from the side. Lay out and drill the 1/4" dia hitch pin hole 1/2" deep 11/16" back from the front edge and 1 1/8" from the side.

Cut the hitch pin (**B**) to length from 1/4" dia dowel. Glue the hitch pin into the hole in the van body.

LIST OF MATERIALS
FINISHED DIMENSIONS IN INCHES

A	BASE	1/2 x 2 x 4 1/4
B	HITCH PIN (2)	1/4 DIA x 11/16
C	CAB	1 1/2 x 2 x 2
D	HEADLIGHT (2)	1/4 DIA x 1/4
E	HITCH PLATE	1/4 x 3/4 x 3/4
F	HITCH	1/4 x 1 1/8 x 2
G	HITCH BLOCK	1/2 x 1 1/8 x 1 1/2
H	FRONT HITCH PIN	3/16 DIA x 1/2
I	TRACTOR AXLE (2)	1/4 DIA x 2
J	TANDEM BLOCK	1/2 x 1 1/8 x 2 3/8
K	VAN BLOCK (6)	3/4 x 2 1/2 x 6
L	WHEEL (14)	1 1/4 DIA x 1/2
M	TRAILER HITCH PLATE	1/2 x 3/4 x 3/4
N	TANDEM AXLE BLOCK	1/2 x 1 1/8 x 3 1/16
O	AXLE BLOCK	1 x 1 1/8 x 2 3/8
P	TRAILER AXLE (5)	1/4 DIA x 2 1/4

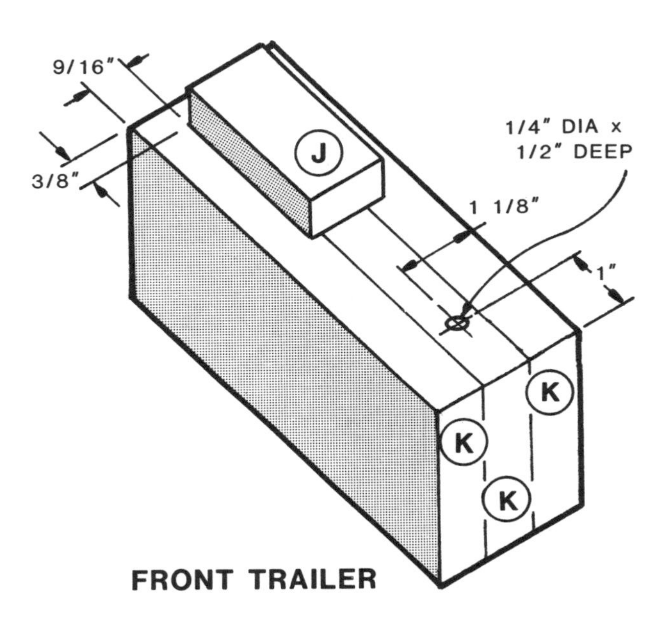

FRONT TRAILER

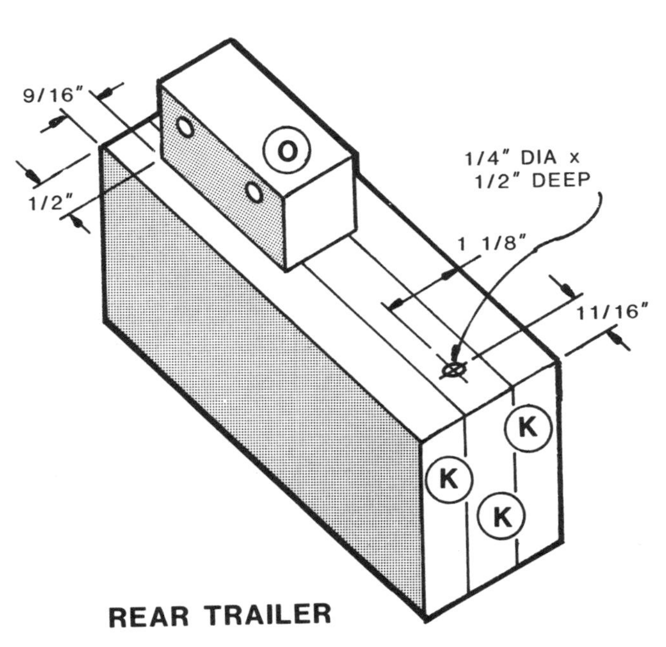

REAR TRAILER

FINAL ASSEMBLY

Cut out all fourteen wheels (**L**) with a 1 3/8" dia hole saw, from 1/2" stock. Sand the cut surfaces smooth and round over the edges. Cut the two tractor axles (**I**) and the five trailer axles (**P**) to length from 1/4" dia dowel. Glue one wheel to each axle.

Sand the pieces with medium grit sandpaper followed with fine grit sandpaper. Remove the dust with a tack cloth and apply two coats of a child-safe finish. After the finish dries, slide the axle wheel assemblies through the axle holes and glue the other wheels in place. Leave about a 1/16" gap between the wheel and base.

Put the hitch pins into their proper holes and the big rigs pair of doubles is ready to roll.

OLD TIMER

Coupe

This toys of wood vehicle has captured that charm of the old time automobile that everyone feels when they see the real thing. The coupe makes a nice size toy for any child.

First cut all the pieces as indicated in the list of materials. After cutting the pieces to size, take the base (**A**) and lay out the axle hole centers as shown on the drawing. Drill the 7/16" dia holes through making sure they are both straight and parallel to each other.

Add the two 1/4 by 45 degree chamfers to the top of the hood (**B**). Lay out and drill the 1/4" dia hole 1/4" deep for the radiator cap (**E**). Glue the radiator cap into the hole.

Lay out the center of the door knob hole on the two doors (**C**). Mark the 1/4" dimension from the front face of one door and the other from the rear face. This will give you a right and left hand door. Drill the 1/4" dia hole 1/4" deep. Glue the door knob (**D**) into the holes.

Chamfer the top of the roof (**F**) on the two sides and the front. The remaining 3" wide end does not get chamfered.

Study the fender detail before cutting the angles on the 1/2" by 3/4" pieces, these pieces are cut to finished length. Take the top rear fender (**G**) and layout the two 30 degree cuts. The back cut is 1/8" up from the bottom. Now carefully sand these angles on a disc sander. Check the angle with an adjustable square. Lay out the two 30 degree angles on the rear fender (**H**) making sure the angles are on opposite sides of the 1/2" face. Lay out the top front fender (**I**) and the front fender (**K**) for 45 degree cuts. The running board (**J**) has a 30 degree angle at one end and a 45 degree at the other end. Sand all the ends to the lines and check the angle of each piece. Glue the fender pieces together on a flat surface. Repeat all the angles for the other fender and glue together.

Lay out the five 2 7/16" dia wheels (**L**) on a piece of 3/4" stock using a compass. Cut the tire outline for the wheels with a 1 1/2" dia hole saw in a drill press. Make the saw cut about 1/16" deep. Cut the

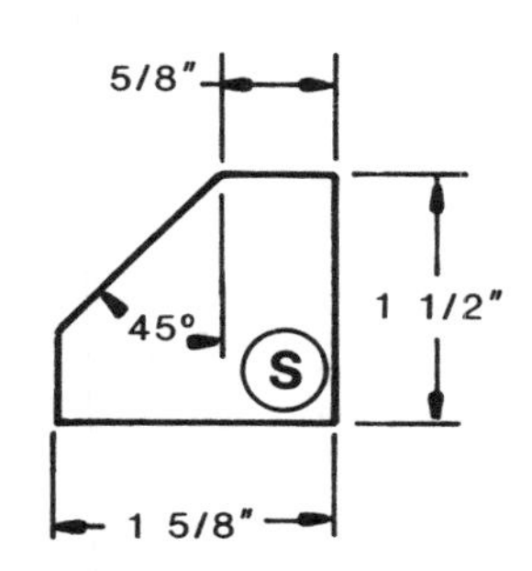

FRONT INSIDE FENDER DETAIL

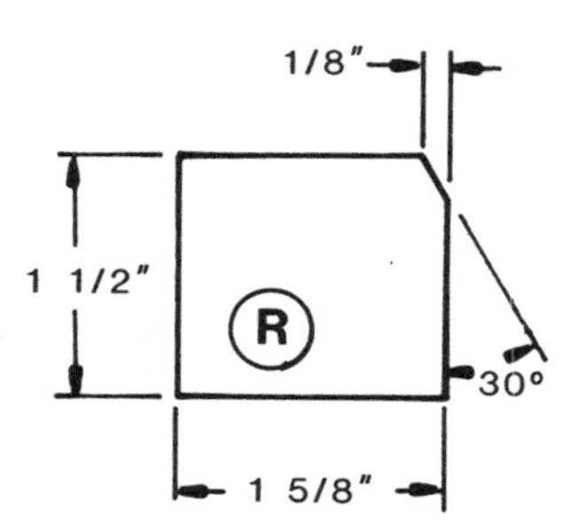

REAR INSIDE FENDER DETAIL

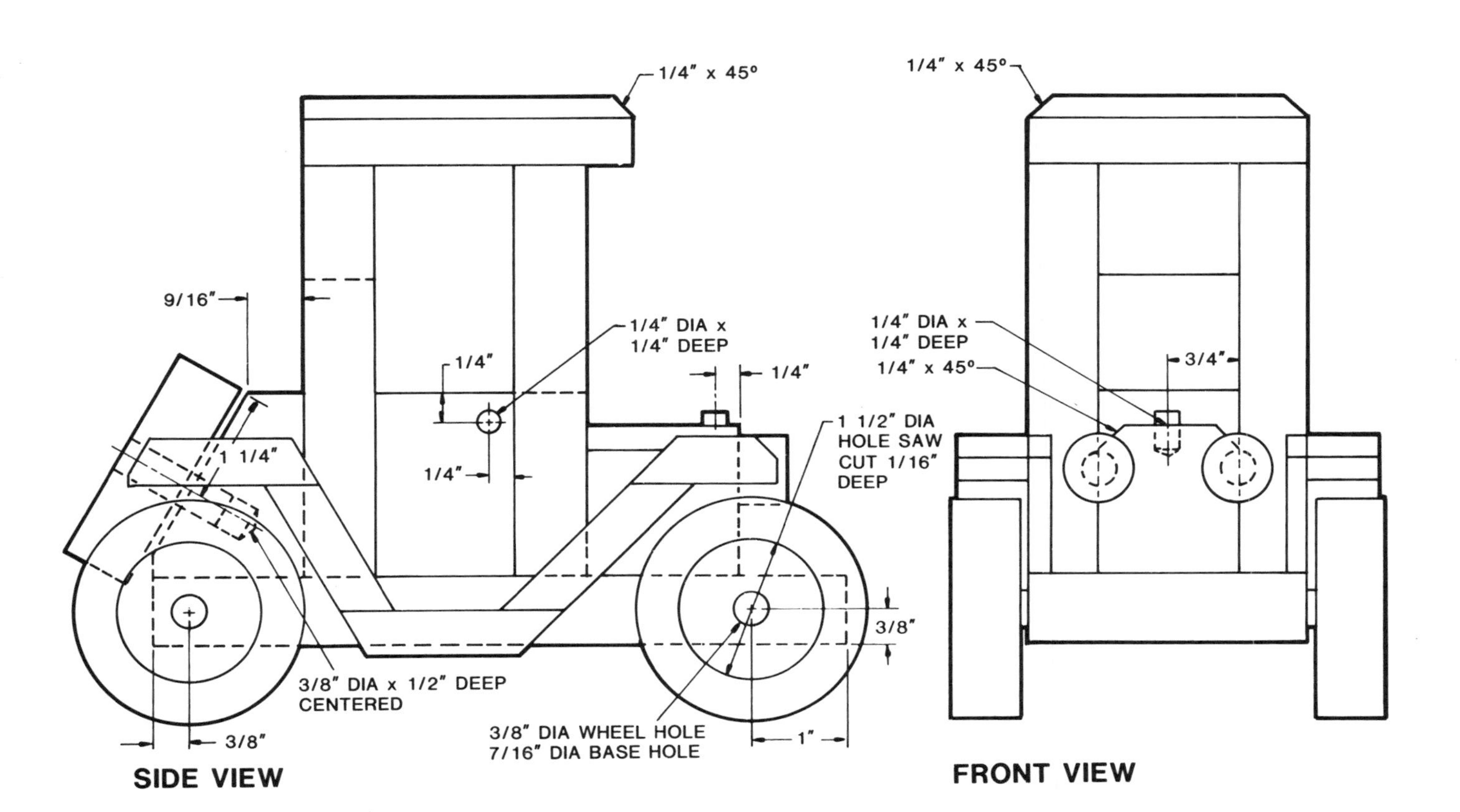

SIDE VIEW

FRONT VIEW

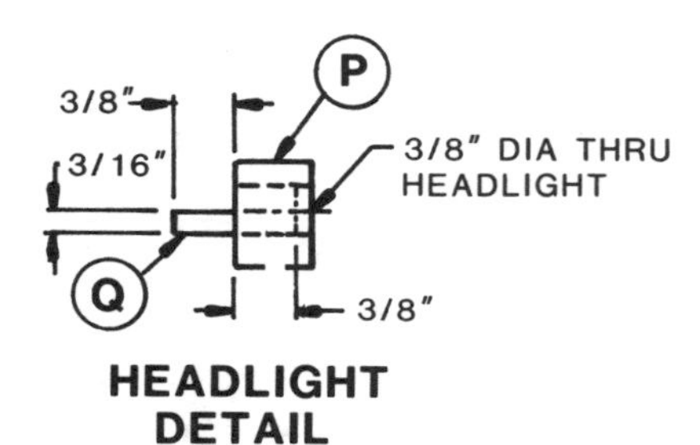

HEADLIGHT DETAIL

wheel out and sand all wheels the same size. Round over the edges with a router.

Glue one wheel to each of the axles (**N**) and one wheel to the spare tire dowel (**M**). The dowels are flush with the outside (tire outline) face of the wheel.

Drill a 3/8" dia hole through the center of each headlight (**P**). Notch the headlight post (**Q**) to the center and 3/8" from the end of the dowel. Glue the post into the headlight hole up to the notch. Glue the headlights to the hood with the centerline of the headlights 1 3/16" up from the bottom of the hood.

Chamfer the two rear inside fenders (**R**) and the two front inside fenders (**S**) as shown in the detail drawings.

The trunk (**U**) is 2" tall with a sloping face 1/4" from the bottom and 9/16" from

LIST OF MATERIALS

FINISHED DIMENSIONS IN INCHES

A	BASE	3/4 x 3 x 7 3/8
B	HOOD	1 1/2 x 1 5/8 x 1 5/8
C	DOOR (2)	3/4 x 1 1/2 x 2
D	DOOR KNOB (2)	1/4 DIA x 3/8
E	RADIATOR CAP	1/4 DIA x 3/8
F	ROOF	3/4 x 3 x 3 1/2
G	TOP REAR FENDER (2)	1/2 x 3/4 x 2
H	REAR FENDER (2)	1/2 x 3/4 x 1 7/8
I	TOP FRONT FENDER (2)	1/2 x 3/4 x 1 9/16
J	RUNNING BOARD (2)	1/2 x 3/4 x 2 3/8
K	FRONT FENDER (2)	1/2 x 3/4 x 2 7/16
L	WHEEL (5)	3/4 x 2 7/16 DIA
M	DOWEL	3/8 DIA X 1 1/4
N	AXLE (2)	3/8 DIA x 4 5/8
O	FIREWALL	3/4 x 1 1/2 x 2
P	HEADLIGHT (2)	3/4 DIA x 1/2
Q	HEADLIGHT POST (2)	3/8 DIA x 3/4
R	REAR INSIDE FENDER (2)	1/4 x 1 1/2 x 1 5/8
S	FRONT INSIDE FENDER (2)	1/4 x 1 1/2 x 1 5/8
T	POST (4)	3/4 x 3/4 x 4 1/2
U	TRUNK	1 1/2 x 1 5/8 x 2
V	BACK	3/4 x 1 1/2 x 3 1/4

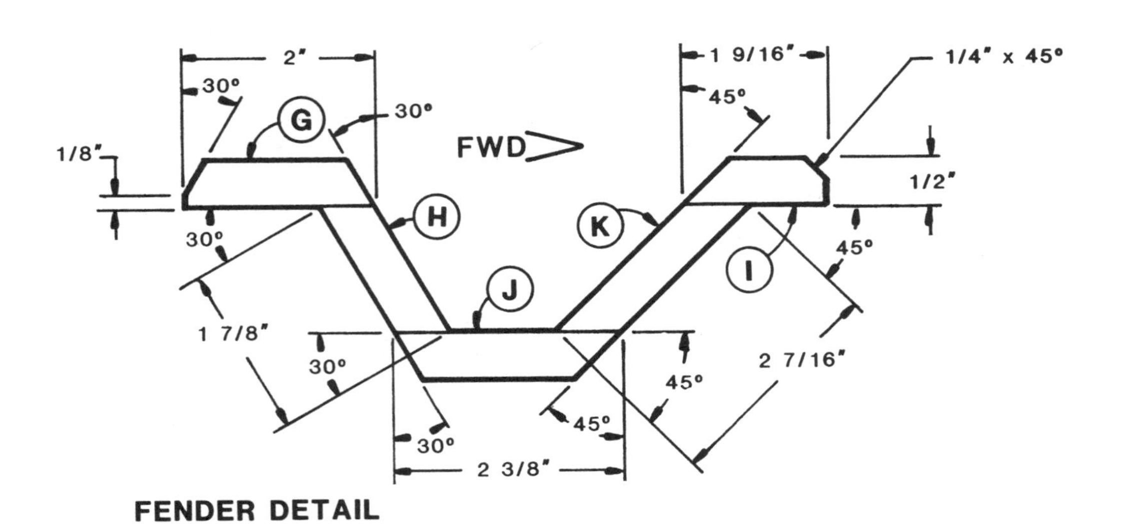

FENDER DETAIL

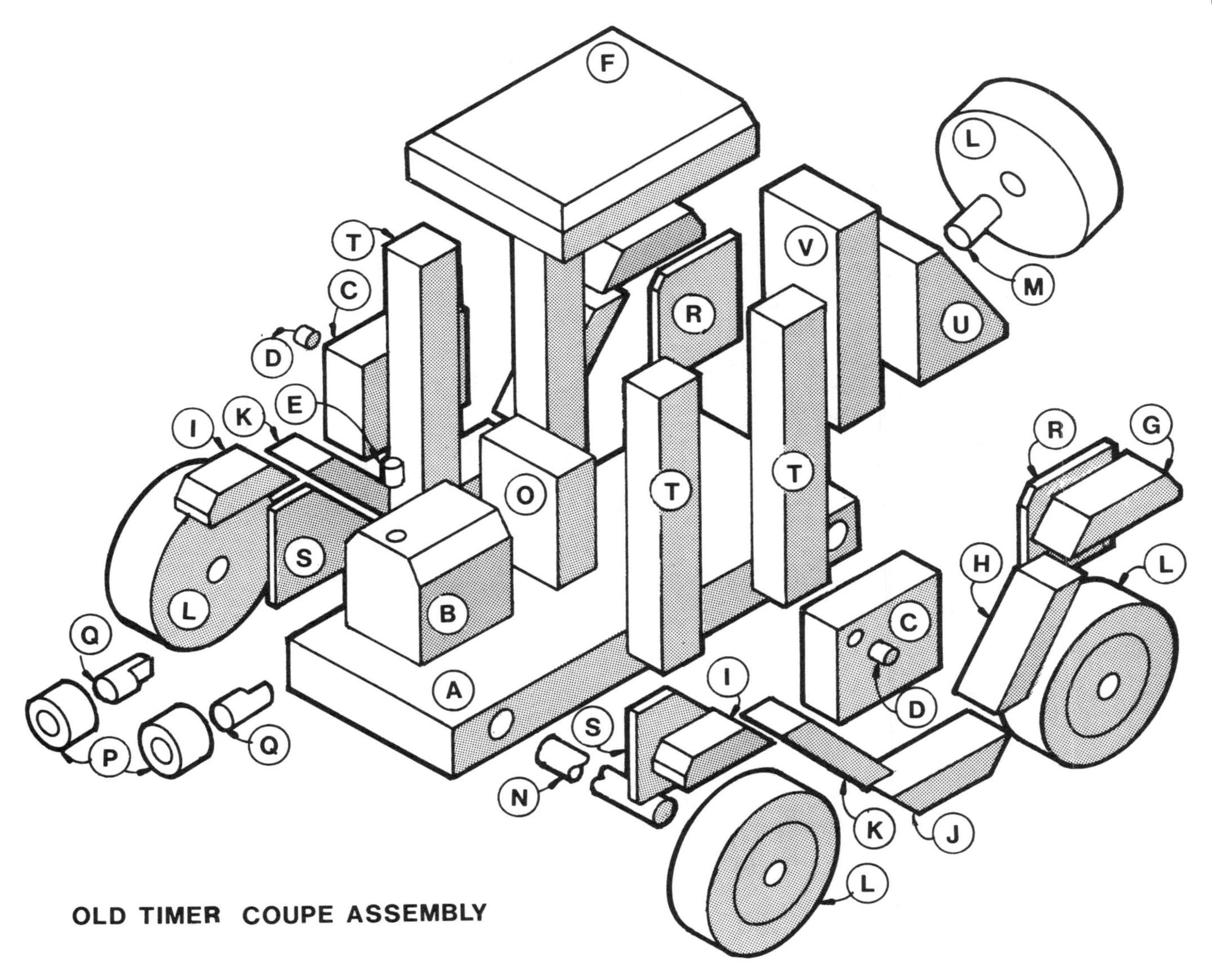

OLD TIMER COUPE ASSEMBLY

the inside face. Lay out the angle and cut away from this line. Sand to the line and check the dimensions. Lay out the spare tire hole centered in the sloping surface and 1 1/4" down from the top. Drill the 3/8" dia hole 1/2" deep.

Glue the trunk to the base flush with the back and centered on the base. Glue the back (**V**) and two posts (**T**) together. Glue the other two posts to the sides of the firewall (**O**). When dry, glue the back post assembly to the base and the trunk. Glue one door on each side to the base and the post. Make sure the door knobs are forward. Glue the firewall post assembly to the base and doors. Glue the roof to the top of the posts and allow to dry.

Attach the fenders to the base and the posts with a small amount of glue. Clamp together with scraps of wood between the fenders and the clamp to prevent marking the fenders. Check the fit of the front and rear inside fenders and make any adjustments necessary before gluing to the base and fender. Glue the hood assembly, with the radiator forward, to the firewall and base. Allow everything to dry overnight.

Sand the finished coupe body and the wheel assemblies with fine grit sandpaper. Remove the dust with a tack cloth, apply a child-safe finish and allow to dry overnight.

Slide the axles through the axle holes and glue the other wheel to the end of the dowel. Glue the spare tire peg into the hole in the trunk.

The old timer coupe is now ready for that child or as a nice decoration on a desk or shelf.

TOY

Hot Rod

The toy hot rod will bring back fond memories of those teenager years. The toy is not difficult to build of pine and maple dowels.

Cut the base (**A**) to size as indicated in the list of materials. Mark and drill the 9/32" dia axle hole and the 1/8" dia by 1/4" deep shift hole.

Lay out the two sides (**B**) on 1/2" stock. Mark the center of the cutouts to clear the wheel and draw the 2 1/4" dia circle. Make the cuts with a band saw and cut the wheel openings with a 2" dia hole saw. Sand the wheel opening to the line with a 2" dia drum sander. Sand a 3/8" by 5/8" chamfer on the front of both sides. Mark the taillight hole on each side as shown in the side detail drawing. Drill the 1/4" dia holes 3/16" deep for the taillight in each side.

Cut the body (**C**) and sand the 1 1/8" radius to the top back edge. Glue the body to the base. Keep the back flush with the back edge of the base. Clamp and allow to dry.

The firewall (**D**) is cut to size. Lay out and drill the 1/4" dia hole for the steering column. Cut the steering wheel (**S**) 3/16" thick from 3/4" dia dowel. Drill a 1/4" dia hole in the center and sand the cut surfaces smooth. Cut the steering column (**T**) to length from 1/4" dia dowel. Glue the steering wheel to the column and the column into the hole in the firewall. Allow the glue to dry.

Glue one side to the base and the body. Glue the firewall to the base and side. Glue the other side to the base, body and firewall and clamp overnight. Put a scrap of wood between the side and the clamp

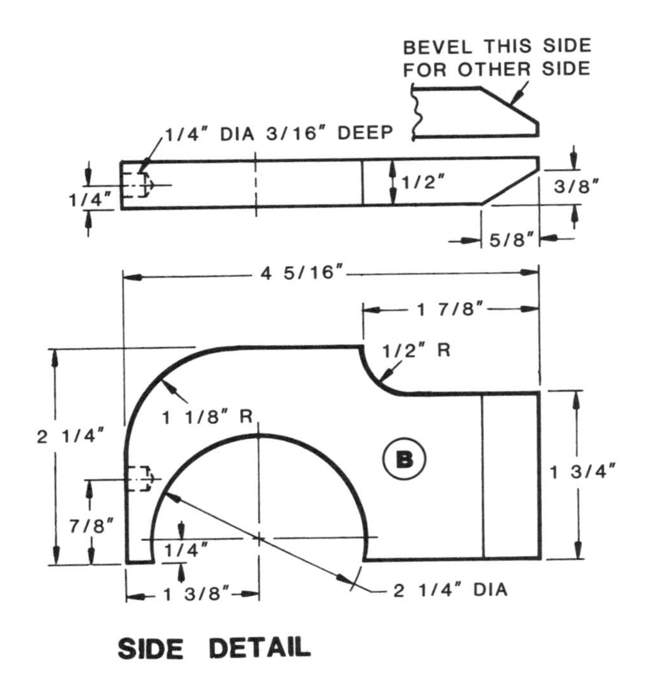

SIDE DETAIL

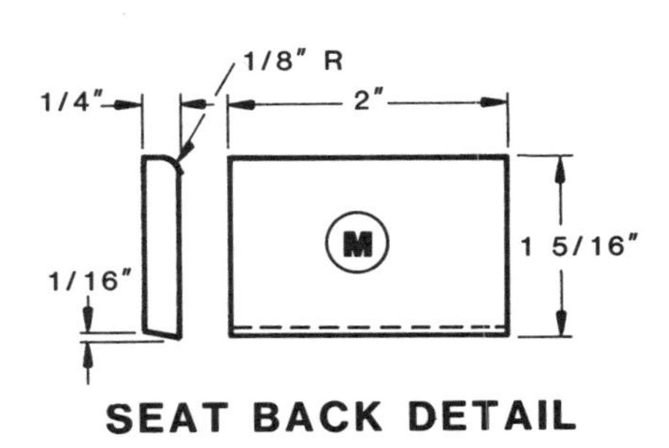

SEAT BACK DETAIL

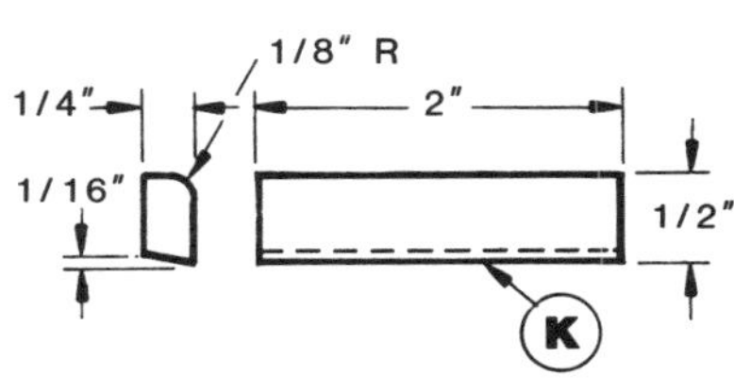

SEAT DETAIL

to prevent marks by the clamp. When dry, sand any mismatch of the body and the sides.

Cut the axle block (**E**) to the size as listed in the list of materials. Glue the axle block to the bottom of the base with the center of the block 3/4" back from the front edge of the base. Drill the 9/32" dia axle hole through the end of the block 1/4" up from the bottom of the block.

Cut the shift (**O**) to length from 1/8" dia dowel. Glue the shift into the hole in

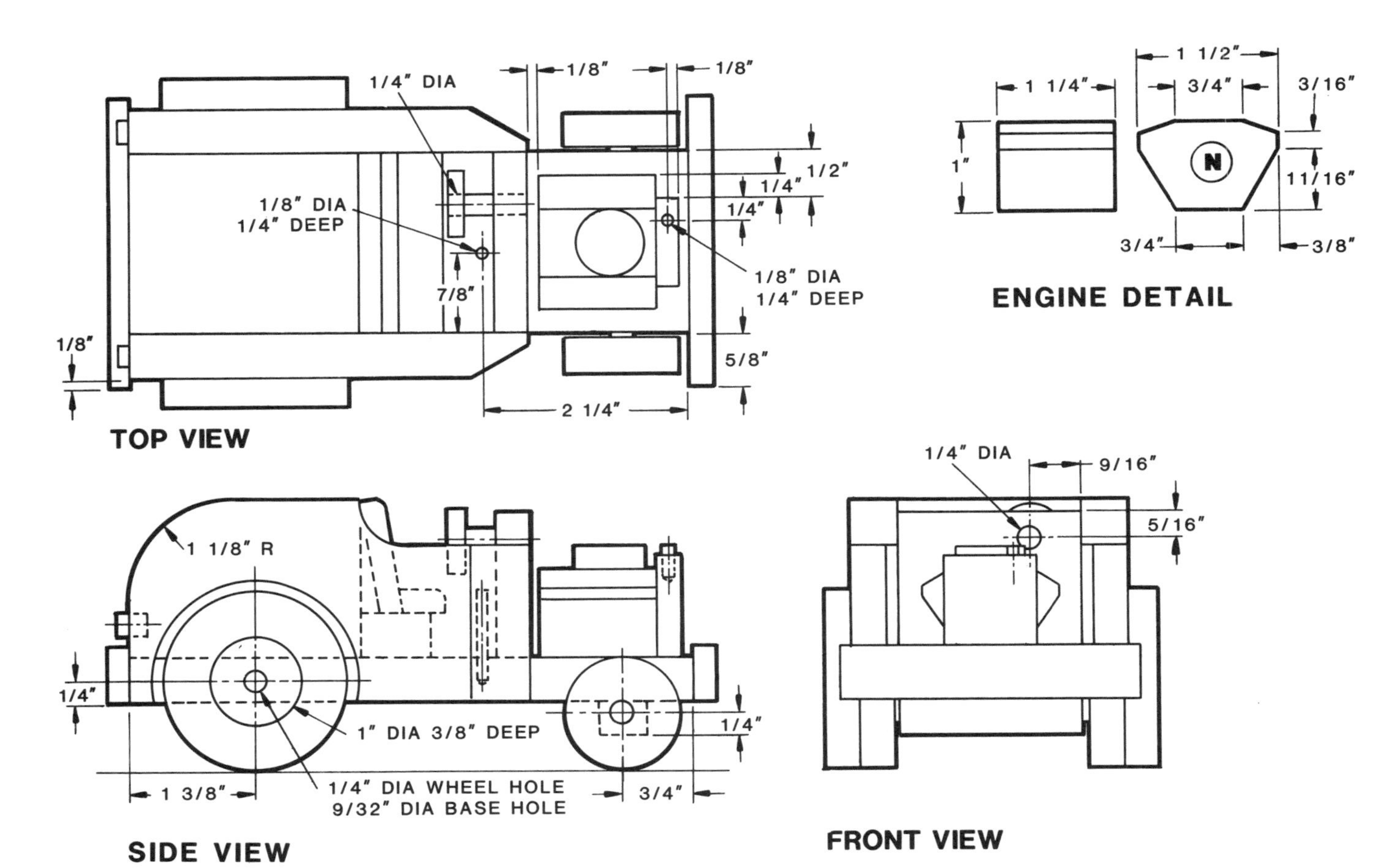

the base. Cut out the seat spacer (**J**), seat (**K**) and seat back (**M**) to size as shown in the list of material. Sand the chamfer and 1/8" radius on the seat and seat back. Glue the pieces in place as shown in the side view drawing.

Cut the two bumpers (**L**) to size. Glue both pieces in place flush with the bottom of the base and with an equal overhang on each side.

The engine (**N**) is made from a block 1" by 1 1/2" by 1 1/4" long. Lay out the angles on each end and carefully sand to the lines. Cut a 1/4" slice of 3/4" dia dowel for the carburetor (**R**). Glue the engine to the base and

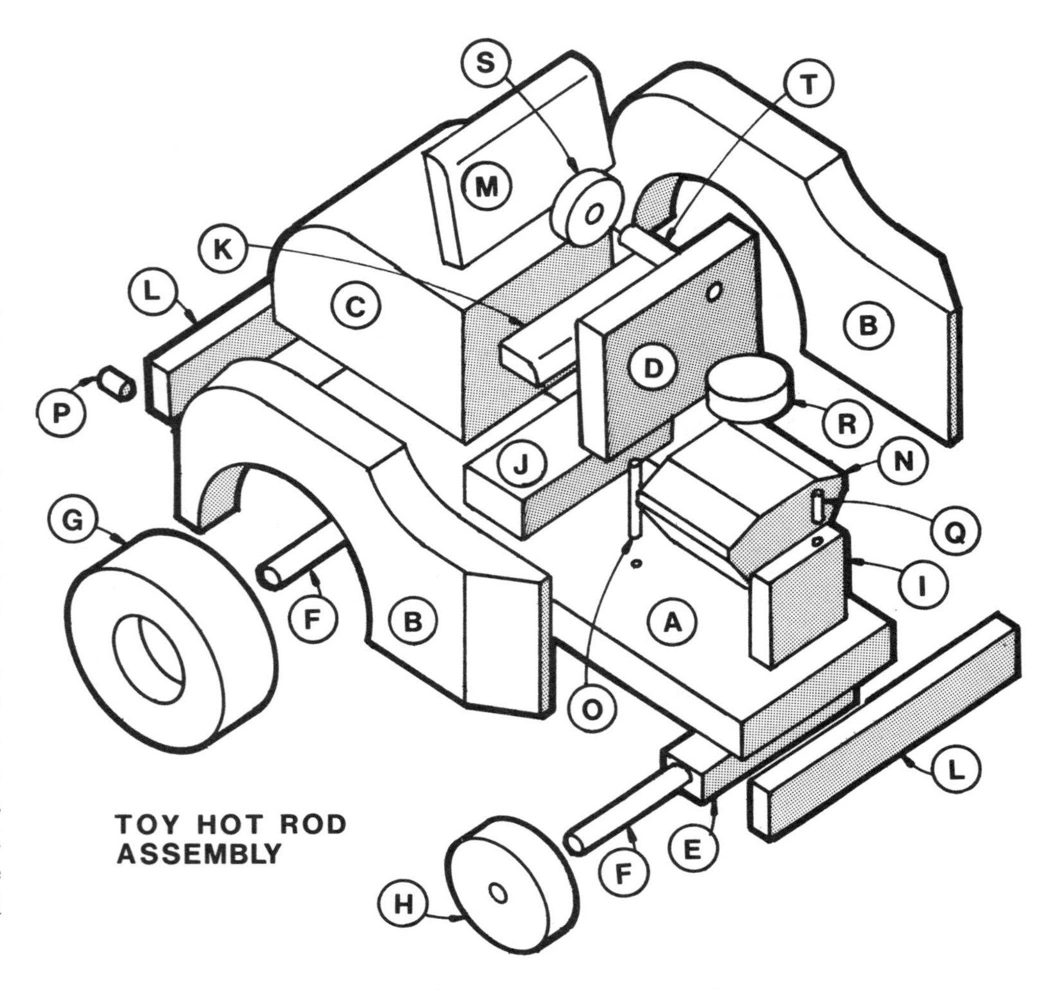

TOY HOT ROD ASSEMBLY

LIST OF MATERIALS

FINISHED DIMENSIONS IN INCHES

A	BASE	1/2 x 2 x 6 1/8
B	SIDE (2)	1/2 x 2 1/4 x 4 5/16
C	BODY	1 3/4 x 2 x 2 1/2
D	FIREWALL	3/8 x 1 5/8 x 2
E	AXLE BLOCK	3/8 x 1/2 x 2
F	AXLE (2)	1/4 DIA x 2 7/8
G	REAR WHEEL (2)	3/4 x 2 DIA
H	WHEEL (2)	3/8 x 1 1/4 DIA
I	RADIATOR	1/4 x 1 x 1 1/8
J	SEAT SPACER	1/2 x 3/4 x 2
K	SEAT	1/4 x 1/2 x 2
L	BUMPER (2)	1/4 x 5/8 x 3 1/4
M	SEAT BACK	1/4 x 1 5/16 x 2
N	ENGINE	1 x 1 1/2 x 1 1/4
O	SHIFT	1/8 DIA x 1
P	TAILLIGHT (2)	1/4 DIA x 5/16
Q	CAP	1/8 DIA x 3/8
R	CARBURETOR	3/4 DIA x 1/4
S	STEERING WHEEL	3/4 DIA x 3/16
T	STEERING COLUMN	1/4 DIA x 7/8

the carburetor to the top of the engine. Cut out the radiator (**I**) from 1/4" stock and drill the 1/8" dia hole 1/4" deep. Cut the cap (**Q**) to length from 1/8" dia dowel. Glue the cap into the hole in the radiator and the radiator to the engine and the base.

Lay out the two rear wheels (**G**) on 3/4" stock. Drill the 1" dia hole 3/8" deep with a Forstner bit. Drill the 1/4" dia hole in the center and cut the wheel. Sand the wheel round and round over the edges.

Wheels (**H**) are cut from 3/8" stock with a circle cutter in a drill press. Sand the cut surface smooth and round over the edges. Cut two axles (**F**) to length from 1/4" dia dowel. Cut two taillights (**P**) from 1/4" dia dowel. Glue one wheel onto each axle. Glue the taillights into the holes in the sides.

Allow the glue to dry overnight and then sand to remove all sharp edges. Remove the dust with a tack cloth. Apply a child-safe finish and allow to dry. Slide the axles into the holes in the base and glue the other wheels to the axles.

Biplane

Cut all the parts to finished size as shown in the list of materials. Lay out the fuselage (**A**) as shown in the detail drawing. Drill the holes for the propeller shaft and tail support.

Lay out the rudder (**B**) and the elevator (**C**) on a 1/2 inch grid square to make a full size pattern. Transfer the outline of the parts onto a piece of 5/16" stock using carbon paper between the pattern and the wood. Cut the parts out using a band saw and sand all edges. Glue the elevator to the fuselage. Then, glue the rudder in place.

The two wings (**D**) are the same finished size. Mark and drill all the holes and sand the radius on the four corners. Cut the 1 1/8" radius notch in the top wing only and sand with a small drum sander. Glue the lower wing into the notch in the fuselage. Glue the eight struts (**H**) into the holes in the lower wing. Put glue into the holes in the top wing and put it in place over the struts.

Add the chamfer to the two supports (**E**) and drill the axle holes. Mark the support locations on the underside of the lower wing and glue the supports in place. The straight edges go forward with the chamfers to the rear.

Make the propeller (**K**) and shaft (**I**) as per the detail drawings.

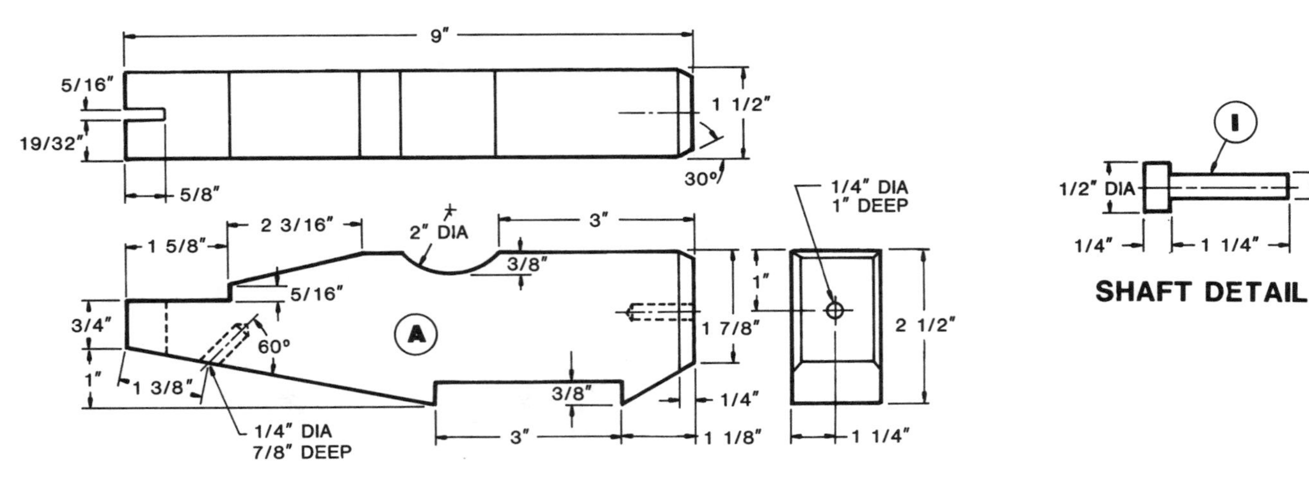

FUSELAGE DETAIL

SHAFT DETAIL

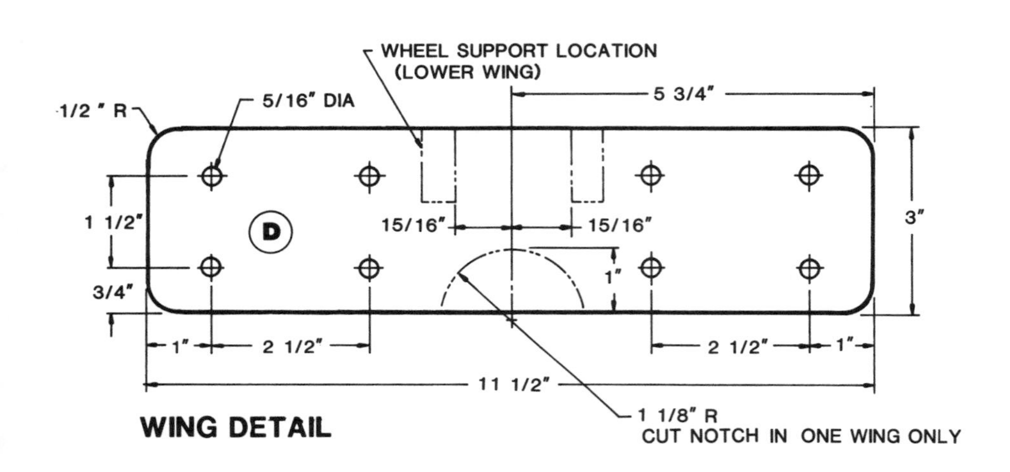

WING DETAIL

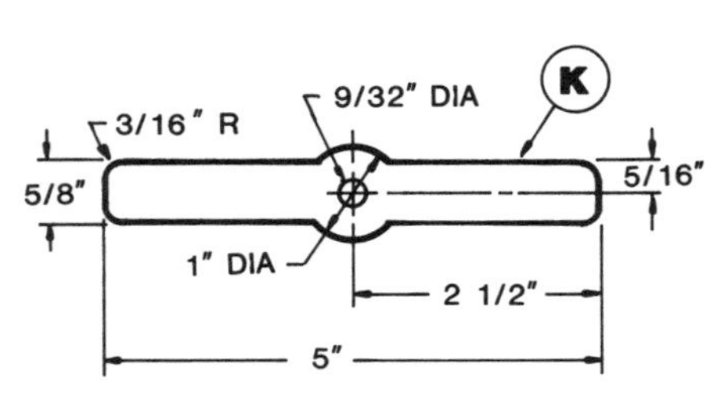

PROPELLER DETAIL

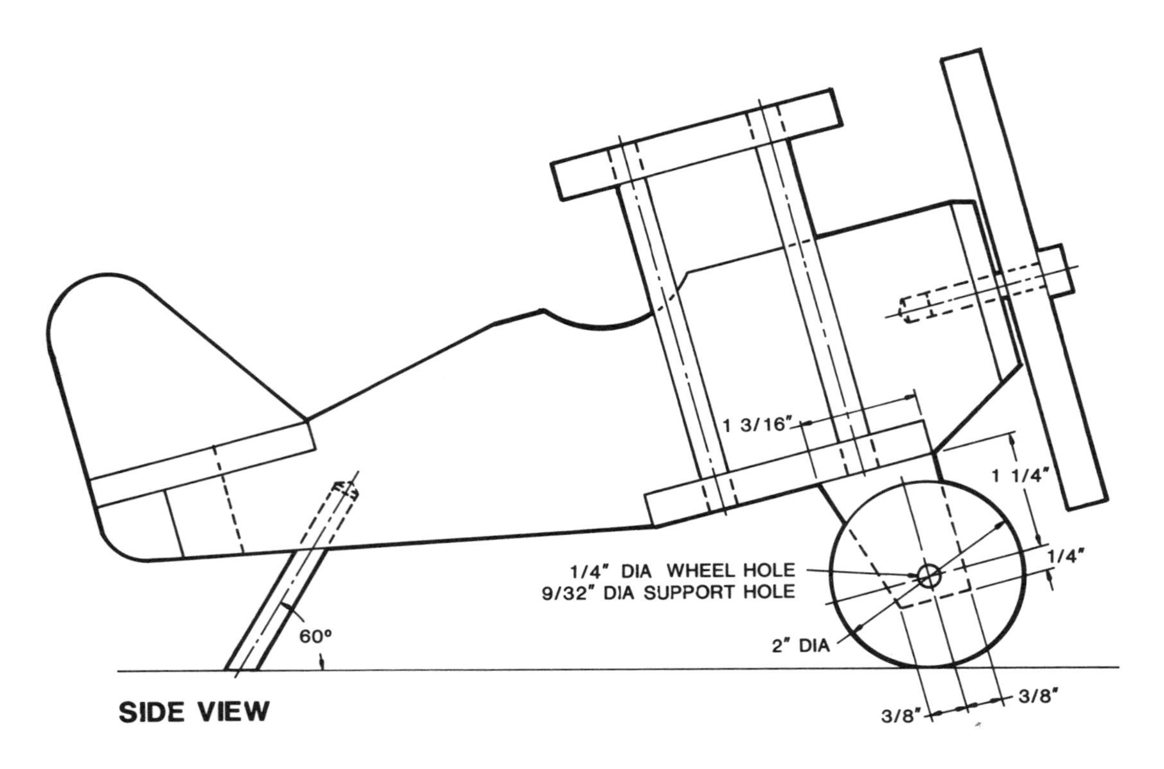

SIDE VIEW

Sand the edges of the two wheels (**J**) and glue one wheel onto the end of the axle (**F**). Cut the 60 degree chamfer on one end of the tail support (**G**). Glue the other end into the hole in the fuselage.

Sand all surfaces with 100-grit sandpaper. Use a tack cloth to remove all the dust. Apply a child-safe finish and allow to dry. Slip the axle into the hole in the support and glue the other wheel to the axle. Leave a small space between the support and the wheel.

Put the propeller onto the shaft and glue the shaft into the hole in the front of the fuselage. Leave about 1/16" gap, so the propeller can turn.

LIST OF MATERIALS

FINISHED DIMENSIONS IN INCHES

A	FUSELAGE	1 1/2 x 2 1/2 x 9
B	RUDDER	5/16 x 2 3/8 x 3 1/8
C	ELEVATOR	5/16 x 2 5/16 x 5 3/4
D	WING (2)	3/8 x 3 x 11 1/2
E	SUPPORT (2)	1/2 x 1 3/16 x 1 1/2
F	AXLE	1/4 DIA x 4
G	TAIL SUPPORT	1/4 DIA x 2 1/4
H	STRUT (8)	5/16 DIA x 4
I	SHAFT	1/2 DIA x 1 1/2
J	WHEEL (2)	1/2 x 2 DIA
K	PROPELLER	3/8 x 1 x 5

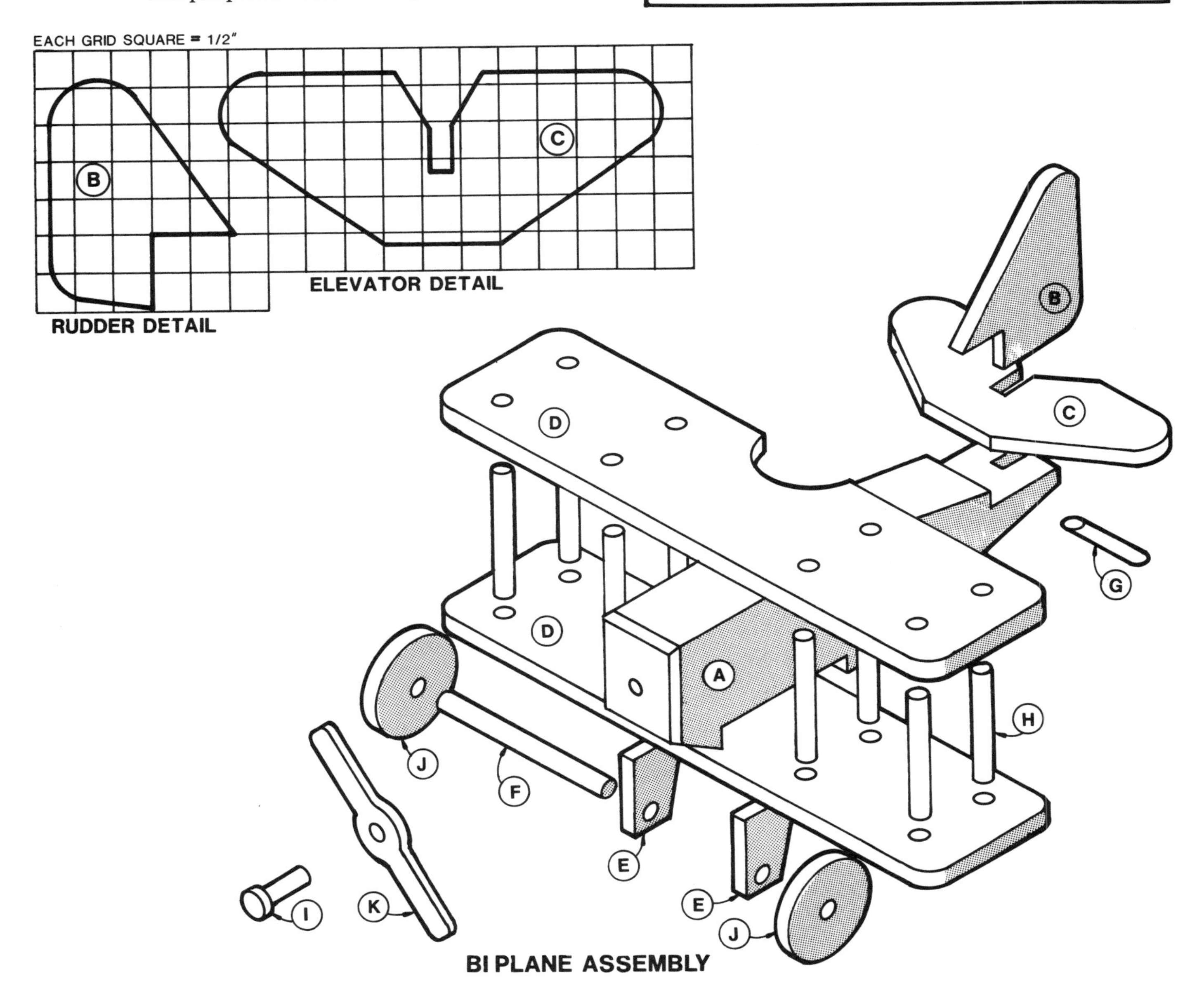

BLOCK'Y

Flatbed Truck

The block'y flatbed truck is not difficult to build since there are only a few parts and all the cuts are straight cuts (except for the wheels). Pine or any hardwood can be used to build this toy. Our toy was built of common 2 pine and maple dowels.

Cut the body (**A**) to size as indicated in the list of materials. Chamfer the body as shown in the drawing. Mark and drill the 9/32" dia axle holes.

Cut the back (**B**) to size. Cut the 1/4" x 45 degree chamfers and sand all edges. Cut the bed (**C**) and sub-bed (**H**) from 1/2" stock.

Cut the cab (**D**) to a block 1 1/2" by 2" by 3 1/2". Cut the cab front face back to form the 1/2" thick roof overhang. Use a band saw and cut away from the line and then sand to the line. Chamfer the roof top as shown in the drawing.

LIST OF MATERIALS
FINISHED DIMENSIONS IN INCHES

A	BODY	3/4 x 1 1/2 x 6 1/4
B	BACK	3/8 x 2 x 3 1/2
C	BED	1/2 x 3 1/2 x 5
D	CAB	1 1/2 x 2 x 3 1/2
E	HOOD	1 x 1 x 1 1/4
F	RADIATOR CAP	1/4 DIA x 1/4
G	WHEEL (6)	1 3/4 DIA x 3/8
H	SUB-BED	1/2 x 1 1/2 x 3 1/4
I	REAR AXLE	1/4 DIA x 3 1/4
J	AXLE	1/4 DIA x 2 3/8

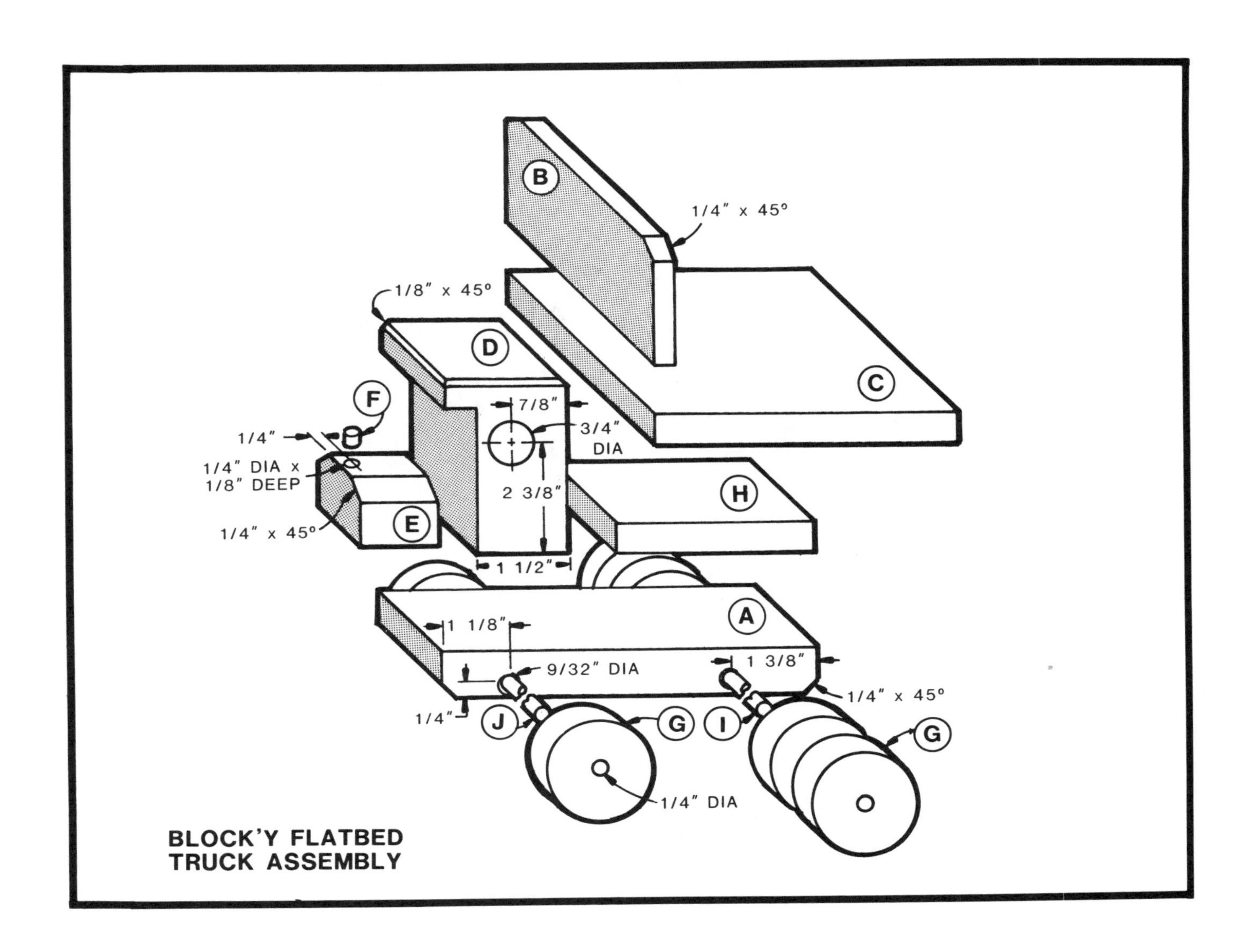

BLOCK'Y FLATBED TRUCK ASSEMBLY

Cut the hood (**E**) to size. Use a disc sander to add the chamfer along both side top edges. Mark and drill a 1/4" dia by 1/8" deep hole for the radiator cap.

Cut the six wheels (**G**) with a 1 7/8" dia hole saw, from 3/8" stock. Sand the cut surface smooth and round over the edges. Cut the rear axle (**I**) and front axle (**J**) to length from 1/4" dia dowel. Cut the radiator cap (**F**) from the same size dowel.

Sand all surfaces with 80-grit sandpaper. Do not round over the exposed edges yet. Then sand with 100-grit followed with 150-grit sandpaper. Use a tack cloth to dust all the wood parts.

Glue the sub-bed to the body flush with the back edge. Allow to dry, then glue the cab to the body and the hood to the body and the cab. Next glue the bed on top of the sub-body keeping equal overhang on both sides. Glue the back on edge to the bed and to the back of the cab. Glue a wheel on one end of each axle. Leave a slight gap between the tandem rear wheels. Allow to dry at least 24 hours.

Finally, round over all exposed edges with sandpaper and remove the dust with a tack cloth. Apply a child-safe finish and allow to dry. Slip the axles into the holes in the body and glue the other wheels to the axles. Leave a slight space between the base and the wheels, and again a slight gap between the tandem rear wheels.

WORK EQUIPMENT
Bulldozer

Construction equipment is a favorite toy for any youngster and this bulldozer wood toy will also fit the bill.

Cut all the parts to finished size as shown in the list of materials. Drill the holes in the base (**A**) and the deck (**B**). Glue the base to the underside of the deck 15/16" from the side and 3/4" from the back.

Chamfer the two base ends (**C**) and the hood top (**D**). Glue the base ends to the base and the underside of the deck. Glue the hood top to the hood (**I**) and then glue the assembly to the top of the deck. Sand full radius on both ends of the tracks (**E**) and drill the 1/4" dia hole. Set the tracks aside for now.

Lay out the two blade supports (**F**) as shown in the blade support detail drawing. Cut and sand to the lines and drill the 1/4" dia hole. Turn down the two 1/2" dia blade pins (**K**) to 1/4" dia for a length of 1 1/2". Draw a diagonal line on one end of the blade bottom (**L**) from one corner to the opposite corner. Cut and then sand the cut surface. Glue the blade bottom to the blade (**J**) and when dry, glue the supports to the back of the blade.

Glue the seat back (**M**) to the back of the seat (**O**). Glue this assembly to the deck. Apply a small amount of glue into the three holes in the deck and the two holes in the hood top. Insert the three levers (**P**) into the deck holes. Insert the

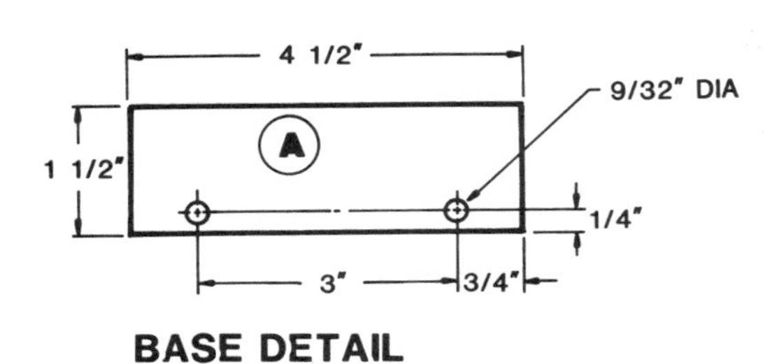

BASE DETAIL

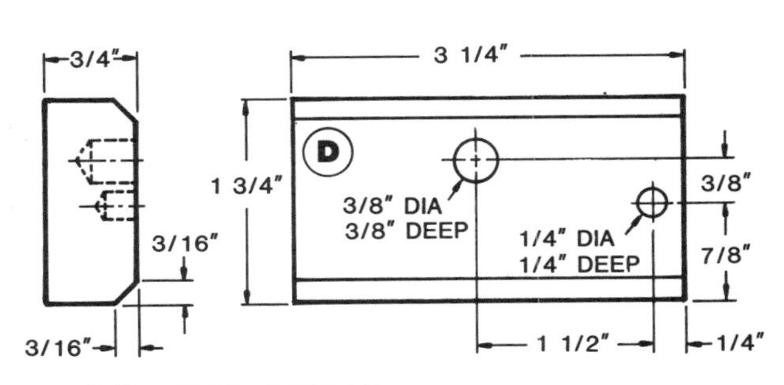

HOOD TOP DETAIL

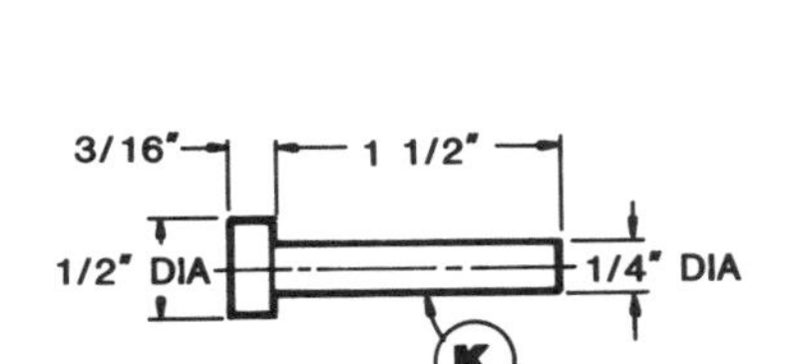

BLADE PIN DETAIL

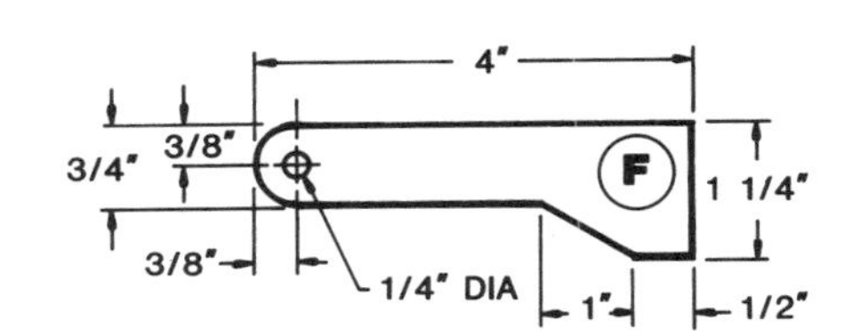

BLADE SUPPORT DETAIL

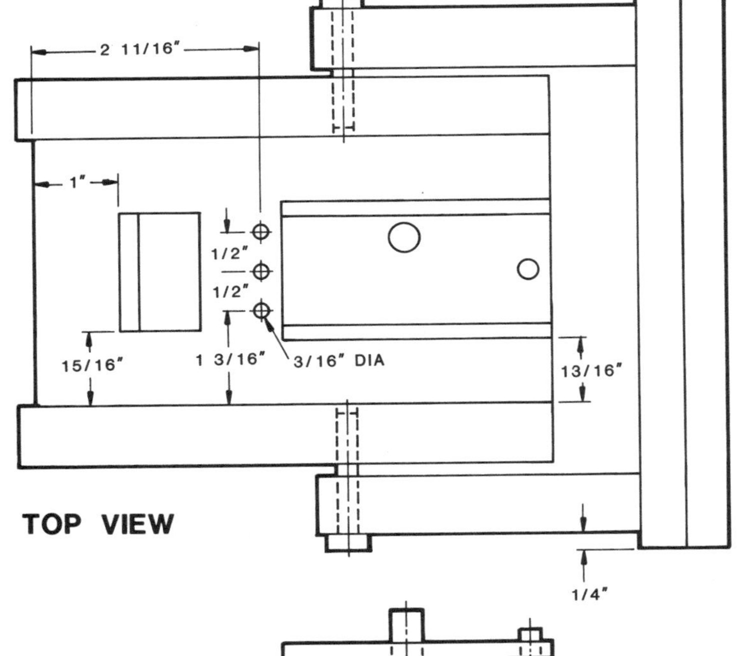

TOP VIEW

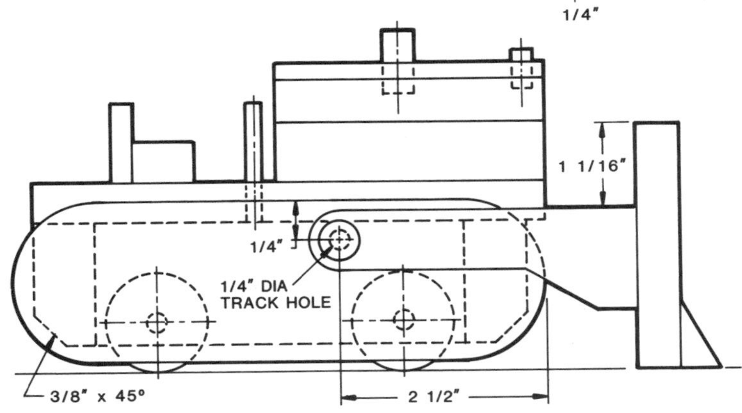

SIDE VIEW

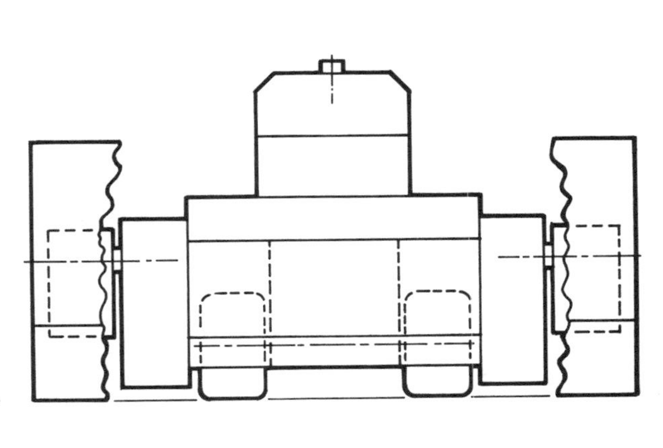

FRONT VIEW

stack (**N**) and the radiator cap (**Q**) into the hood top holes. Glue one wheel (**H**) to each of the axles (**G**).

Sand all surfaces with a fine grit sandpaper. Use a tack cloth to remove all the dust. Apply a child-safe finish and allow to dry. Do not put any finish on the ends of the base ends nor the inside of the track. Slip the axle into the hole in the base and glue the other wheel to the axle. Leave a small space between the base and the wheel. Glue the tracks to the end of the base ends. When dry, insert the blade pins and test the up and down movement of the blade. If the blade pins are a snug fit in the support holes, the blade will stay in the up position when raised. If it does not stay up, make a new blade pin.

Now the bulldozer is ready to be rolled onto the low-boy trailer found elsewhere in this book. They make a fine beginning to the fleet of work equipment.

LIST OF MATERIALS

FINISHED DIMENSIONS IN INCHES

A	BASE	1 1/2 x 1 1/2 x 4 1/2
B	DECK	1/2 x 3 3/8 x 6 3/16
C	BASE ENDS (2)	3/4 x 1 1/2 x 3 3/8
D	HOOD TOP	3/4 x 1 3/4 x 3 1/4
E	TRACK (2)	3/4 x 2 x 6 1/2
F	BLADE SUPPORT (2)	3/4 x 1 1/4 x 4
G	AXLE (2)	1/4 DIA x 3 1/8
H	WHEEL (4)	3/4 x 1 1/4 DIA
I	HOOD	3/4 x 1 3/4 x 3 1/4
J	BLADE	1/2 x 3 x 7
K	BLADE PIN (2)	1/2 DIA x 1 11/16
L	BLADE BOTTOM	1/2 x 7/8 x 7
M	SEAT BACK	1/4 x 1 x 1 1/2
N	STACK	3/8 DIA x 3/4
O	SEAT	1/2 x 3/4 x 1 1/2
P	LEVER (3)	3/16 DIA x 1 3/8
Q	RADIATOR CAP	1/4 DIA x 3/8

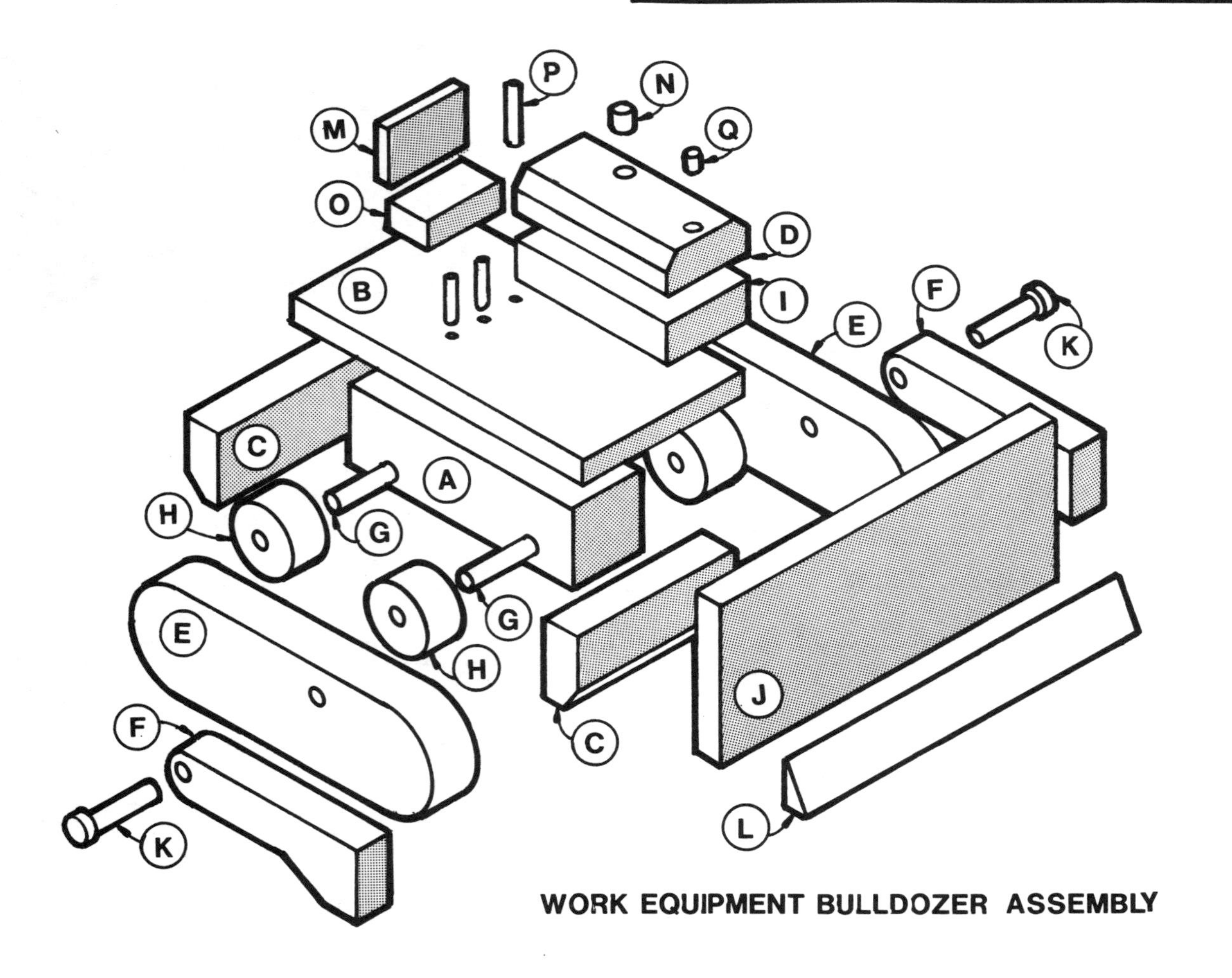

WORK EQUIPMENT BULLDOZER ASSEMBLY

OLD TIMER Delivery

This old timer delivery truck has a charm all its own with the large headlights and enclosed panel sides. It is a perfect companion for the old timer coupe.

Cut base (**A**) 3" wide by 8 1/2" long from 3/4" stock. Lay out the axle hole centers 3/8" from the bottom, 1" from the front edge and 1 1/2" from the back edge. Drill the 7/16" dia holes through the base, making sure they are both straight and parallel to each other.

Next cut the roof (**C**) 3" wide by 6 1/4" long from 3/4" stock. Chamfer the top of the roof 1/4" by 45 degrees on the two sides and the front. The remaining 3" wide back edge does not get chamfered.

Study the fender detail before cutting the angles on the 1/2" by 3/4" stock. First cut all these pieces to finished length as indicated in the list of material. Take the top rear fender (**D**) and lay out the two 30 degree cuts. The back cut is 1/8" up from the bottom. Now carefully sand these an-

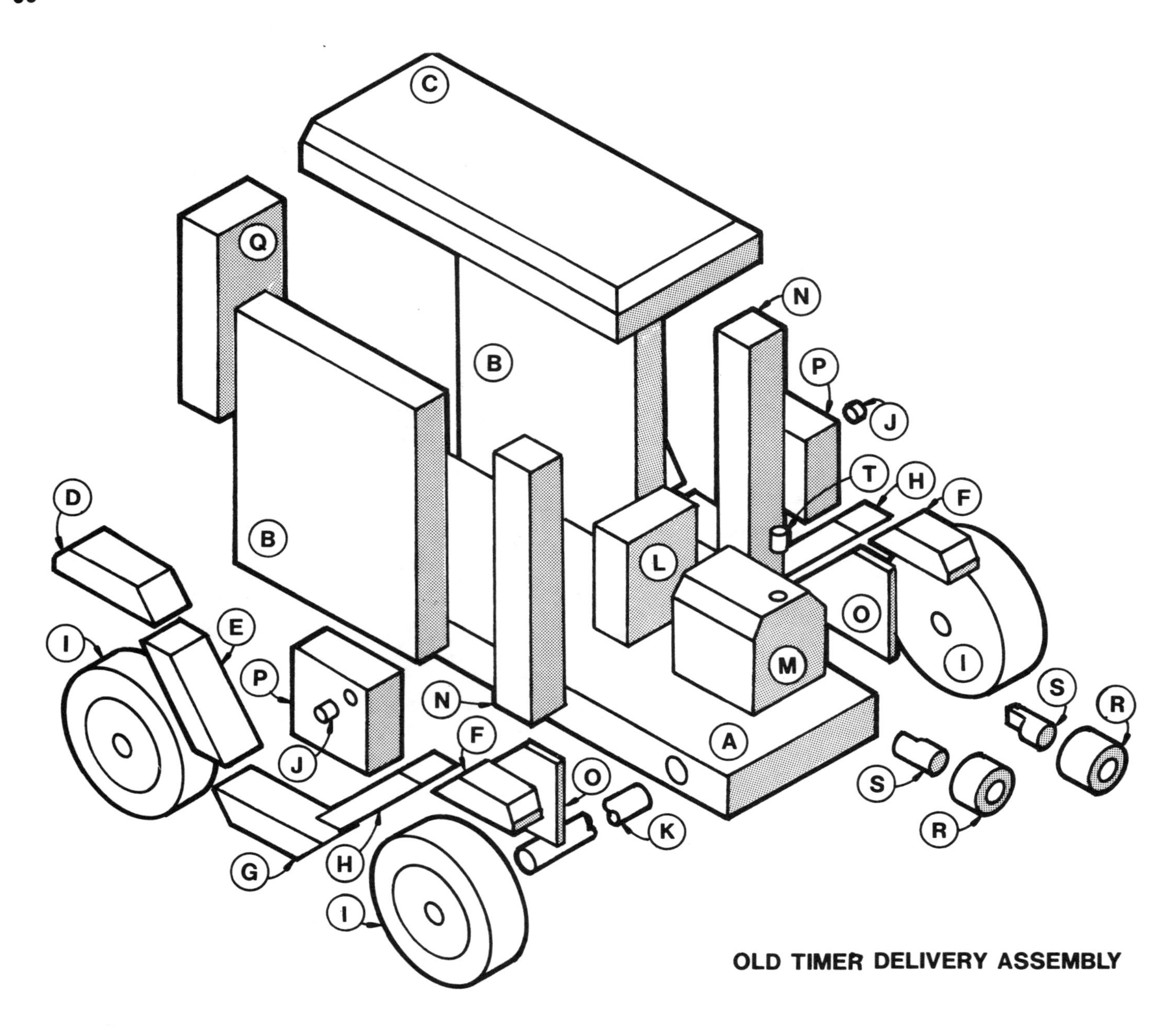

OLD TIMER DELIVERY ASSEMBLY

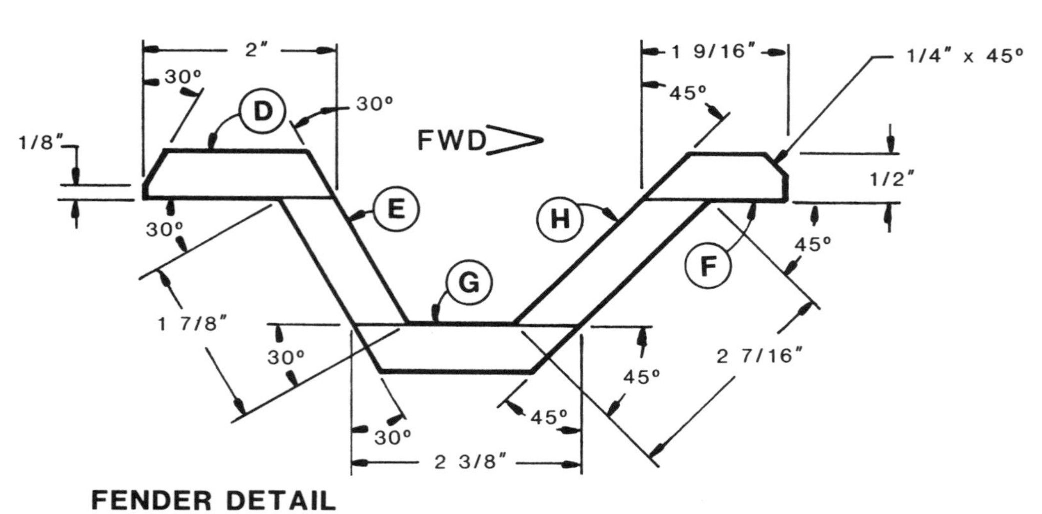

FENDER DETAIL

gles on a disc sander. Check the angle with an adjustable square. Lay out the two 30 degree angles on the rear fender (**E**) making sure the angles are on opposite sides of the 1/2" face. Lay out the top front fender (**F**) and the front fender (**H**) for 45 degree cuts. The running board (**G**) has a 30 degree angle at one end and a 45 degree at the other end. Sand all the ends to the lines and check the angle of each piece. Glue the fender pieces together on a flat surface. Repeat all the angles for the other fender and glue together.

Lay out the four 2 7/16" dia wheels (**I**) on a piece of 3/4" stock using a compass. Cut the tire outline for the wheels with a 1 1/2" dia hole saw in a drill press. Make the saw cut about 1/16" deep. Glue one wheel to each of the axles (**K**). The dowels are flush with the outside (tire outline) face of the wheel.

Next cut the hood (**M**) 1 1/2" by 1 5/8" by 1 5/8" long. Add the two 1/4" by 45 degree chamfer to the top of the hood. Lay

LIST OF MATERIALS

FINISHED DIMENSIONS IN INCHES

A	BASE	3/4 x 3 x 8 1/2
B	SIDE (2)	3/4 x 3 1/2 x 4 1/2
C	ROOF	3/4 x 3 x 6 1/4
D	TOP REAR FENDER (2)	1/2 x 3/4 x 2
E	REAR FENDER (2)	1/2 x 3/4 x 1 7/8
F	TOP FRONT FENDER (2)	1/2 x 3/4 x 1 9/16
G	RUNNING BOARD (2)	1/2 x 3/4 x 2 3/8
H	FRONT FENDER (2)	1/2 x 3/4 x 2 7/16
I	WHEEL (4)	3/4 x 2 7/16 DIA
J	DOOR KNOB (2)	1/4 DIA x 3/8
K	AXLE (2)	3/8 DIA x 4 5/8
L	FIREWALL	3/4 x 1 1/2 x 2
M	HOOD	1 1/2 x 1 5/8 x 1 5/8
N	POST (2)	3/4 x 3/4 x 4 1/2
O	FRONT INSIDE FENDER (2)	1/4 x 1 1/2 x 1 5/8
P	DOOR (2)	3/4 x 1 1/2 x 2
Q	BACK	3/4 x 1 1/2 x 3 1/4
R	HEADLIGHT (2)	3/4 DIA x 1/2
S	HEADLIGHT POST (2)	3/8 DIA x 3/4
T	RADIATOR CAP	1/4 DIA x 3/8

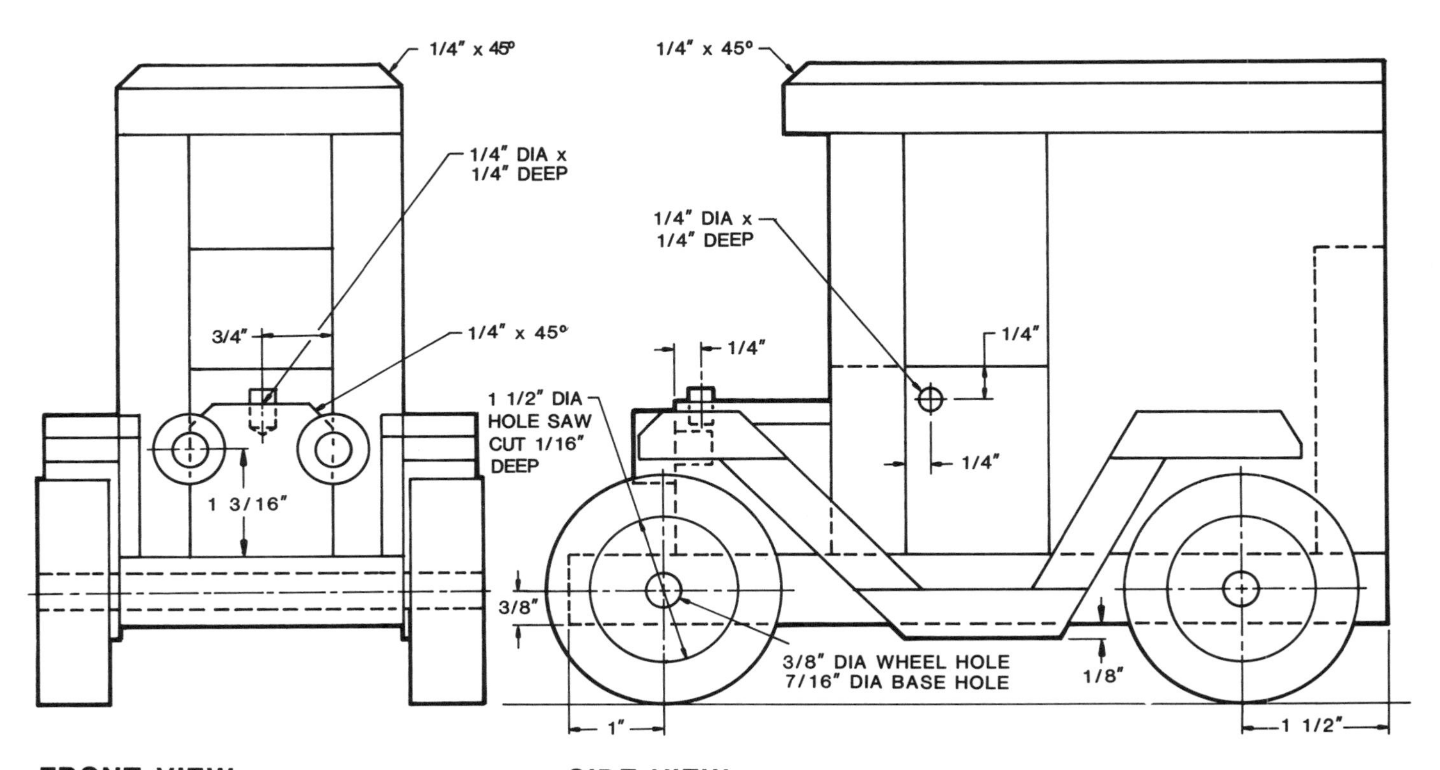

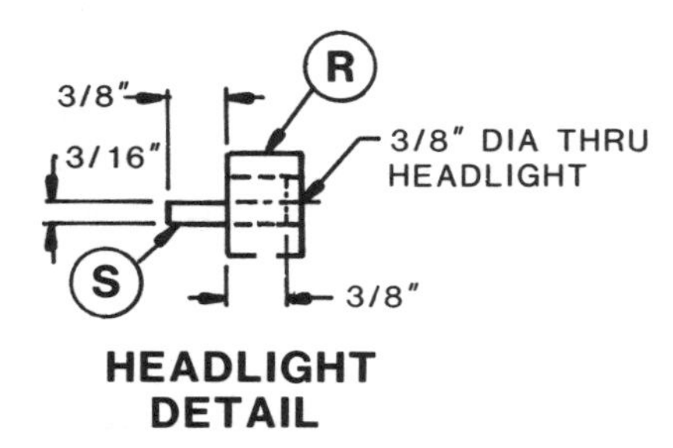

HEADLIGHT DETAIL

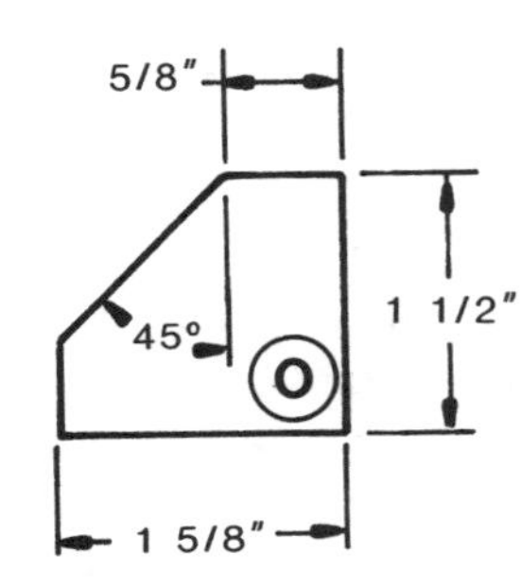

FRONT INSIDE FENDER DETAIL

out the center for the radiator cap hole 1/4" from the front edge and 3/4" from the side. Drill the 1/4" dia hole 1/4" deep. Cut the radiator cap (**T**) 3/8" long from 1/4" dia dowel. Glue the radiator cap into the hole.

Next cut the two front inside fenders (**O**) 1 1/2" by 1 5/8" from 1/4" stock. Lay out the chamfer for the back edge of each piece as shown in the detail drawings. Cut away from the line and then sand to the line of each piece.

Cut the two doors (**P**) 1 1/2" by 2" from 3/4" stock. Lay out the center of the door knob hole 1/4" below the top edge. Mark the 1/4" dimension from the front face of one door and the other from the rear face. This will give you a right and left hand door. Drill the 1/4" dia hole 1/4" deep. Cut the two door knobs (**J**) 3/8" long from 1/4" dia dowel. Glue the door knobs into the holes in each door.

Cut the back (**Q**) 1 1/2" wide by 3 1/4" long from 3/4" stock. Glue the back to the base flush with the back of the base and centered on the base. Next cut two sides (**B**) 3 1/2" wide by 4 1/2" long from 3/4" stock. Glue the sides to the base and back. Cut two posts (**N**) 4 1/2" long from 3/4" x 3/4" stock. Cut the firewall (**L**) 1 1/2" wide by 2" long from 3/4" stock. Glue one post to each side of the firewall. Glue one door on each side to the base and the post. Make sure the door knobs are forward. Glue the firewall post assembly to the base and doors. Glue the roof to the top of the posts and allow to dry.

Cut two headlights (**R**) 1/2" long from 3/4" dia dowel. Drill a 3/8" dia hole through the center of each headlight. Cut two headlight posts(**S**) 3/4" long from 3/8" dia dowel. Notch each post 3/8" from one end to the center of the dowel. Glue the post into the headlight hole up to the notch. Next glue the headlights to the front of the hood with the centerline of the headlights 1 3/16" up from the bottom of the hood.

Attach the fenders to the base, side and post with a small amount of glue. Clamp together with scraps of wood between the fenders and the clamp to prevent marking the fenders. Check the fit of the front inside fenders and make any adjustments necessary before gluing to the base and fender.

Glue the hood assembly to the firewall and base and allow everything to dry overnight.

Sand the finished delivery body and the wheel assemblies with fine grit sandpaper. Remove the dust with a tack cloth, apply a child-safe finish and allow to dry for several days.

Slide the axles through the axle holes and glue the other wheels to the end of the dowels.

The old timer delivery is now ready for that special child or for a quick sale at that next crafts show. This wood toy will also make a nice addition to the desk or display shelf.

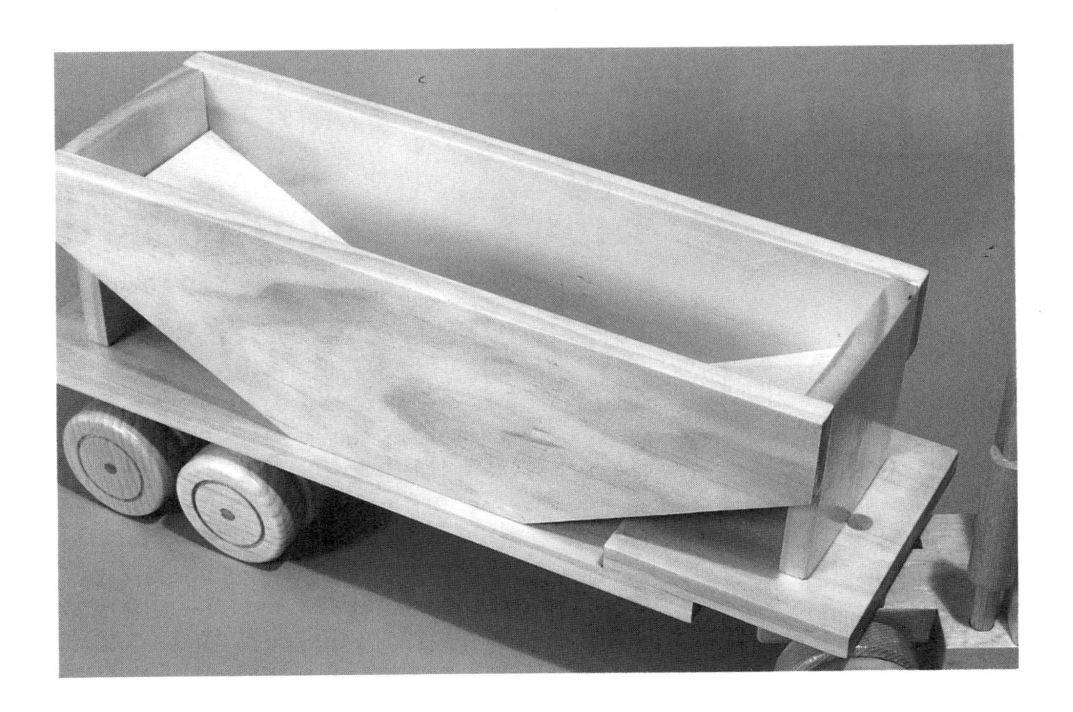

HEAVY HAULERS

Gravel Trailer

The heavy haulers long hood tractor can use this heavy haulers gravel trailer. The trailer can be used outdoors to haul gravel or indoors to haul marbles.

Cut the base (**A**) 4 3/4" wide by 13" long from a piece of 1/2" stock. Cut the hitch base (**B**) 4 3/4" wide by 4" long from 1/2" stock. Lay out and drill the 3/8" dia hitch pin hole at the front of the bed. Glue the hitch base to the bed with a 1 1/2" overlap.

Two sides (**C**) are cut from 1/2" stock. Lay out and cut the two chamfers to each side.

Cut the back (**D**) and the front (**I**) to size. Two bottoms (**E**) are cut from 1/2" stock. Cut the chamfers at both ends. Glue the back and one bottom to one of the sides. Glue the front and the other bottom to the same side. Then glue the other side to the front, back and bottoms. Clamp the parts together and let the glue dry. Then glue the assembly to the base and hitch base.

Cut the bumper (**F**) 1/2" wide by 4 3/4" long from 1/2" stock. Glue the bumper to the bottom of the base.

Cut the hitch pin (**H**) 1 1/8" long from 3/8" dia dowel. Sand a slight chamfer on one end of the dowel. Glue the hitch pin with the chamfered end out into the hole in the hitch base.

Cut a piece of 1 1/2" stock to 1 3/4" wide by 3 1/2" long for the axle block (**J**). Mark the axle hole locations using the dimensions and drill the two 9/32" dia holes through the axle block. Glue the block to the underside of the base 1 1/2" from the base back and 1 5/8" from the side.

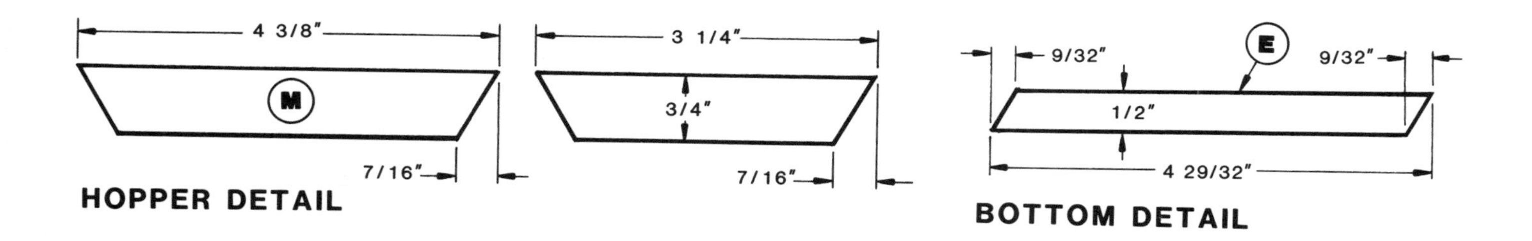

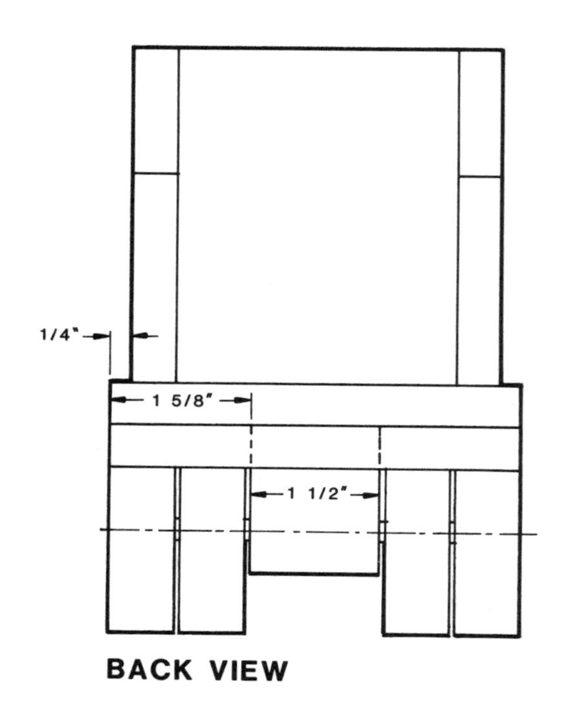

Next cut the hopper (**M**) 3 1/4" wide by 4 3/8" long from 3/4" stock. Cut the chamfers on both ends and sides. Glue the hopper to the underside of the base 3" from the front edge.

There are two different types of wheels needed for the trailer. Lay out the eight 2 1/4" dia wheels on a piece of 3/4" stock using a compass. Cut the tire outline for the four wheels (**K**) with a 1 1/2" dia hole saw. Make the saw cut about 1/16" deep. The four inside wheels (**L**) do not have the tire outline. Cut the eight wheels out with a 2 3/8" dia hole saw. Sand the cut surfaces smooth and round over the edges of the wheels.

Cut the two axles (**G**) from 1/4" dia dowel. Glue one wheel to each axle so the end of the dowel is flush with the outside. Glue the inner wheel to the axle and keep a 1/16" gap between it and the outer wheel.

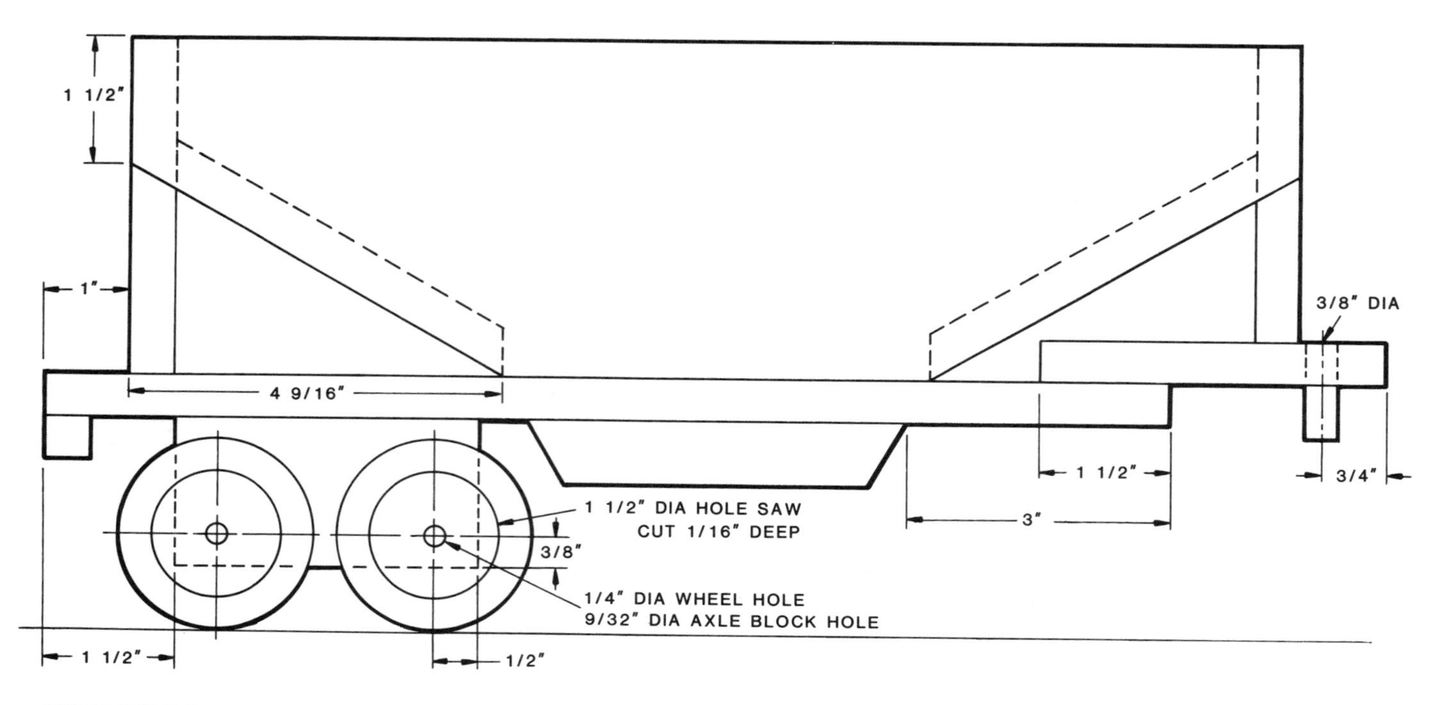

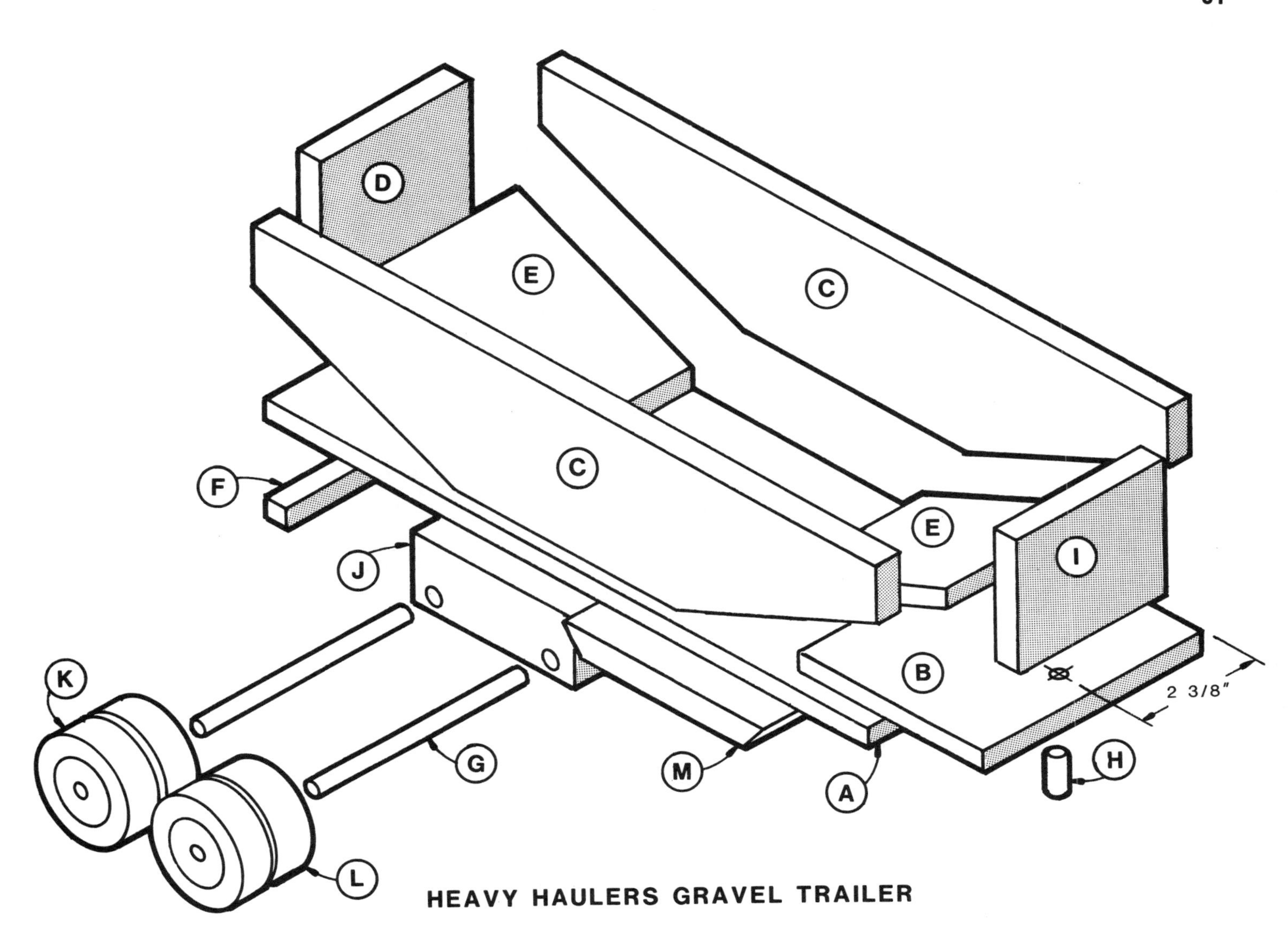

HEAVY HAULERS GRAVEL TRAILER

LIST OF MATERIALS

FINISHED DIMENSIONS IN INCHES

A	BASE	1/2 x 4 3/4 x 13
B	HITCH BASE	1/2 x 4 3/4 x 4
C	SIDE (2)	1/2 x 4 x 13 1/2
D	BACK	1/2 x 3 1/4 x 4
E	BOTTOM (2)	1/2 x 3 1/4 x 4 29/32
F	BUMPER	1/2 x 1/2 x 4 3/4
G	AXLE (2)	1/4 DIA x 4 3/4
H	PIN	3/8 DIA x 1 1/8
I	FRONT	1/2 x 3 1/4 x 3 1/2
J	AXLE BLOCK	1 1/2 x 1 3/4 x 3 1/2
K	WHEEL (4)	3/4 x 2 1/4 DIA
L	WHEEL (4)	3/4 x 2 1/4 DIA
M	HOPPER	3/4 x 3 1/4 x 4 3/8

Sand the assembly and wheels with fine sandpaper. Wipe the parts with a tack cloth to remove all the dust left from sanding. Apply a good grade of child-safe finish. Allow to dry and then slip the axles through the holes in the axle block and glue the other inner wheels to the axle. Leave enough clearance between the bed and the inside wheels so they turn easily. Glue the outer wheels to the axle flush with the face of the outside. This should leave a 1/16" gap between the two wheels. If a gap is not present, move the inner wheel on the axle to get this gap.

Add the gravel trailer to your fleet of heavy haulers. To use this trailer with the cab-over tractor the hitch base should be lengthened to 4 1/2" long.

Low Wing Plane

A WWII fighter plane was the inspiration for this low wing toy plane. The guns are not on the toy. It will be a perfect companion for the biplane found elsewhere in this book.

Cut all the parts to finished size as shown in the list of materials. Lay out the fuselage (**A**) and locate the center of the two holes. Clamp a scrap of wood, that is 1 1/2" thick, to the top of the fuselage. Locate and drill the 2" dia hole for the cockpit. Cut out the notches for the wing and elevator. Cut the bottom sloping surface at the back. Sand the four chamfers at the nose of the fuselage and all the fresh cut surfaces. Drill the two holes with a 1/4" bit.

Using the dimensions shown in the side view drawing, lay out the rudder (**B**). Lay out the elevator (**C**) using the dimensions shown in the detail drawing. Cut with a band saw away from the lines, then sand to the lines. Using the dimensions in the side view drawing, lay out the two supports (**E**).

Lay out the 10 degree end cuts and the 3/8" radius on the wing (**D**) and mark the location for the wheel supports. Cut and then sand the edges and the four corners to form the radius. Glue the wing and the elevator to the fuselage. Allow to dry, then glue the wheel supports to the wing. Slip the axle through the holes in the supports to make sure everything is correct. Glue the rudder to the elevator.

Cut two wheels (**I**) with a 2 1/8" dia hole saw, from 1/2" stock. Sand the cut surface and round over the edges.

Draw the propeller (**J**) on a 1/2 inch grid square to make a full size pattern.

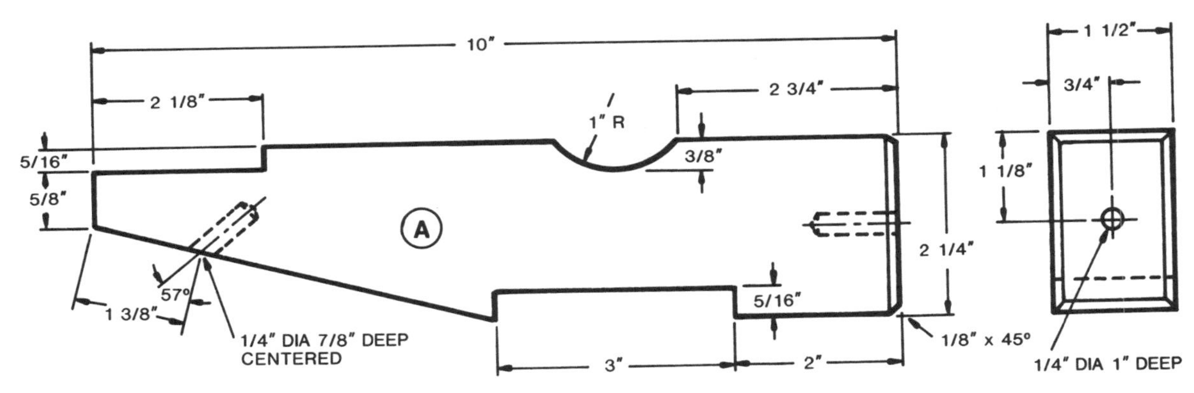

FUSELAGE DETAIL

Transfer the outline and the hole center onto a piece of 3/8" stock using carbon paper between the pattern and the wood. Cut the part out using a scroll saw. Drill the shaft hole with a 9/32" bit.

Glue one wheel to the axle (**F**) and temporarily slip the axle into the support holes and the other wheel to the axle. Insert the tail support (**G**) into the hole in the fuselage. Place the plane on a flat surface and mark the end of the tail support. Remove the tail support and sand the end. Put a small amount of glue into the hole and slip the tail support into the hole. Place on the flat surface again and make final adjustments to the tail support. Remove the wheel and the wheel axle assembly.

Turn the shaft (**H**) diameter down to 1/4" for a length of 1 1/4". Sand all surfaces with sandpaper and wipe with a tack cloth to remove all the dust left from sanding. Apply a good grade of child-safe finish. Allow to dry, then slip the axle through the support holes and glue the other wheel to the axle. Put some glue into the hole in the front of the fuselage. Slip the propeller onto the shaft and the shaft into the hole.

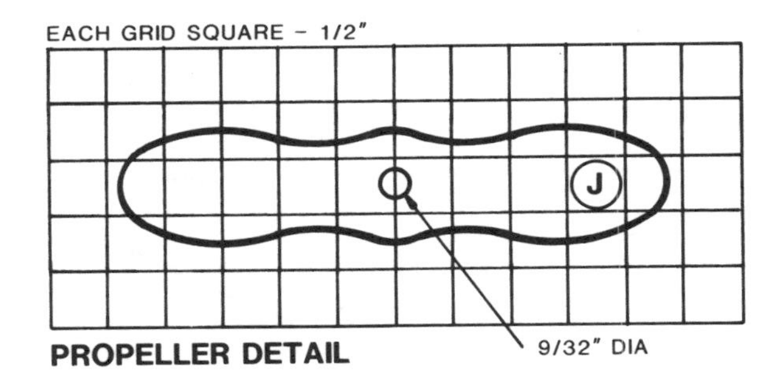

PROPELLER DETAIL

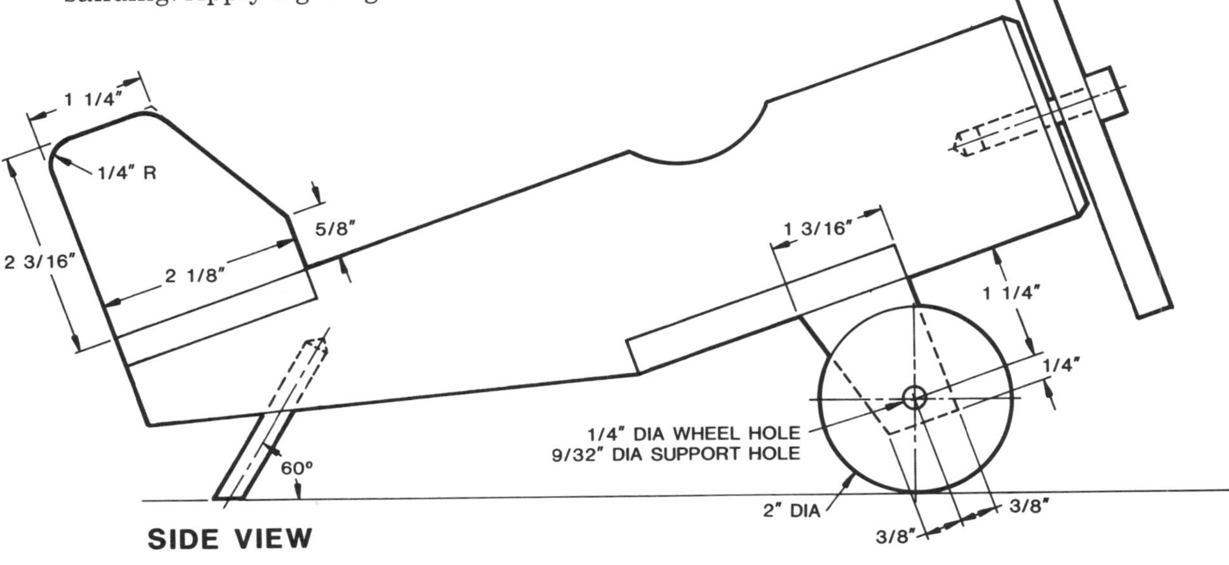

SIDE VIEW

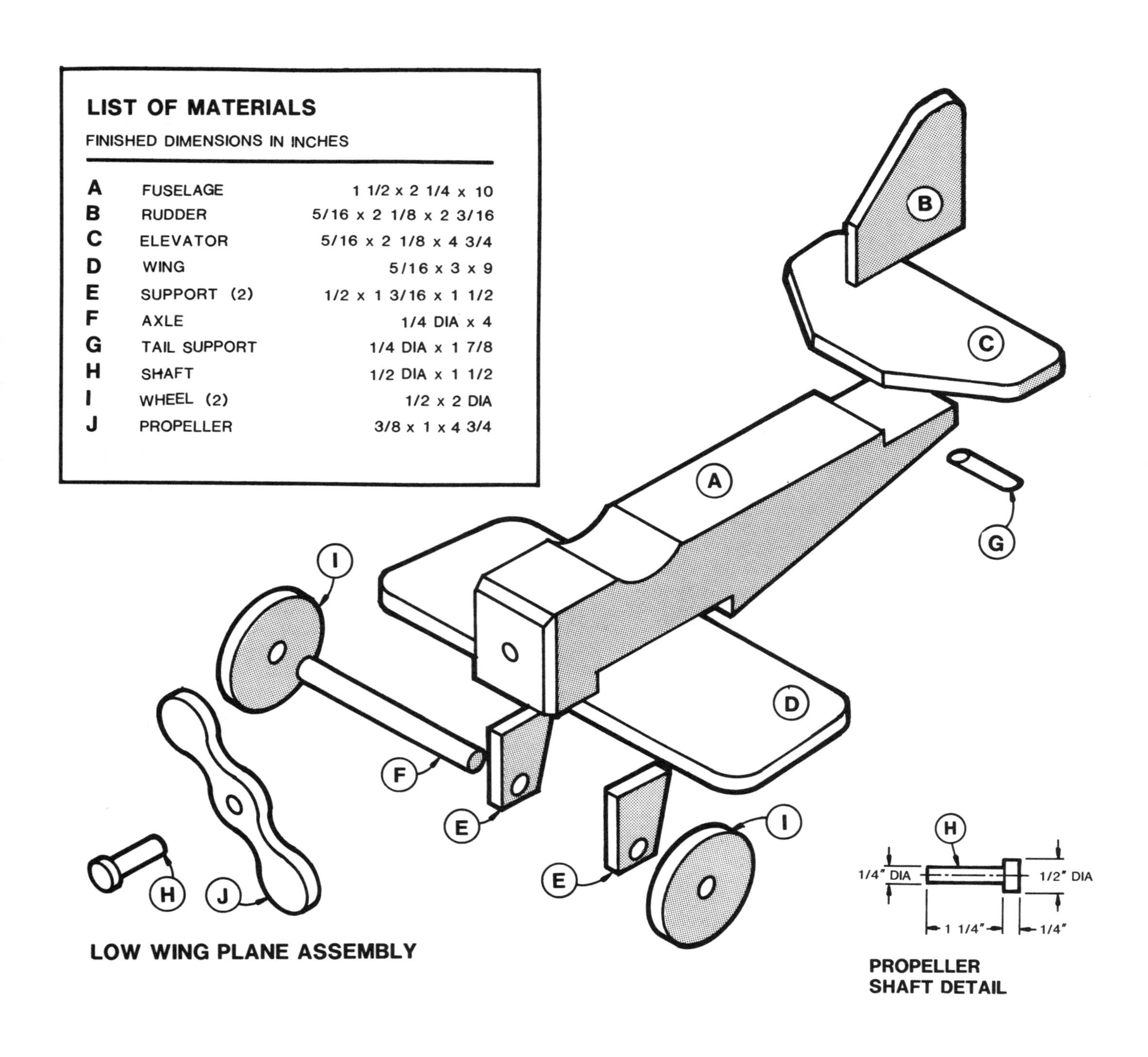

LIST OF MATERIALS

FINISHED DIMENSIONS IN INCHES

A	FUSELAGE	1 1/2 x 2 1/4 x 10
B	RUDDER	5/16 x 2 1/8 x 2 3/16
C	ELEVATOR	5/16 x 2 1/8 x 4 3/4
D	WING	5/16 x 3 x 9
E	SUPPORT (2)	1/2 x 1 3/16 x 1 1/2
F	AXLE	1/4 DIA x 4
G	TAIL SUPPORT	1/4 DIA x 1 7/8
H	SHAFT	1/2 DIA x 1 1/2
I	WHEEL (2)	1/2 x 2 DIA
J	PROPELLER	3/8 x 1 x 4 3/4

LOW WING PLANE ASSEMBLY

PROPELLER SHAFT DETAIL

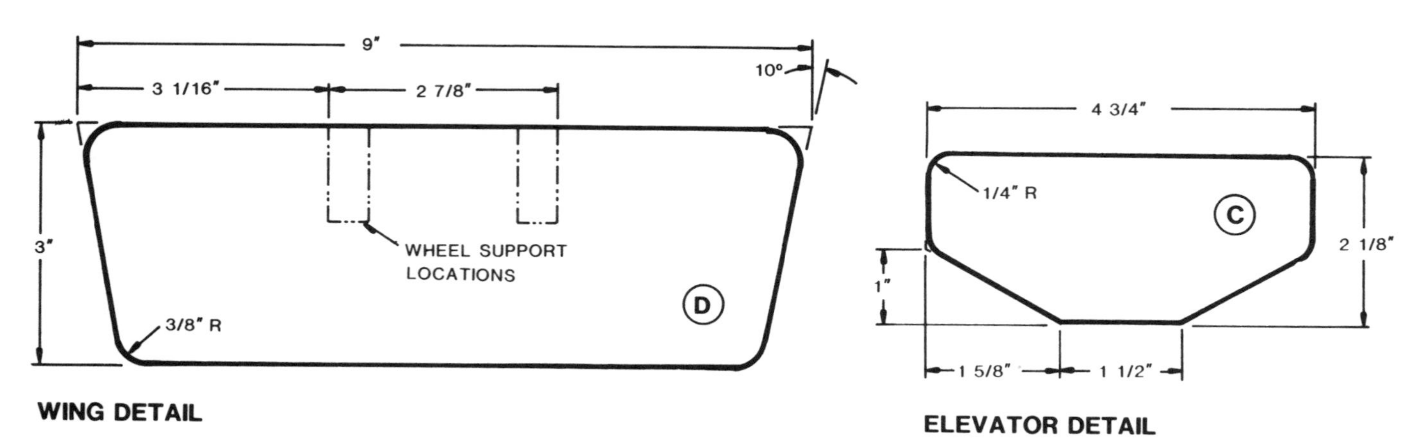

WING DETAIL

ELEVATOR DETAIL

HEAVY HAULERS

Cab-Over Tractor

The heavy haulers van and tank trailers in this book can use this cab-over tractor. In particular, it looks good pulling the tank trailer. By eliminating one axle and the wheels of the rear tandem wheel assembly and making the base shorter, a six-wheel tractor is possible.

Cut the base (**A**) from 3/4" stock to 3" wide by 9 3/4" long. Lay out the notch on both sides at the rear and cut with a band saw. Cut away from the line and sand to the line with a 1" wide belt sander. Lay out and mark the exhaust stack hole with an awl and drill the 3/8" dia hole.

Cut the front axle block (**K**) and the rear axle block (**L**) from 3/4" stock. Mark and drill the 9/32" dia axle holes in each block as shown in the drawing.

Mark the underside of the base for the axle blocks. The front axle block is 1 1/8" back from the front and the rear axle block is 7/8" from the back. Glue the blocks to the base and check the squareness with a square before clamping. Place scraps of wood under the clamp head to prevent denting the part. Check the squareness of the axle blocks again and loosen the clamps and make adjustments if necessary, then re-clamp the parts.

Glue up stock for the 3" wide cab (**E**) and allow the glue to dry. Lay out the 3"

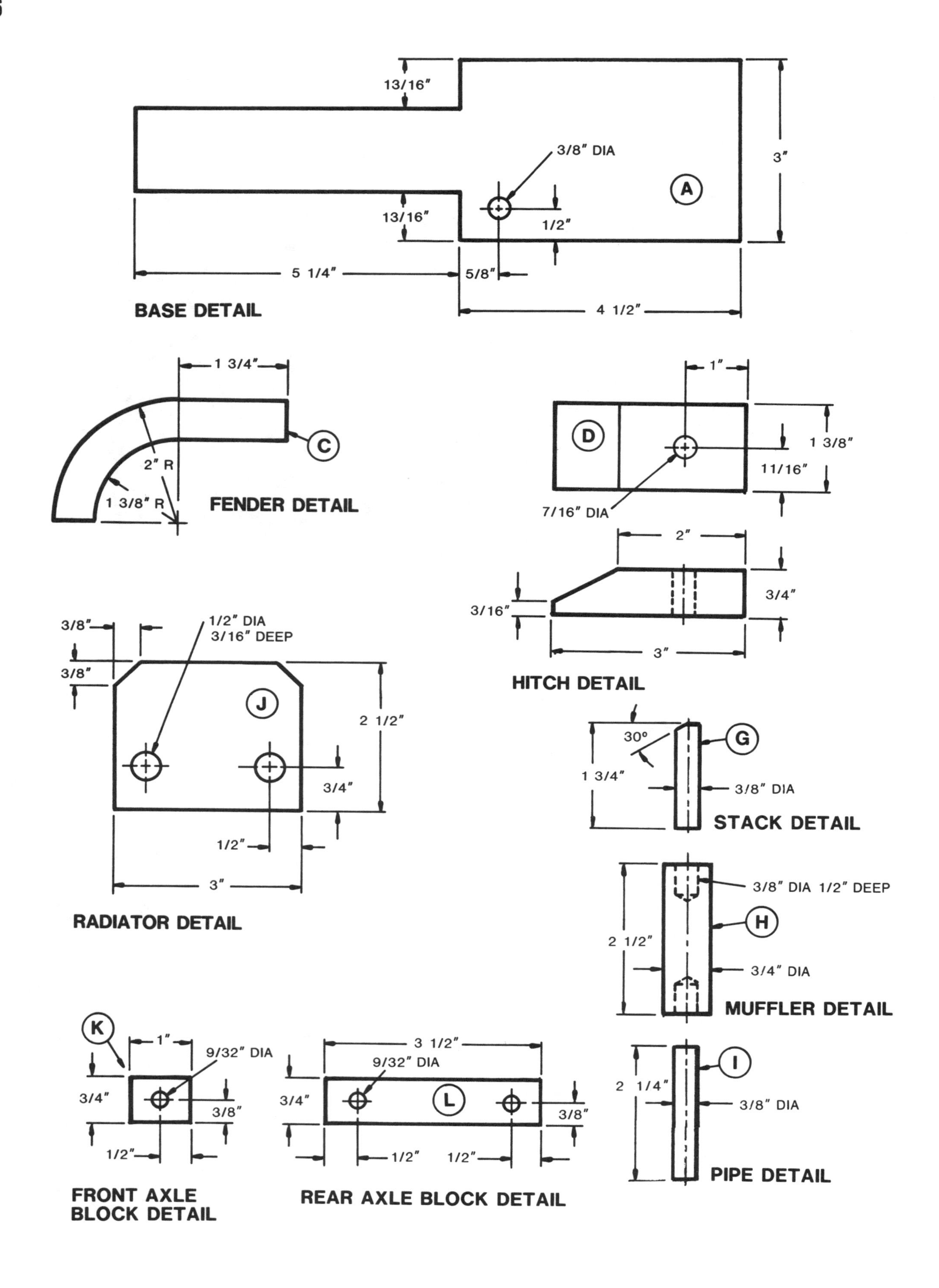
13/16"
3/8" DIA
3"
A
13/16"
1/2"
5 1/4"
5/8"
BASE DETAIL
4 1/2"
1 3/4"
C
2" R
1 3/8" R
FENDER DETAIL
1"
D
1 3/8"
11/16"
7/16" DIA
2"
3/4"
3/16"
3"
HITCH DETAIL
3/8"
1/2" DIA
3/16" DEEP
3/8"
J
2 1/2"
3/4"
1/2"
3"
RADIATOR DETAIL
30°
G
1 3/4"
3/8" DIA
STACK DETAIL
3/8" DIA 1/2" DEEP
H
2 1/2"
3/4" DIA
MUFFLER DETAIL
K
1"
9/32" DIA
3/4"
3/8"
1/2"
FRONT AXLE
BLOCK DETAIL
3 1/2"
9/32" DIA
3/4"
L
3/8"
1/2"
1/2"
REAR AXLE BLOCK DETAIL
I
2 1/4"
3/8" DIA
PIPE DETAIL

length and 4 3/8" height on the block and then draw the windshield slope 1 7/8" from the top and 3/4" from the front. Cut out with a band saw and sand all cut surfaces. Round over all edges except where the cab joins the base and the radiator.

Cut the radiator (**J**) to size from 1/2" stock. Cut a 3/8" by 3/8" chamfer off the top corners. Mark and drill the two 1/2" dia headlight holes 3/16" deep.

Glue the radiator to the front of the cab making sure the bottom and edges are flush. Clamp the parts together and allow to dry. When dry, remove the clamp and glue the cab to the base. The front of the radiator is flush

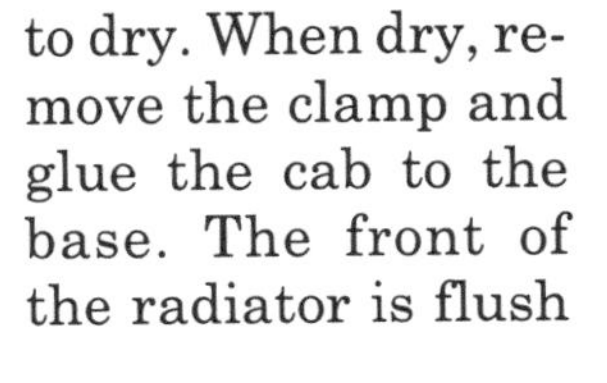

LIST OF MATERIALS

FINISHED DIMENSIONS IN INCHES

A	BASE	3/4 x 3 x 9 3/4
B	HEADLIGHT (2)	1/2 DIA x 3/8
C	FENDER (2)	3/4 x 2 x 3 3/4
D	HITCH	3/4 x 1 3/8 x 3
E	CAB	3 x 3 x 4 3/8
F	AXLE (3)	1/4 DIA x 4 5/8
G	STACK	3/8 DIA x 1 3/4
H	MUFFLER	3/4 DIA 2 1/2
I	PIPE	3/8 DIA x 2 1/4
J	RADIATOR	1/2 x 2 1/2 x 3
K	FRONT AXLE BLOCK	3/4 x 1 x 3
L	REAR AXLE BLOCK	3/4 x 1 3/8 x 3 1/2
M	CAB LIGHT (3)	3/8 DIA x 5/8
N	BUMPER	3/8 x 1 1/8 x 4 1/2
O	WHEEL (6)	3/4 x 2 1/4 DIA
P	PLAIN WHEEL (4)	3/4 x 2 1/4 DIA

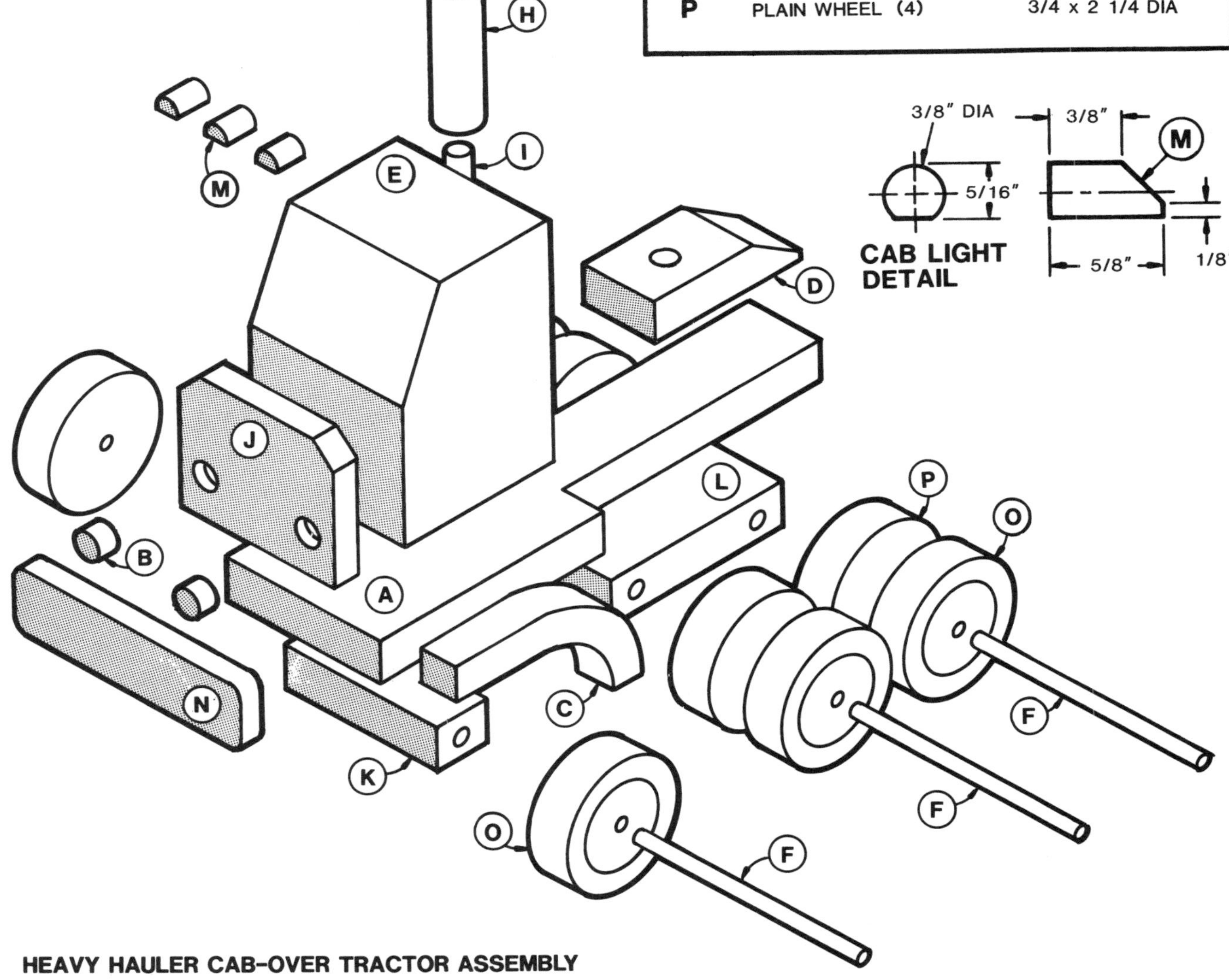

HEAVY HAULER CAB-OVER TRACTOR ASSEMBLY

with the front edge of the base.

Cut the bumper (**N**) to size. Sand the edges and the 3/16" radius at the four corners. Glue the bumper to the front of the base.

Cut the hitch block (**D**) from 3/4" stock. Mark and cut the slope at the rear. Then, drill the 7/16" dia hole for the trailer hitch pin. Sand the block and glue to the base 3/8" from the back edge.

Build up exhaust stack from sections of dowels. Cut the muffler (**H**) 2 1/2" long from 3/4" dia dowel. Mark the center of each end and drill 3/8" dia 1/2" deep. From a piece of 3/8" dia dowel cut the exhaust pipe (**I**) 2 1/4" long and the stack (**G**) 1 3/4" long. Cut a 30 degree chamfer at one end of the stack. Glue the stack, muffler and pipe together and allow to dry. Then glue the exhaust stack into the hole in the base. Make sure the chamfer at the top faces forward.

Cut two headlights (**B**) 3/8" long from 1/2" dia dowel. Glue the headlights into the holes in the radiator. Make three cab lights (**M**) from 3/8" dia dowel and glue to the top of the cab.

There are two different types of wheels needed for the tractor. First lay out the ten 2 1/4" dia wheels on a piece of 3/4" stock using a compass. Cut the tire outline for the six wheels (**O**) with a 1 1/2" dia hole saw. Make the saw cut about 1/16" deep. The four inside rear wheels (**P**) do not have the tire outline. Cut the wheels out with a 2 3/8" dia hole saw. Sand the cut surface and round over the edges of the tires.

Cut the three axles (**F**) from 1/4" dia dowel. Glue one wheel to each axle so the end of the dowel is flush with the outside (tire saw cut face) of the wheel. Put glue on the two rear axles near the outside wheel and slide the inside wheel up to the other wheel. Keep a 1/16" gap between the wheels.

Lay out the two fenders (**C**) on 3/4" stock. Cut out with a scroll saw and sand the edges with a 2" dia drum sander. Slip the front wheel axle into the axle hole and then glue the fender to the base and cab. Keep about 1/4" gap between the wheel and fender. Do the other fender the same way.

Sand the pieces with medium grit sandpaper, followed by fine grit sandpaper. Remove the dust with a tack cloth and apply a child-safe, clear finish. After the finish dries, slide the front axle assembly through the axle hole. Glue the front wheel to the end of the dowel. The tire saw cut is to the outside. Slide the rear axle assemblies through the axle holes, and then glue the inner and outer rear wheels to the dowels. If all measurements are correct the axles should be flush with the wheel face and a 1/16" gap between each wheel and the base.

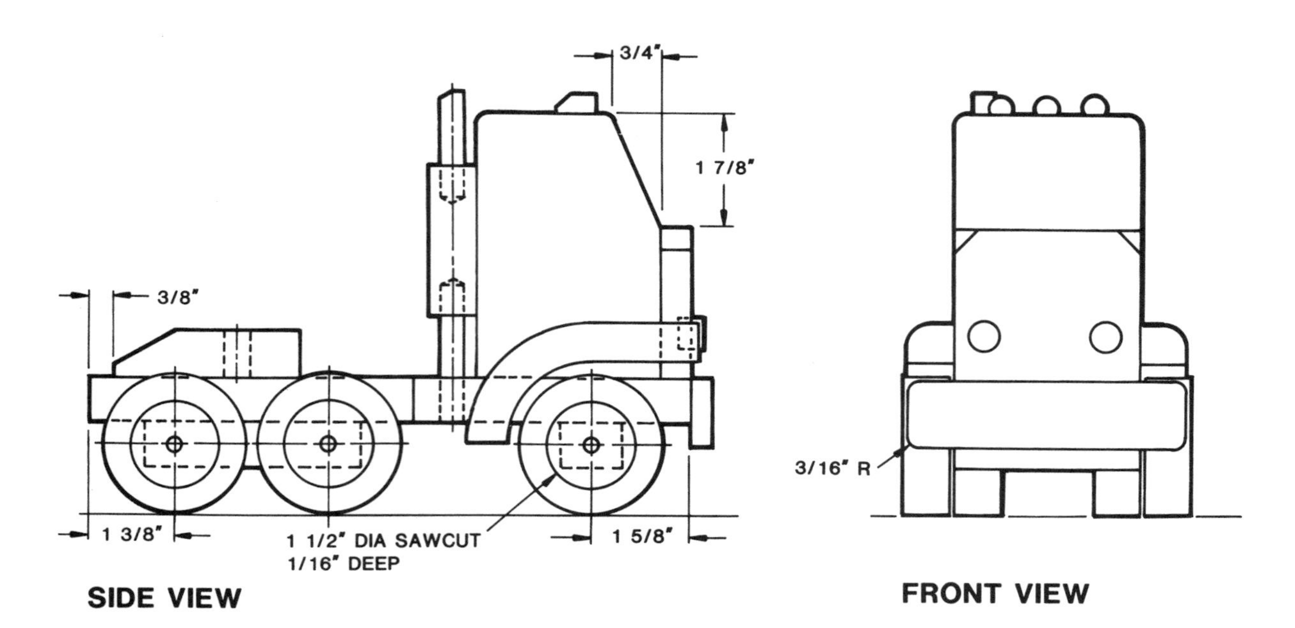

HEAVY HAULERS

Low-boy Trailer

The heavy haulers long hood tractor and the work equipment bulldozer can use this heavy haulers low-boy trailer. By making the bed longer this trailer can haul the road grader or road roller.

Cut the bed (**A**) 6" wide by 12 5/8" long from a piece of 3/4" stock. Lay out and cut the two notches for the wheels and the two notches for the ramps. Lay out and drill the ramp pin hole at the rear of the bed.

Two ramps (**C**) are cut from 1/2" thick stock. Drill the 1/4" dia hole and sand the two chamfers. Cut the ramp pin (**E**) to length from 1/4" dia dowel.

Cut the apron (**B**) and the support (**J**) to size. Lay out and drill the 3/8" dia 1/2" deep hitch pin hole in the apron. Drill two 3/8" dia holes through after marking their location from the drawing. Glue the support to the front of the bed and the apron on top, positioning the hole down and to the front. Clamp the parts together and let the glue dry.

To strengthen the apron joint, drill two 3/8" dia holes through the support and bed using the apron holes as a guide. Cut the two 3/8" dia dowels (**I**) 2 3/4" long. Glue the dowels into the holes and allow to dry.

Cut the hitch pin (**H**) 1 1/8" long from 3/8" dia dowel. Sand a slight chamfer on one end of the dowel. Glue the hitch pin with the chamfer end out into the hole in the apron.

Cut a piece of 1/2" stock to 2 3/4" wide by 3 3/4" long for the axle block (**F**). Mark the axle hole locations using the dimensions on the detail drawing. Drill the 9/32" dia holes through the axle block. Glue the block to the underside of the bed.

Cut the eight wheels (**G**) from 1/2" stock with a 1 5/8" dia hole saw. Sand the cut surfaces smooth and round over the edges of the wheels.

Cut the two axles (**D**) from 1/4" dia dowel. Glue one wheel to each axle so the end of the dowel is flush with the outside. Glue the inner wheel to the axle and keep a 1/16" gap between it and the outer wheel.

Sand the bed assembly and wheels with fine sandpaper. Wipe the parts with a tack cloth to remove all the dust left from sanding. Apply a good grade of child-safe finish. Allow to dry and then slip the axles through the holes in the axle block and glue the other inner wheels to the

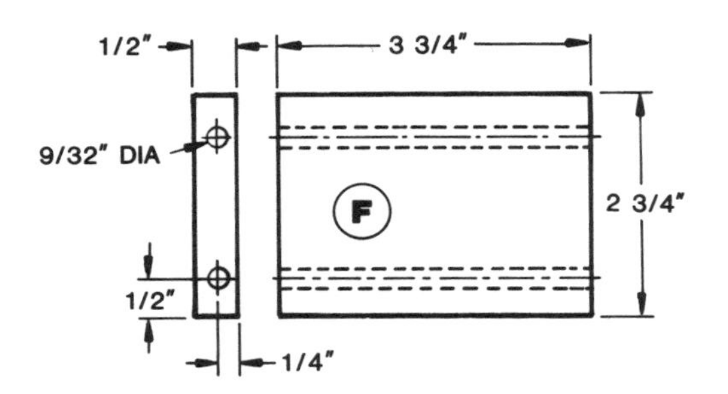

AXLE BLOCK DETAIL

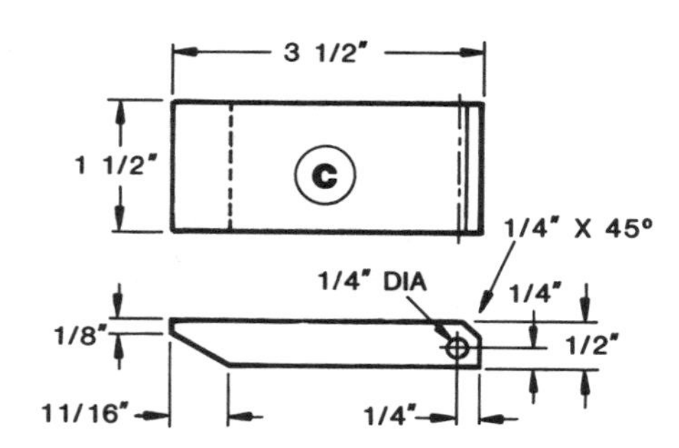

RAMP DETAIL

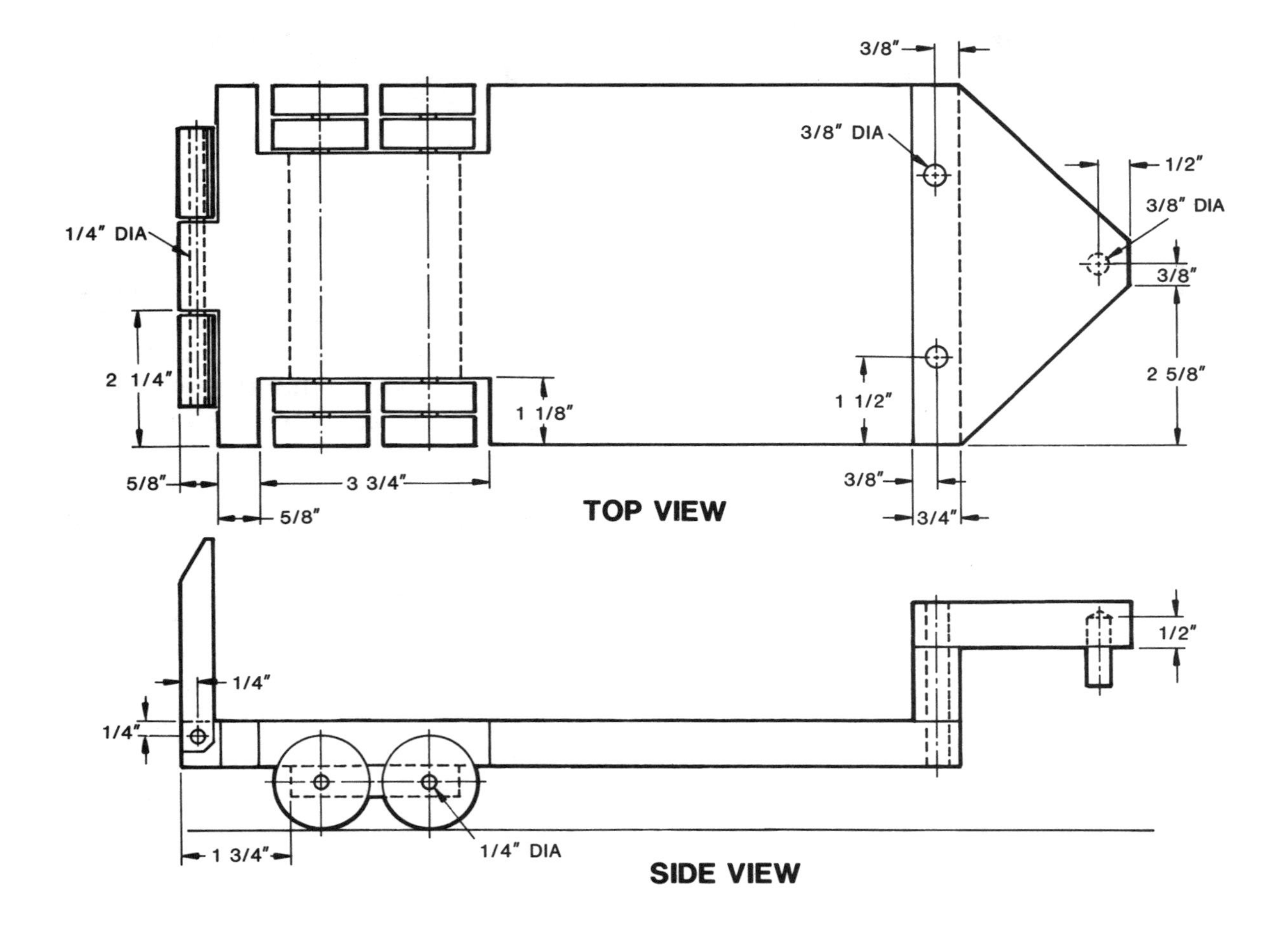

LIST OF MATERIALS

FINISHED DIMENSIONS IN INCHES

A	BED	3/4 x 6 x 12 5/8
B	APRON	3/4 x 3 1/2 x 6
C	RAMP (2)	1/2 x 1 1/2 x 3 1/2
D	AXLE (2)	1/4 DIA x 6
E	RAMP PIN	1/4 DIA x 4 5/8
F	AXLE BLOCK	1/2 x 2 3/4 x 3 3/4
G	WHEEL (8)	1/2 x 1 1/2 DIA
H	PIN	3/8 DIA x 1 1/8
I	DOWEL (2)	3/8 DIA x 2 3/4
J	SUPPORT	3/4 x 1 1/4 x 6

axle. Leave enough clearance between the bed and the inside wheels so they turn easily. Glue the outer wheels to the axle again flush with the face of the outside. This should leave a 1/16" gap between the two wheels. Move the inner wheel on the axle to get this gap if needed.

This trailer will fit the long hood tractor and with lengthening, it will fit the cab-over tractor. The distance from the hitch block hole to the rear of the frame is greater for the dual rear axle tractor. Add 1 1/8" to the 3 1/2" dimension of the apron for a 4 5/8" total. Cut and assemble the same as the regular apron.

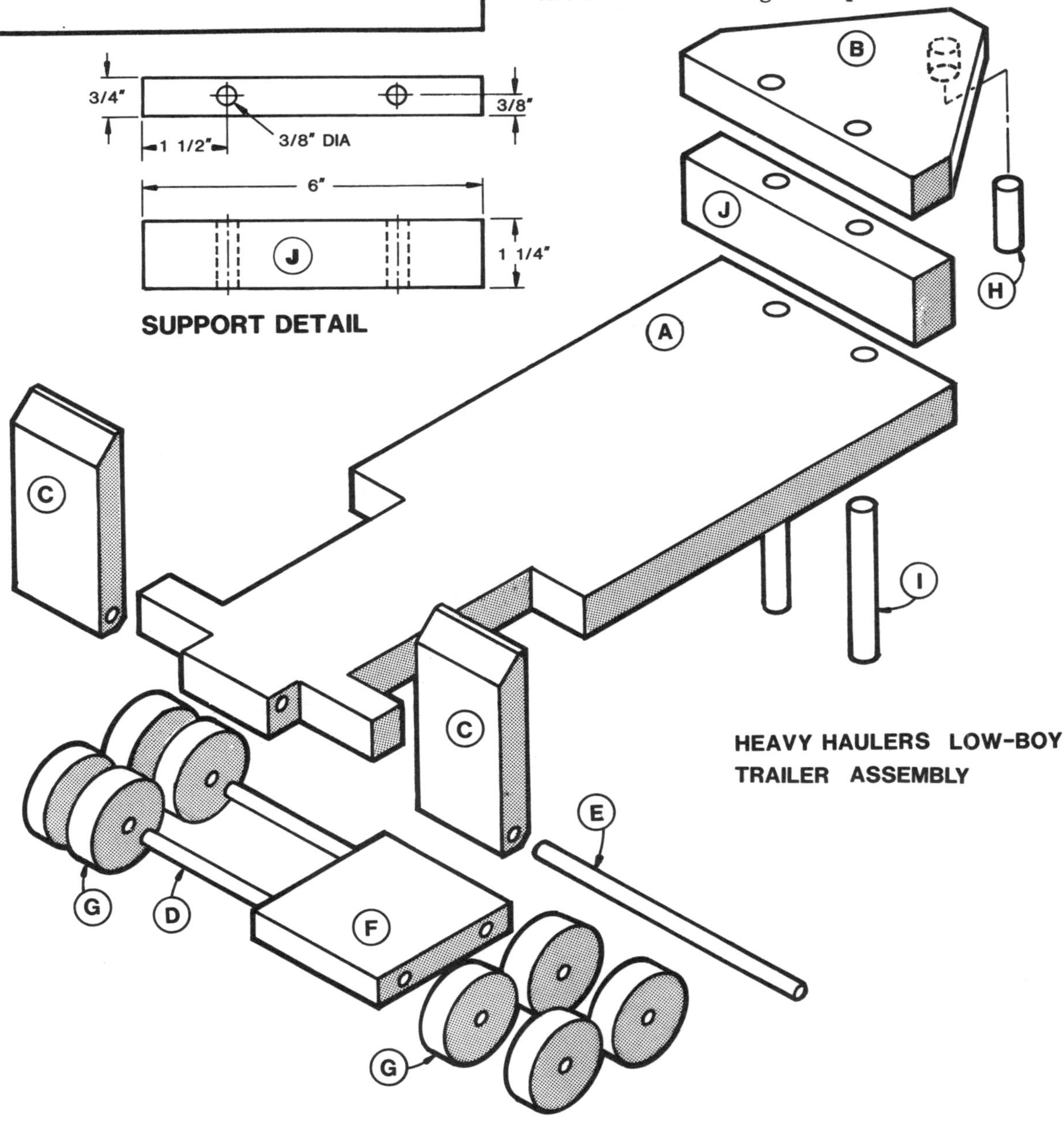

HEAVY HAULERS LOW-BOY TRAILER ASSEMBLY

Helicopter

This tear drop shaped helicopter is an unusual wood toy and is a lot of fun to build.

Lay out the two inner bodies (**E**) and the two outer bodies (**F**) on 3/4" stock. Cut the four pieces out on a band saw keeping away from the lines. Then, sand to the lines rotating the parts when sanding the round areas. We will add the holes later.

Cut the boom (**A**) to size and lay out the chamfer and the hole center for the rotor pin. Drill the hole with a 1/4" bit and sand the chamfer to the line. To get the proper radius for the other end of the boom, hold the four body parts together with the boom between upside down on a flat surface. Make sure the boom edge is flush with the front radius of the body. Draw the arc of the outer body on both sides of the boom. Cut the arc keeping away from the line and then sand to the line. Glue the four body parts and the boom together, clamp and allow to dry.

Lay out the block (**B**) and locate the center for the hole. Cut the front two chamfers on a band saw. Sand the two cuts just made. Then sand all the beveled surfaces. Drill the 1/4" dia hole through the block.

Cut the tail rotor (**C**) 1/4" thick from a piece of 1 1/2" dia dowel. Make the rotor pin (**D**) from 1/2" dia dowel as shown on the rotor pin detail drawing.

The two skids (**G**) are 1/2" dia dowels. Lay out the centers for the 1/4" dia holes and drill them 1/4" deep. With the holes

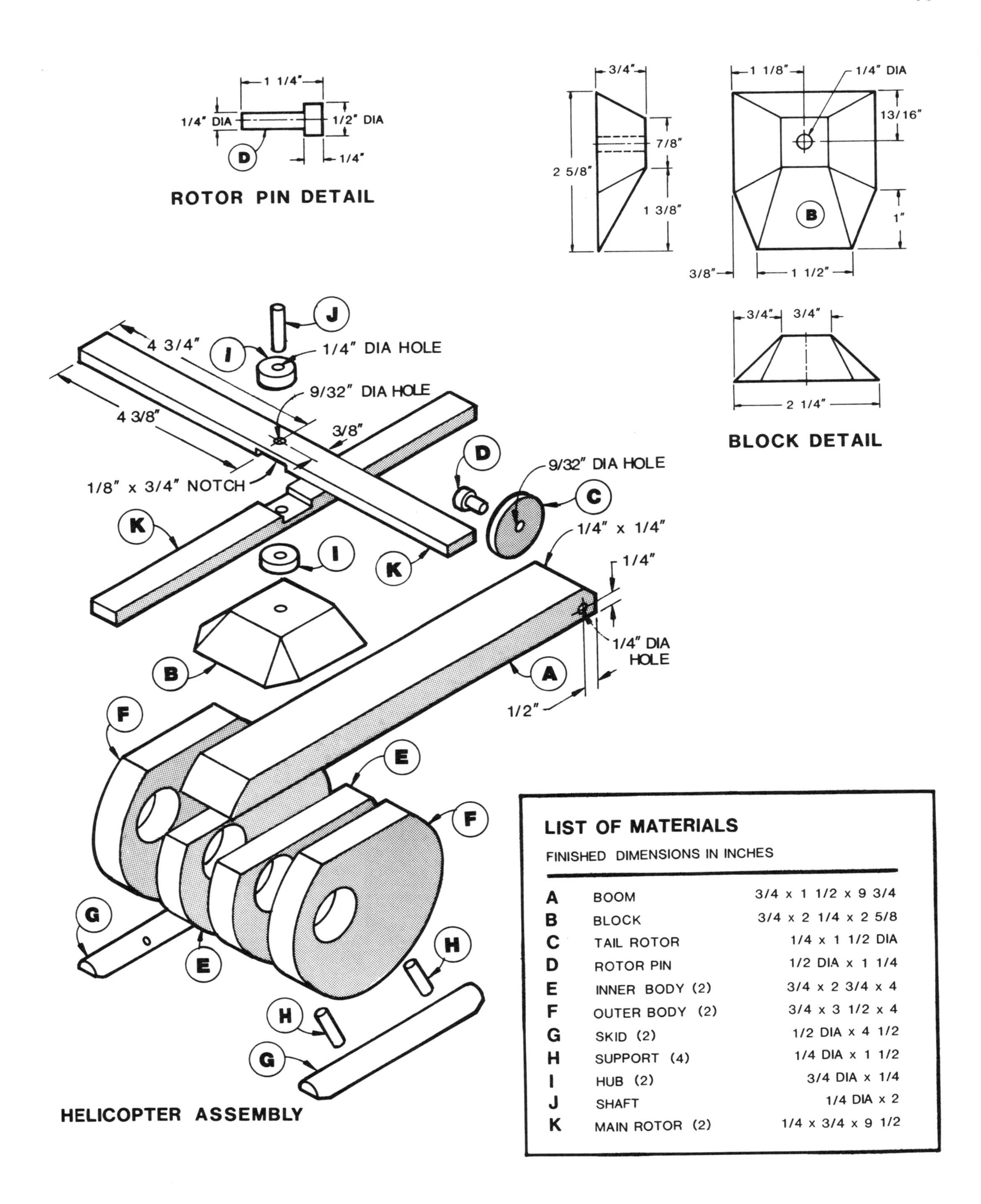

LIST OF MATERIALS

FINISHED DIMENSIONS IN INCHES

A	BOOM	3/4 x 1 1/2 x 9 3/4
B	BLOCK	3/4 x 2 1/4 x 2 5/8
C	TAIL ROTOR	1/4 x 1 1/2 DIA
D	ROTOR PIN	1/2 DIA x 1 1/4
E	INNER BODY (2)	3/4 x 2 3/4 x 4
F	OUTER BODY (2)	3/4 x 3 1/2 x 4
G	SKID (2)	1/2 DIA x 4 1/2
H	SUPPORT (4)	1/4 DIA x 1 1/2
I	HUB (2)	3/4 DIA x 1/4
J	SHAFT	1/4 DIA x 2
K	MAIN ROTOR (2)	1/4 x 3/4 x 9 1/2

oriented correctly, chamfer the end of each skid. Remember you must make a right and left hand skid.

Next, we will work on the main rotor. Cut two hubs (**I**) from 3/4" dia dowel and drill the 1/4" dia hole in the center of each. Cut the shaft (**J**) to length from 1/4" dia dowel. Lay out two main rotors (**K**) on 1/4" stock as shown in the isometric drawing. Drill the 9/32" dia hole and cut the 1/8" by 3/4" notch in each rotor.

The glued up body and boom should be dry by now, so we can begin final assembly. Lay out the center for the 1 1/4" dia window hole and the center for the four 1/4" dia holes for the skid supports. Adjust your drill press table to 45 degrees and clamp a stop block to the table. Hold the body next to this block, the hole center will be in line. Drill each hole 5/8" deep. Return the table to 90 degrees and drill the large hole with a Forstner bit. Do a final sanding to the round contour of the body to eliminate any small irregularity. Round over the edges with a 1/4" round over router bit.

Glue the block to the top of the body. Put a small amount of glue into the holes in the skids and the body. Insert the supports (**H**) into the holes in the skids and then insert the assembly into the holes in the body. Make sure the helicopter will sit level. Glue one hub to the end of the shaft. Glue the main rotor together.

Finally, round over all exposed edges with sandpaper and remove the dust with a tack cloth. Apply a child-safe finish and allow to dry.

Slip the shaft into the main rotor hole and glue the other hub to the shaft. Leave a small gap, so the main rotor will rotate and when dry glue the shaft into the hole in the block. Add a small amount of glue in the hole in the boom. Slip the tail rotor onto the rotor pin and then insert the pin into the hole. Again, leave a slight gap so the tail rotor will rotate. Before the glue dries check the rotation of both blades.

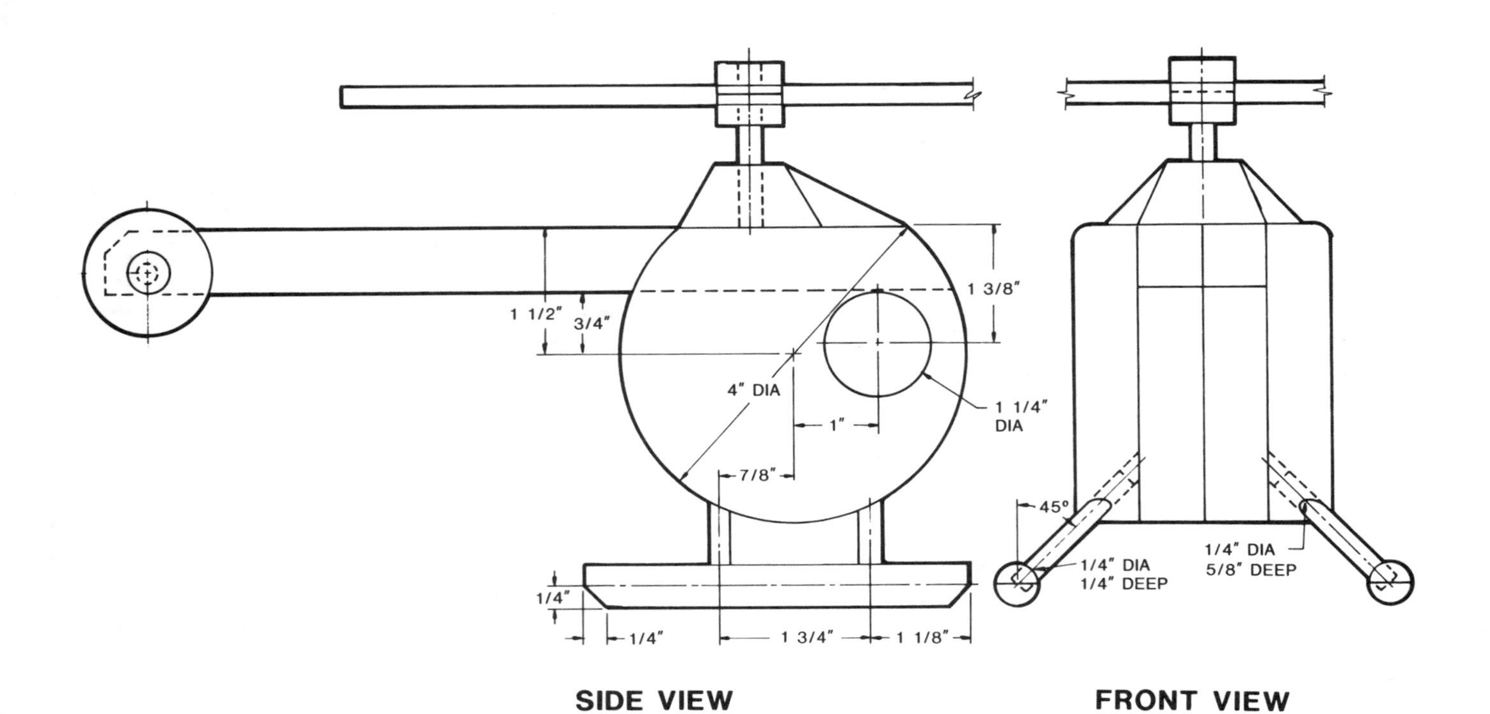

SIDE VIEW

FRONT VIEW

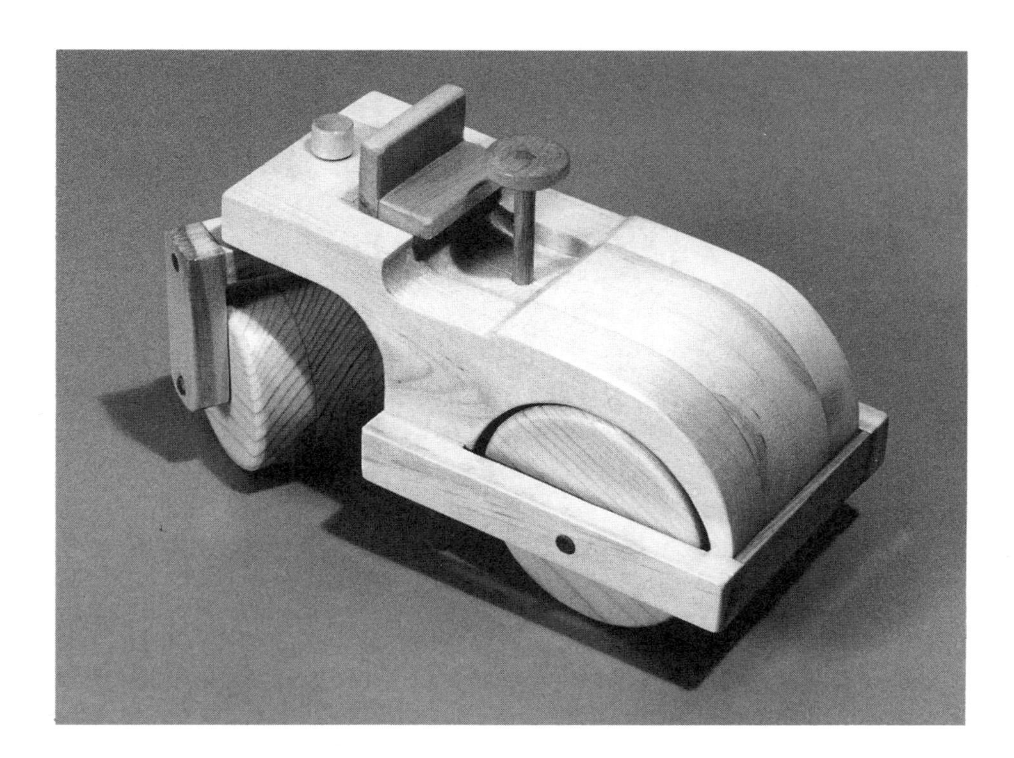

WORK EQUIPMENT

Road Roller

To compact material construction companies use road rollers. This toy will surely compact the hallway rug of the youngster who receives this wood toy. To build this toy we used pine with maple dowels.

Lay out the two body sides (**A**) on two pieces of 3" wide by 7 1/8" long 3/4" stock. Drill a 1/2" dia hole to form the 1/4" radius. Cut the parts out using a band saw and sand all edges with a drum sander chucked into a drill press.

The two bodies (**B**) are similar to the sides and are laid out on two pieces of 3" wide by 5 3/4" long 3/4" stock. Drill the 1/2" dia hole and cut the parts out away from the lines. Sand to the lines and glue the bodies and body sides together. Clamp together and allow to dry. Sometimes when gluing two flat pieces together they will move when applying the clamp pressure. To eliminate this problem drive two small brads into the back of the sides and snip the ends sharp with a pair of side cutters. About 1/16" of the brad is all that's needed. It will dig into the mating part and eliminate the sliding. When the glue dries drill the 1/4" dia by 3/8" deep steering column hole 1" from the recessed edge and in the center of the recess.

Cut the two side supports (**C**) 3/4" wide by 2 3/8" long from 1/2" stock. Lay out the center of the axle hole and drill the 1/4" dia hole. Sand the two 1/8" by 45 degree chamfer to the end with the hole.

The two skirts (**D**) are cut 3/4" wide by 4 7/8" long from 1/2" stock. Lay out the

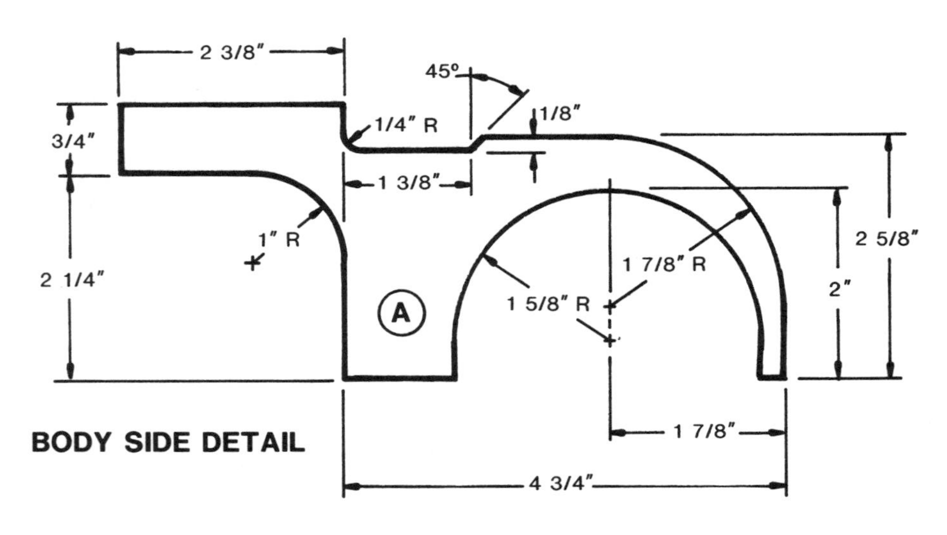

BODY SIDE DETAIL

notches in the sides and the centers of the holes as shown in the skirt detail drawing. Drill the 1/4" dia holes and sand the 1/16" deep notches with a 1/2" wide belt sander. Cut the bumper (**E**) from 1/8" stock. Check the length against the width of the body and make any adjustments. Glue the bumper to the back of the body and the two skirts to the sides.

Lay out the block (**F**) 1 3/8" by 1 1/2" on a piece of 3/4" stock. Mark the center of the hole using the dimensions in the assembly drawing. Drill the 1/4" dia hole thru the block. Glue the block between the sides and to the body.

Cut the support (**G**) 3/4" wide by 3 1/8" long on a piece of 1/2" stock. Lay out the center of the hole 3/8" from the side and 1 9/16" from the end. Drill the 1/4" dia hole through the support. Slip the two side supports onto a 1/4" dia dowel. Lay on edge and separate the parts enough to insert the support between the other ends of the side supports. Apply glue to the ends and between the sides of the supports. Apply a clamp and allow to dry. Strengthen this joint with a dowel if this toy will receive rough handling. When dry drill a 3/16" dia hole 3/4" deep 3/8" from the side and 1/4" down from the top. Drill another hole

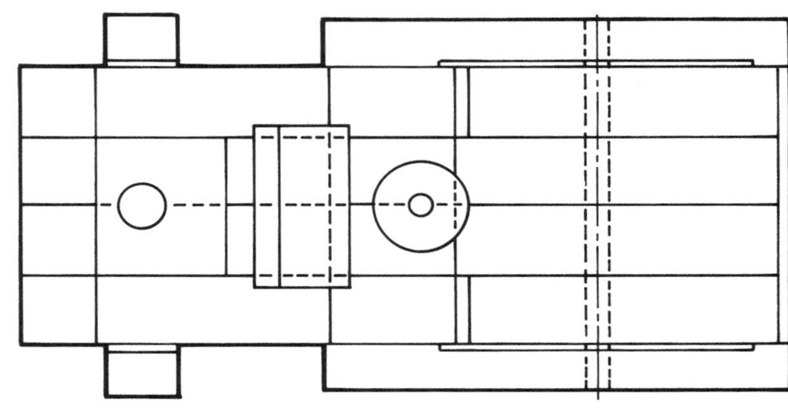
TOP VIEW

REAR VIEW

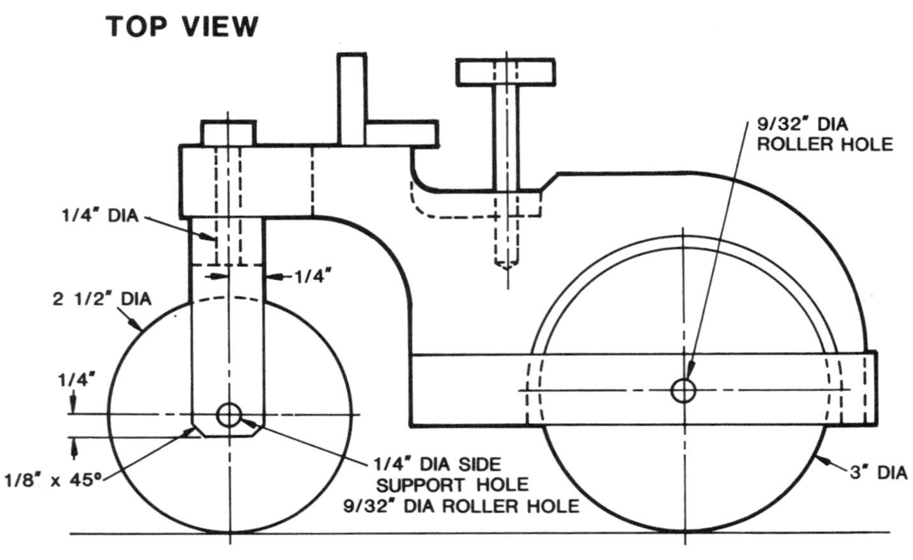

SIDE VIEW

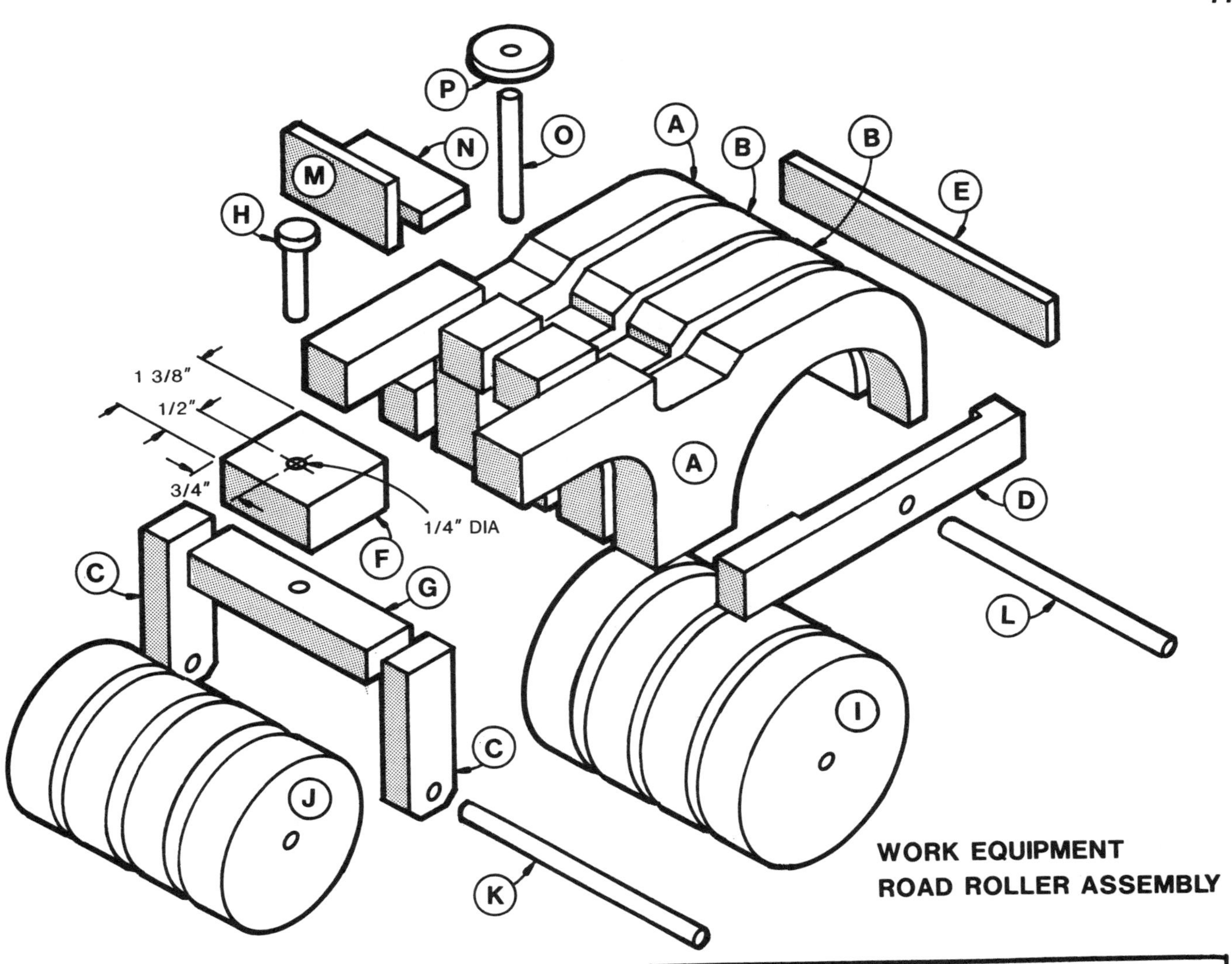

in the other side of the side support. Cut two dowels to length from a 3/16" dia dowel. Apply some glue into the hole and slip the dowel into the hole. Sand the end flush with the side when dry.

Make the pin (**H**) from a 1/2" dia dowel as shown in the pin detail drawing. An easy way to do this is with a v-block and a router mounted in a router table. Use the end of a straight bit and rotate the dowel in the v-block over the bit. A stop block will help to get the proper shoulder length. Cut the pin to an overall length of 1 1/2".

Lay out four rollers (**I**) on a piece of 3/4" stock. Rough cut the 3" dia disks and drill a 1/4" dia hole in each center. With the aid of a sanding jig, sand each of the pieces the same diameter. Glue the four disks together and then slip a 1/4" dia dowel through the holes to line up the

LIST OF MATERIALS

FINISHED DIMENSIONS IN INCHES

A	BODY SIDE (2)	3/4 x 3 x 7 1/8
B	BODY (2)	3/4 x 3 x 5 3/4
C	SIDE SUPPORT (2)	1/2 x 3/4 x 2 3/8
D	SKIRT (2)	1/2 x 3/4 x 4 7/8
E	BUMPER	1/8 x 3/4 x 3
F	BLOCK	3/4 x 1 3/8 x 1 1/2
G	SUPPORT	1/2 x 3/4 x 3 1/8
H	PIN	1/2 DIA x 1 1/2
I	ROLLER (4)	3/4 x 3 DIA
J	ROLLER (4)	3/4 x 2 1/2 DIA
K	AXLE	1/4 DIA x 4 1/8
L	AXLE	1/4 DIA x 4
M	SEAT BACK	1/4 x 1 x 1 3/4
N	SEAT	1/4 x 3/4 x 1 3/4
O	STEERING COLUMN	1/4 DIA x 2 1/8
P	STEERING WHEEL	1 DIA x 1/4

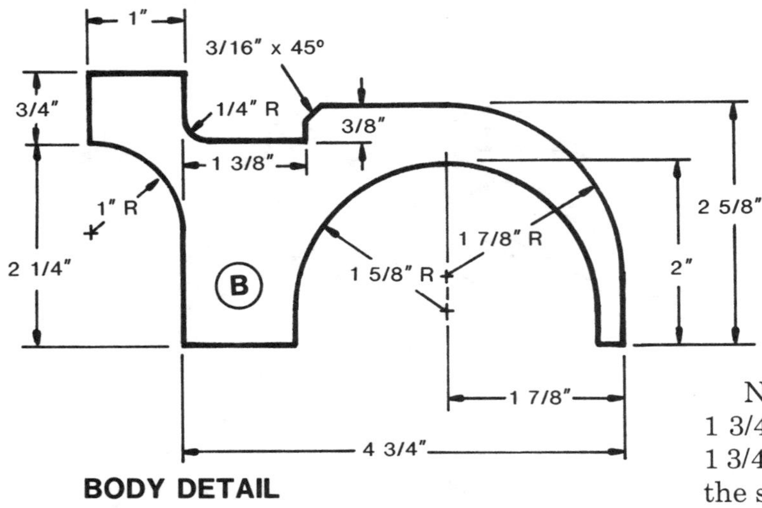

BODY DETAIL

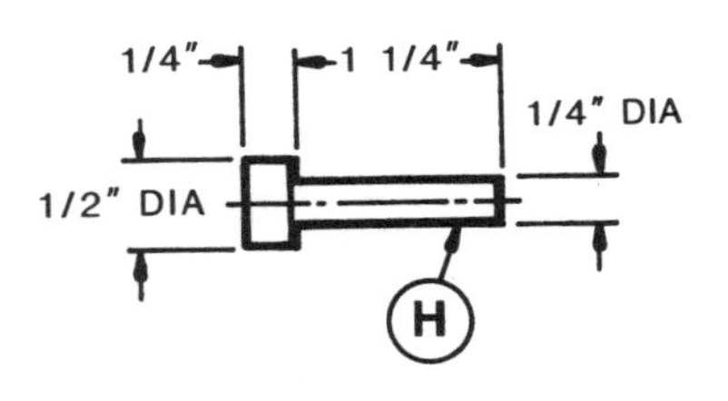

PIN DETAIL

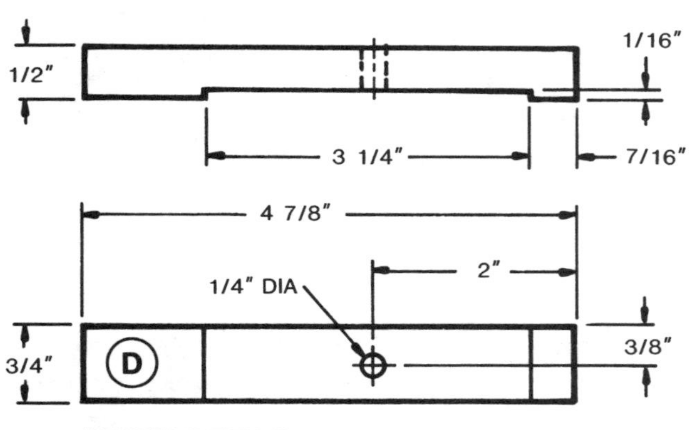

SKIRT DETAIL

disks. Clamp the disks and then slip the dowel from the disks.

The four smaller rollers (**J**) are drawn 2 1/2" dia on a piece of 3/4" stock. Cut the four disks keeping well away from the line and drill a 1/4" dia hole in each center. Use the sanding jig and sand the disks to the same diameter. Glue the four disks together and then slip a 1/4" dia dowel through the holes to line up the disks. Clamp the disks and then slip the dowel from the disks. When the two rollers are dry insert a 1/4" dia bolt with a washer under the head into one of the roller holes. Put another washer and a nut on the end. Chuck into a drill press chuck and sand the dia smooth. Remove the bolt and enlarge the 1/4" dia hole to 9/32" dia.

Cut the axle (**K**) and the axle (**L**) to length from 1/4" dia dowel.

Next cut the seat back (**M**) 1" wide by 1 3/4" long and the seat (**N**) 3/4" wide by 1 3/4" long from a piece of 1/4" stock. Glue the seat to the seat back and then glue it to the body 5/8" from the side and 1 5/8" from the back.

Drill a 1/4" dia hole about 1/2" deep in the center of the end of a 1" dia dowel. Cross cut the dowel 1/4" from the end for the steering wheel (**P**). Cut the steering column (**O**) to length from 1/4" dia dowel. Glue the steering wheel to the column and then glue into the hole in the body.

Finally, round over all exposed edges with sandpaper and remove the dust with a tack cloth. Apply a child-safe finish and allow to dry. Finish only the ends of both axles. Keep the finish out of all the holes.

Now to do the final assembly. Care must be taken not to get glue on any of the moving parts. Apply a small amount of glue into the holes in the skirt. Slip the roller into the opening and slide the 4" long axle into the hole in the other skirt (no glue) and into the roller. With about 1/2" of the axle sticking out apply a small amount of glue to the last 1/8" of the axle. Now push the axle into the hole in the other skirt. Wipe away any excess glue.

Slip the pin into the pivot hole in the body. Apply a small amount of glue into the pivot hole in the support assembly and put the pin into the hole. Slip pieces of index card on each side to maintain a small gap between the body and the support. Use the same method to install the small roller in the support as used on the large roller.

The road roller can now join the fleet of work equipment in this book.

HEAVY HAULERS

Long Hood Tractor

The long hood tractor was built to pull the heavy haulers van trailer in this book, but it can be used with all the heavy hauler trailers. The long hood tractor is similar to the cab-over tractor except for the single rear axle and the longer hood. Many of the parts are the same for both tractors.

Start by laying out the base (**A**) on 3/4" stock. Cut out the notch on both sides at the rear on a band saw. Cut away from the lines and then sand to the lines with a 1" wide belt sander. Lay out and mark the exhaust stack hole and then drill the 3/8" dia hole for the exhaust pipe.

Cut the front axle block (**K**) and the rear axle block (**L**) from 3/4" by 1" stock. The front block is 3" long while the rear block is only 1 3/8" long. Mark and drill the 9/32" dia axle hole in the center of each block end.

Mark the underside of the base for the axle blocks. The front block is 1 1/8" back from the front and the rear axle block is 7/8" from the back. Glue the blocks to the base and check the squareness with a square before clamping. Place scraps of wood under the clamp head to prevent denting the part.

Lay out the cab (**E**) on a piece of 3" by 3" stock to 4 3/8" long. Draw the windshield slope 1 7/8" from the top and 3/4" from the front at the top. Cut with a bandsaw and sand all cut surfaces.

Round over all edges except where the cab joins the base and the hood.

Cut out the hood (**Q**) from the 2 1/2" by 3" stock and add the 3/8" x 3/8" chamfer to both top edges along the length.

Next make a radiator (**J**) from 1/2" stock. Cut a 3/8" x 3/8" chamfer on the top corners. Mark the two headlight hole centers and drill the 1/2" dia holes 3/16" deep.

Glue the radiator to the front of the hood. Glue the other end of the hood to the cab front. Clamp the parts together and allow to dry. When dry, remove the clamp and glue the cab to the base with the front of the radiator flush with the front edge of the base.

Cut the bumber (**N**) to size. Sand the edges and form the 3/16" radius to each corner. Glue the bumper to the front of the base.

Cut the hitch block (**D**) from 3/4" stock. Mark and cut the slope at the rear. Then, drill the 7/16" dia hole for the trailer hitch

LIST OF MATERIALS

FINISHED DIMENSIONS IN INCHES

A	BASE	3/4 x 3 x 9 3/4
B	HEADLIGHT (2)	1/2 DIA x 3/8
C	FENDER (2)	3/4 x 2 x 3 3/4
D	HITCH	3/4 x 1 3/8 x 1 3/4
E	CAB	3 x 3 x 4 3/8
F	AXLE (2)	1/4 DIA x 4 5/8
G	STACK	3/8 DIA x 1 3/4
H	MUFFLER	3/4 DIA 2 1/2
I	PIPE	3/8 DIA x 2 1/4
J	RADIATOR	1/2 x 2 1/2 x 3
K	FRONT AXLE BLOCK	3/4 x 1 x 3
L	REAR AXLE BLOCK	3/4 x 1 x 1 3/8
M	CAB LIGHT (3)	3/8 DIA x 5/8
N	BUMPER	3/8 x 1 1/8 x 4 1/2
O	WHEEL (4)	3/4 x 2 1/4 DIA
P	PLAIN WHEEL (2)	3/4 x 2 1/4 DIA
Q	HOOD	2 1/2 x 3 x 2 1/2
R	STEP	3/8 x 2 x 3 3/4

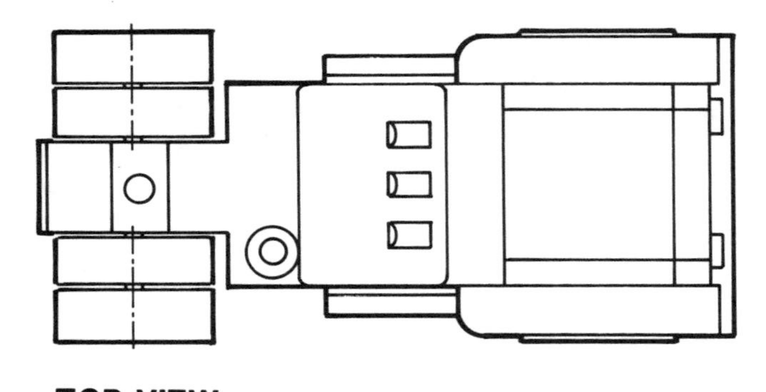

TOP VIEW

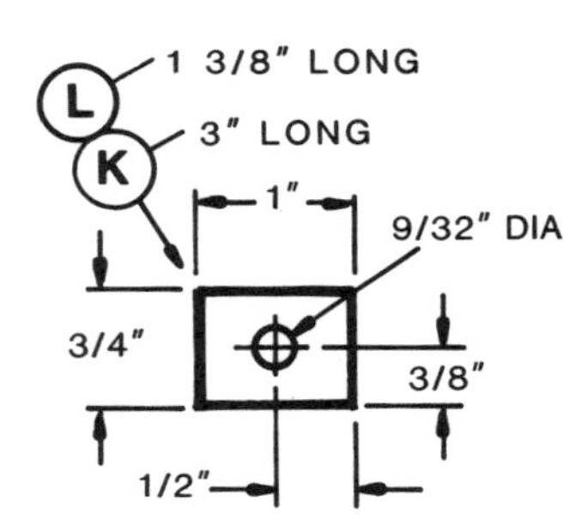

FRONT AXLE & REAR AXLE BLOCK DETAIL

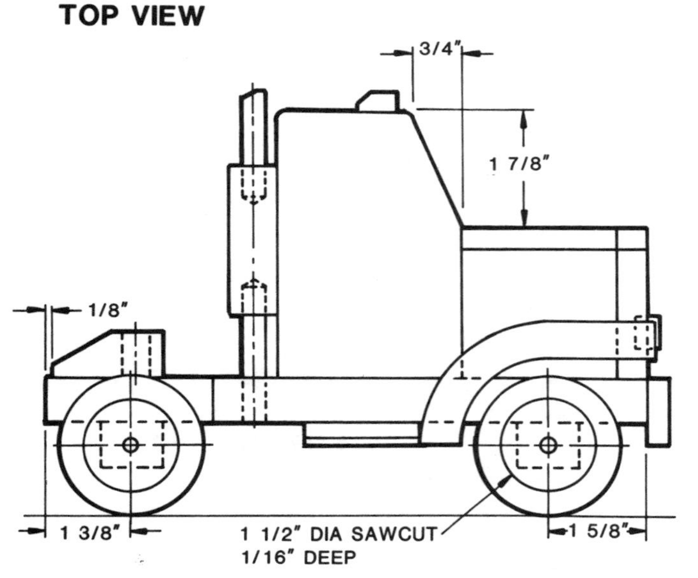

SIDE VIEW

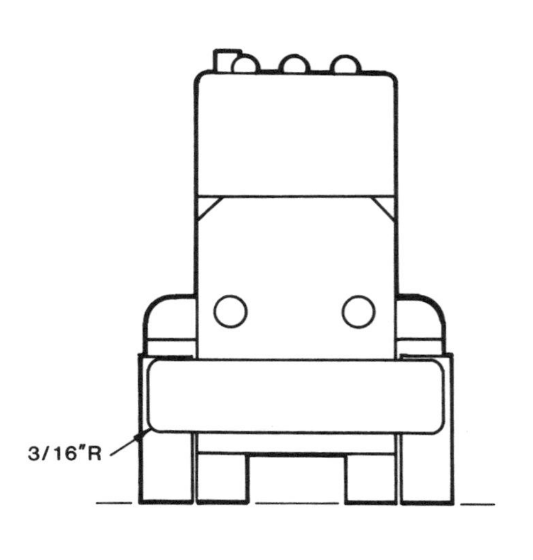

FRONT VIEW

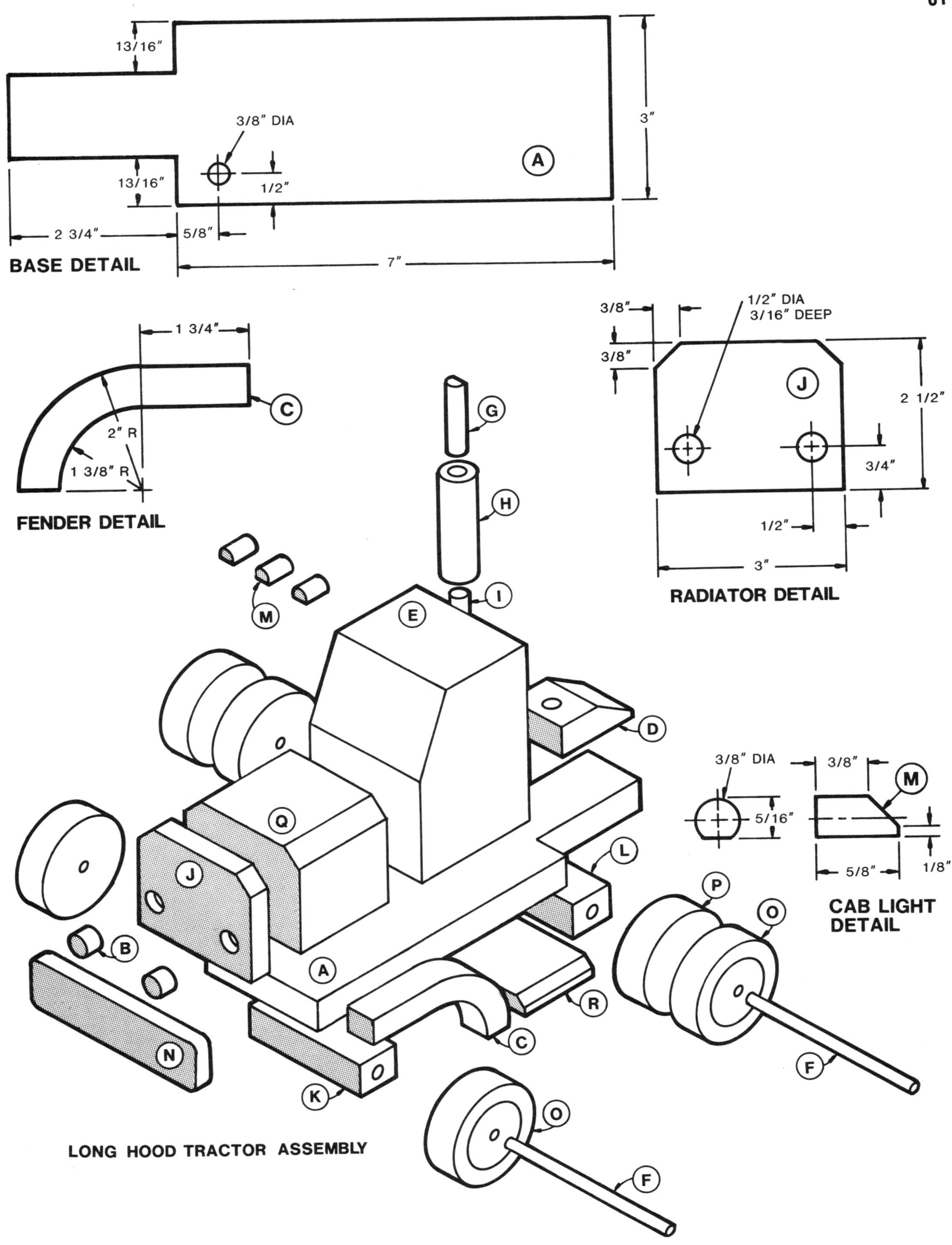
13/16"
3/8" DIA
3"
A
13/16"
1/2"
2 3/4"
5/8"
7"
BASE DETAIL
1 3/4"
C
2" R
1 3/8" R
FENDER DETAIL
3/8"
1/2" DIA
3/16" DEEP
3/8"
J
2 1/2"
3/4"
1/2"
3"
RADIATOR DETAIL
G
H
I
M
E
D
3/8" DIA
3/8"
M
5/16"
1/8"
5/8"
CAB LIGHT DETAIL
Q
J
L
P
O
B
A
R
C
N
K
F
O
F
LONG HOOD TRACTOR ASSEMBLY

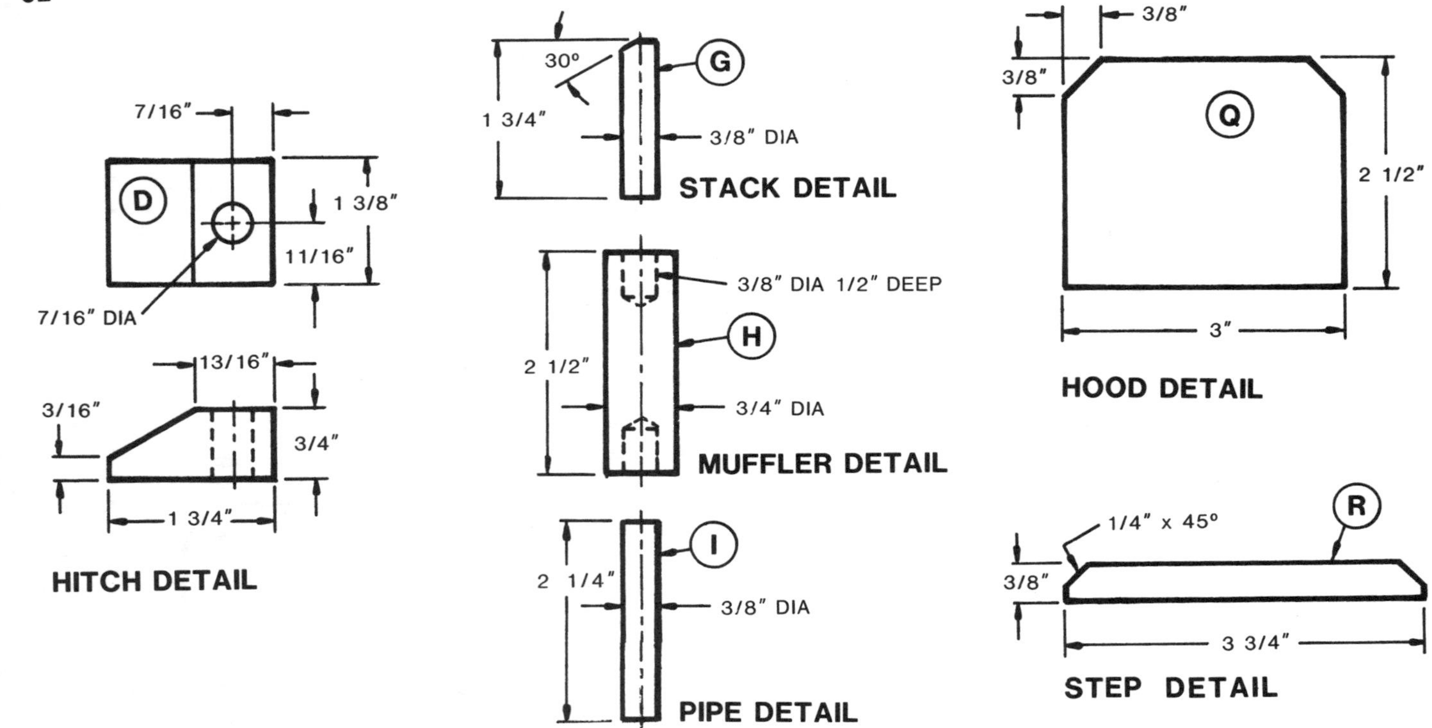

pin. Sand the block and glue it to the base 1/8" from the back edge.

Build up the exhaust stack from sections of dowels. Cut the muffler (**H**) 2 1/2" long from 3/4" dia dowel. Mark the center of each end and drill 3/8" dia hole 1/2" deep in both ends. From a piece of 3/8" dia dowel cut the exhaust pipe (**I**) 2 1/4" long and the stack (**G**) 1 3/4" long. Cut a 30 degree chamfer at one end of the stack. Glue the stack, muffler and pipe together and allow to dry. Then glue the exhaust stack into the hole in the base with the chamfer at the top facing toward the rear.

Cut two headlights (**B**) 3/8" long from 1/2" dia dowel. Glue the headlights into the holes in the radiator. Make three cab lights (**M**) from 3/8" dia dowel and glue to the top of the cab.

There are two different types of wheels needed for this tractor. First lay out the six 2 1/4" dia wheels on a piece of 3/4" stock using a compass. Cut the tire outline for the four wheels (**O**) with a 1 1/2" dia hole saw. Make the saw cut about 1/16" deep. The two remaining wheels (**P**) do not need the tire outline since it will not be seen. Cut all the wheels out with a 2 3/8" dia hole saw. Sand the cut surface and round over the edges of the wheels.

Cut the two axles (**F**) from 1/4" dia dowel. Glue one front wheel to one axle with the outside (saw cut face) of the wheel. Glue one plain wheel and one with the tire outline on the other axle keeping a 1/16" gap between the pair of wheels.

Lay out the two fenders (**C**) on 3/4" stock. Cut out with a scroll saw and sand the edges with a 2" dia drum sander. Slip the front wheel axle assembly into the axle hole and then glue the fender to the base and cab. Keep about 1/4" gap between the wheel and fender. Do the other fender the same way.

Make the step (**R**) from 3/8" stock and bevel the two ends. Glue the step to the underside of the base.

Sand the pieces with fine grit sandpaper. Remove the dust with a tack cloth and apply a child-safe finish. After the finish dries, slide the front axle assembly through the axle hole. Glue the front wheel to the end of the dowel, again with the saw cut face to the outside. Slide the rear axle assembly through the axle holes and then glue the inner (plain) and outer (saw cut) wheel to the dowel.

The long hood tractor looks good pulling the low-boy trailer with the bulldozer load.

HEAVY HAULERS
Van Trailer

The heavy haulers long hood and cab-over tractors found elsewhere in this book can pull this heavy haulers van trailer. Both tractors can use this trailer since the underside is free of obstacles behind the hitch pin.

Cut two pieces of 3/4" stock to 4 3/4" wide by 15" long for the bottom (**J**) and top (**A**). Mark the hole centers on the bottom 3/4" from the front and 2 3/8" from the side. Drill the 3/8" dia hole 1/2" deep in the bottom.

Cut two pieces of 3/4" stock to 3 1/2" wide by 15" long for the sides (**B**). Cut the front (**F**) from 3/4" stock to fit between the sides, top and bottom. Cut two doors (**C**) from 1/2" stock to 1 5/8" wide by 3 1/2" long. Glue the front to the bed and the sides to the front and bed. Glue the doors to the bed and side. Glue the top in place.

Cut the axle block (**I**) to size. Mark the axle hole centers with an awl. Drill the 9/32" dia axle holes. Glue the axle block to the underside of the bed 1" from the back and 1 11/16" from the side. Make sure the 3/8" dimension of the axle holes are away from the bottom of the trailer.

Lay out the eight 2 1/4" dia wheels on a piece of 3/4" stock using a compass. Cut the tire outline for the four outside

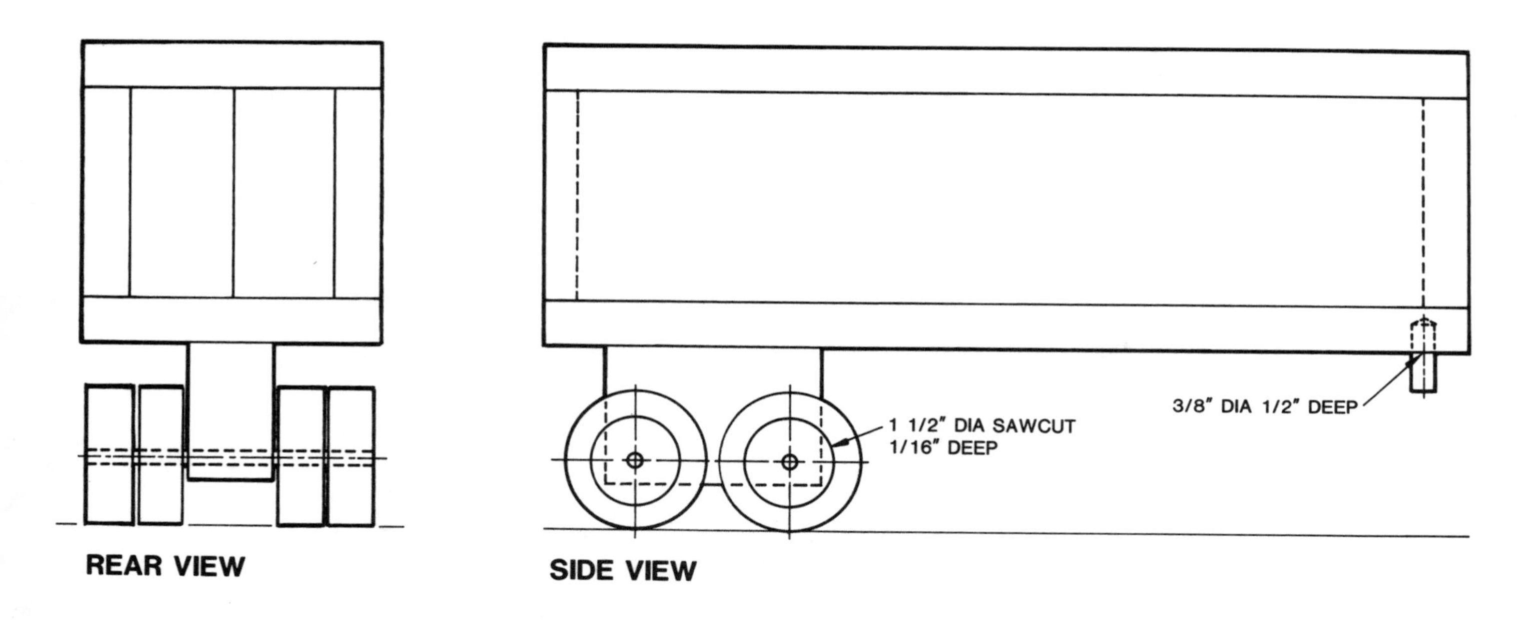

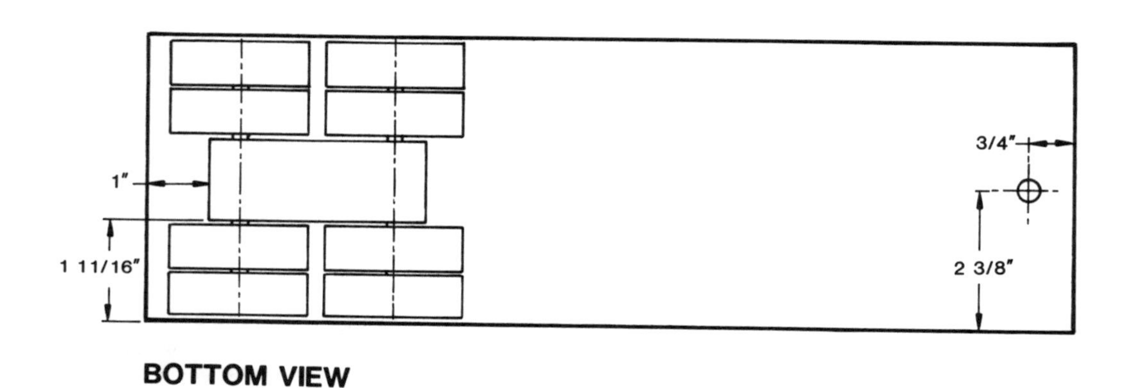

wheels (**G**) with a 1 1/2" dia hole saw. Make the saw cut about 1/16" deep. The four inner wheels (**H**) do not have the tire outline since it would not show. Cut the wheels out with a 2 3/8" dia hole saw. Sand the cut surface and round over the edges of the wheels.

Cut two axles (**D**) 4 5/8" long from 1/4" dia dowel. Glue one inner wheel and one outer wheel to each axle. The tire outline face is flush with the end of the dowel.

Chamfer the end of a piece of 3/8" dia dowel by rotating it at an angle against a belt sander. Cut to a length of 1 1/8" for the hitch pin (**E**). Glue the dowel with the

LIST OF MATERIALS

FINISHED DIMENSIONS IN INCHES

A	TOP	3/4 x 4 3/4 x 15
B	SIDE (2)	3/4 x 3 1/2 x 15
C	DOOR (2)	1/2 x 1 5/8 x 3 1/2
D	AXLE (2)	1/4 DIA x 4 5/8
E	PIN	3/8 DIA x 1 1/8
F	FRONT	3/4 x 3 1/4 x 3 1/2
G	WHEEL (4)	3/4 x 2 1/4 DIA
H	WHEEL (4)	3/4 x 2 1/4 DIA
I	AXLE BLOCK	1 3/8 x 2 1/4 x 3 1/2
J	BOTTOM	3/4 x 4 3/4 x 15

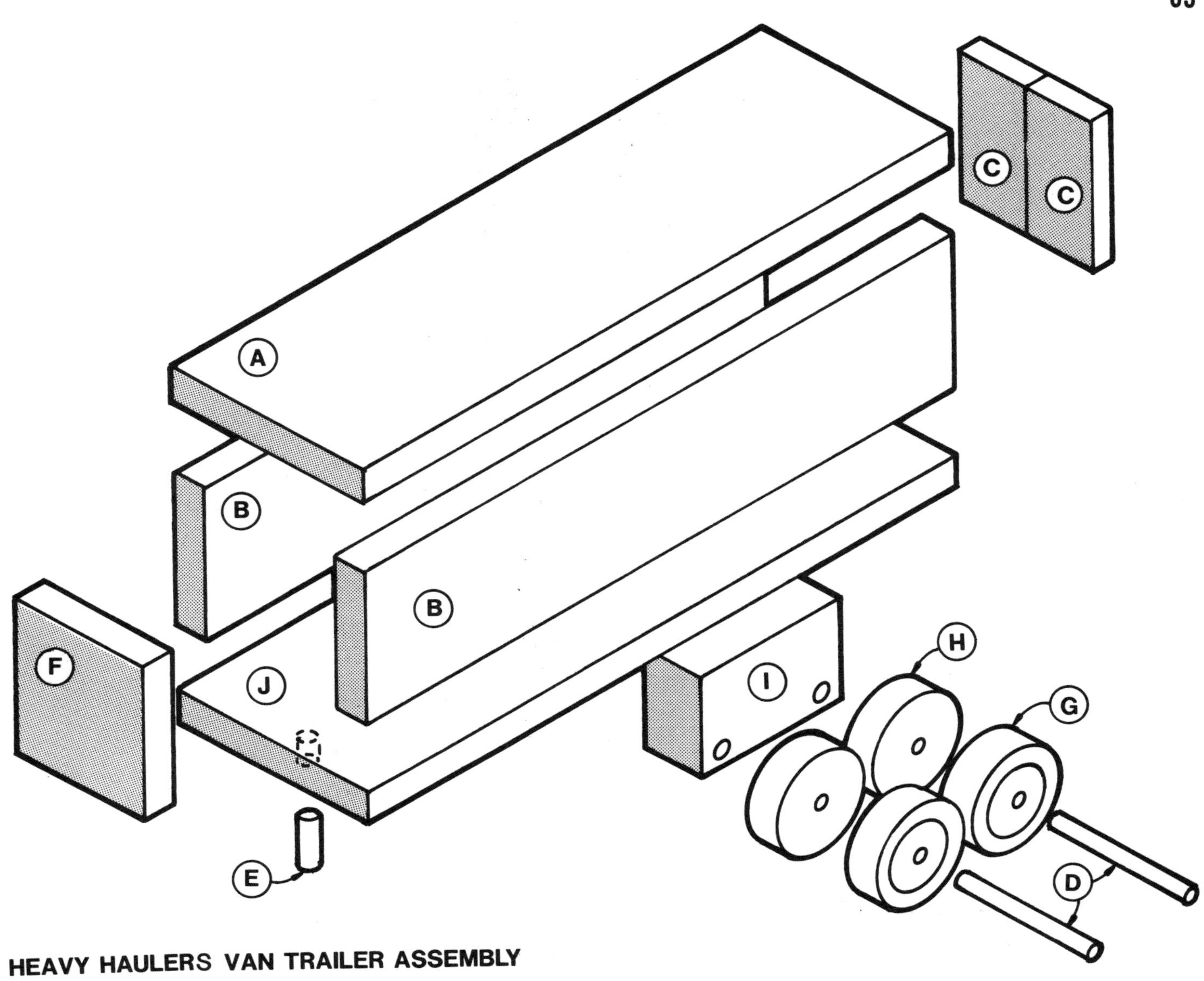

HEAVY HAULERS VAN TRAILER ASSEMBLY

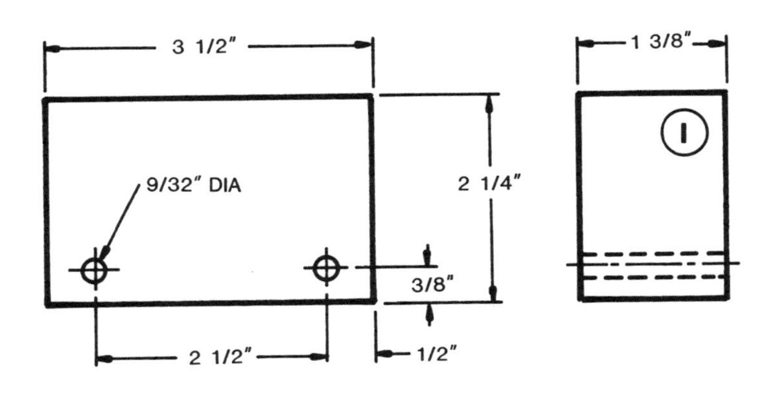

AXLE BLOCK DETAIL

chamfer end out into the hole in the bottom of the trailer.

Sand the pieces with fine grit sandpaper. Remove the sanding dust with a tack cloth, apply a child-safe finish and allow to dry.

Slide the axle assemblies through the axle holes and glue the inner and outer wheels to the dowel. Keep about a 1/16" gap between the inner wheel and the axle block and the inner and outer wheel. This should make the axle flush with the outside face (tire outline) of the outer wheel.

You can now add the van trailer to your fleet of heavy haulers.

WORK EQUIPMENT

Road Grader

This scaled down version of a road grader will thrill that youngster. The blade can be turned or raised and lowered.

Cut all the pieces as indicated in the list of materials. After the pieces have been cut to size take the base (**A**) and lay out the 5/8" relief on both sides. Measure 2 1/4" from the back edge for the relief and cut both sides (the 1 3/8" R will be added later). Lay out the angle on the top of the back (**H**), cut and sand to shape. Glue the back to the base 2 1/4" from the back edge of the base. Lay out the axle hole center as shown on the base detail drawing. Drill the 9/32" dia hole.

Lay out and cut a template from card-stock as shown in the template detail drawing. Lay the template on the edge of the base back assembly and trace the arc with a sharp pencil. Draw another arc on the other side. Chuck a 2 3/4" dia sanding

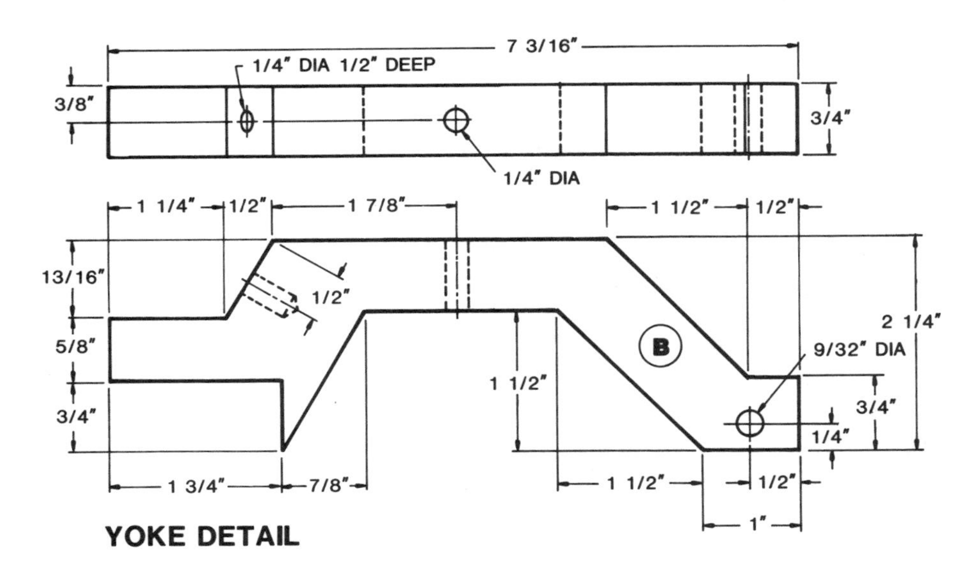

YOKE DETAIL

drum in the drill press and lock to the height needed. Sand the arc to the line and then sand the other side.

Lay out the yoke (**B**) as shown in the yoke detail drawing. Cut out with a band saw and then sand the edges. Drill the 1/4" dia hole through for the blade pin and the 1/4" dia hole 1/2" deep for the steering column.

Glue the two blocks (**F**) to the front of the yoke. When dry lay out the axle center and drill the 9/32" dia hole.

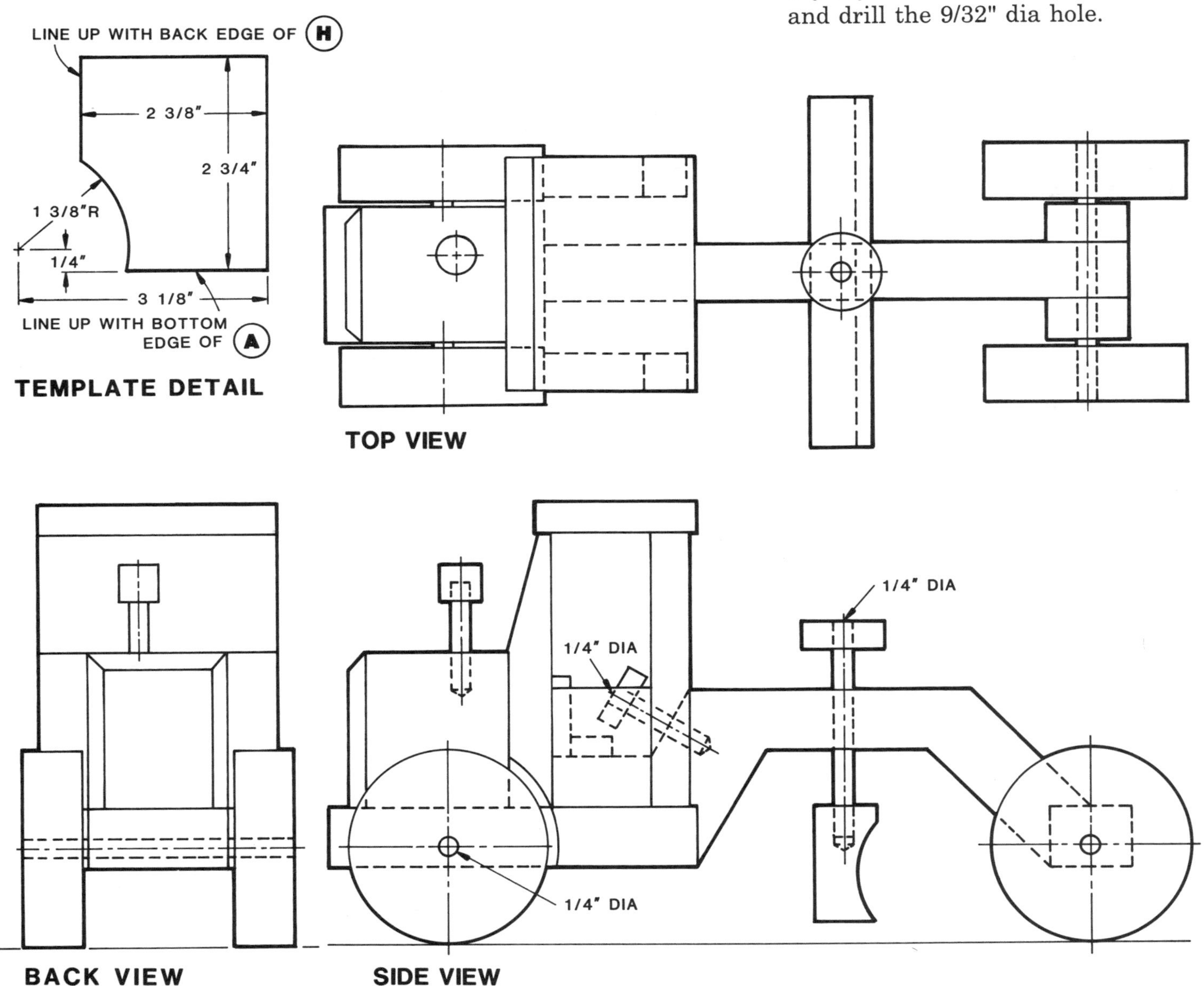

TEMPLATE DETAIL

TOP VIEW

BACK VIEW

SIDE VIEW

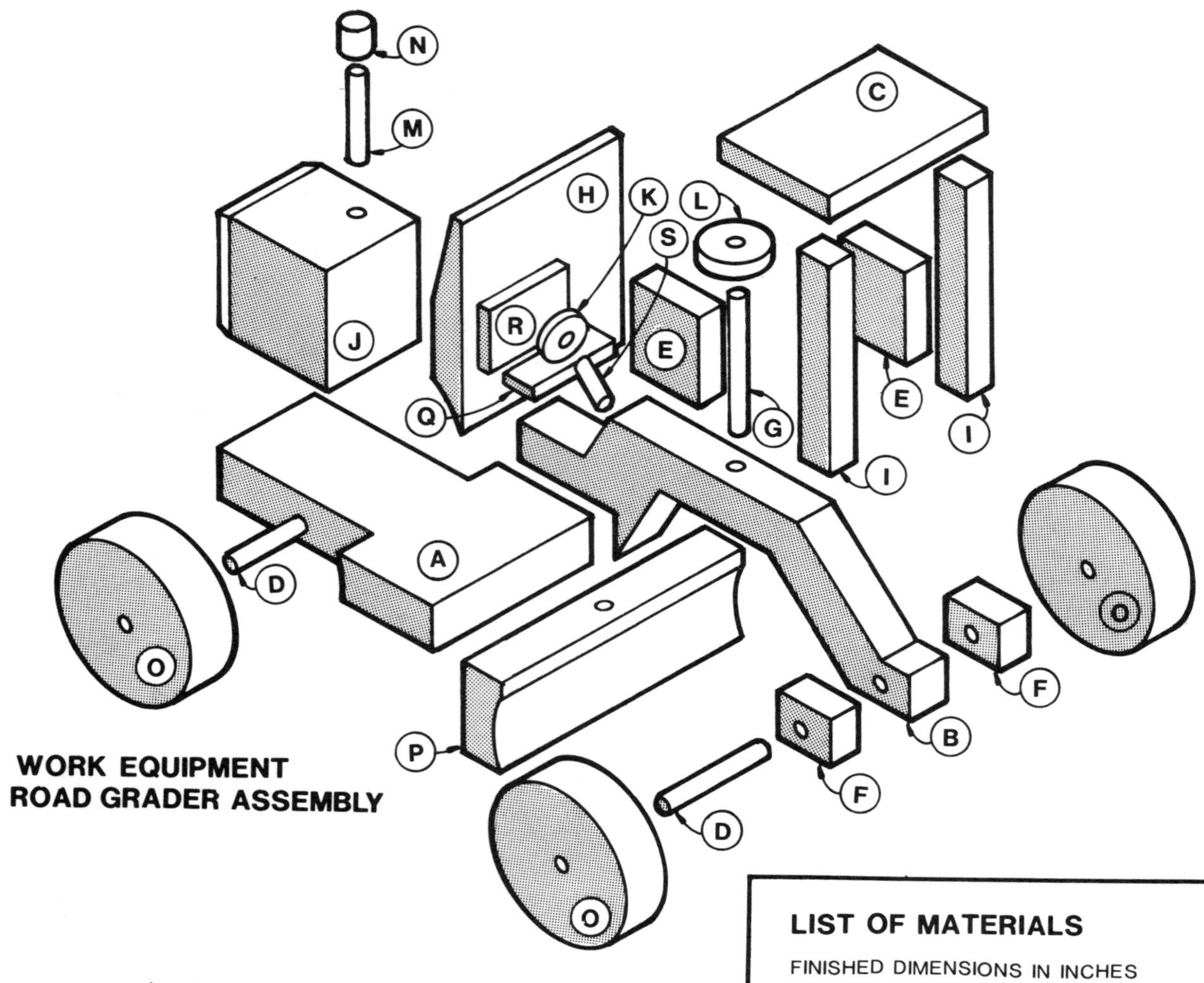

WORK EQUIPMENT
ROAD GRADER ASSEMBLY

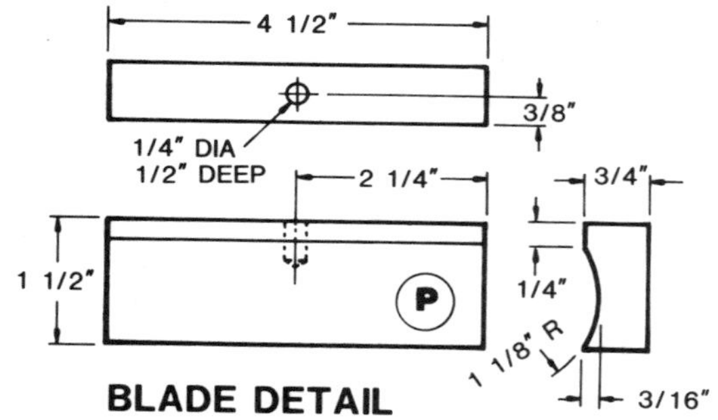

BLADE DETAIL

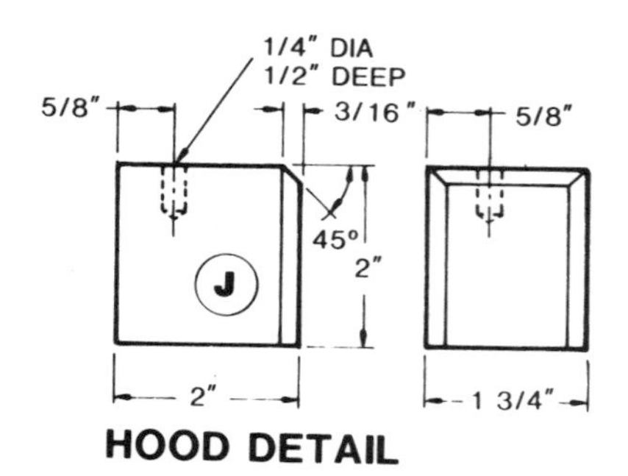

HOOD DETAIL

LIST OF MATERIALS

FINISHED DIMENSIONS IN INCHES

A	BASE	3/4 x 3 x 4 5/8
B	YOKE	3/4 x 2 1/4 x 7 3/16
C	ROOF	3/8 x 2 x 3
D	AXLE (2)	1/4 DIA x 3 3/8
E	DOOR (2)	1/2 x 1 1/4 x 1 1/2
F	BLOCK (2)	1/2 x 3/4 x 1
G	BLADE PIN	1/4 DIA x 2 3/4
H	BACK	1/2 x 3 x 3 1/2
I	POST (2)	1/2 x 1/2 x 3 1/2
J	HOOD	1 3/4 x 2 x 2
K	STEERING WHEEL	3/4 DIA x 1/4
L	WHEEL	1 DIA x 3/8
M	STACK	1/4 DIA x 1 3/8
N	CAP	1/2 DIA x 1/2
O	WHEEL (4)	3/4 x 2 1/2 DIA
P	BLADE	3/4 x 1 1/2 x 4 1/2
Q	SEAT	1/4 x 1/2 x 1 1/2
R	SEAT BACK	1/4 x 1 x 1 1/2
S	STEERING COLUMN	1/4 DIA x 1 1/4

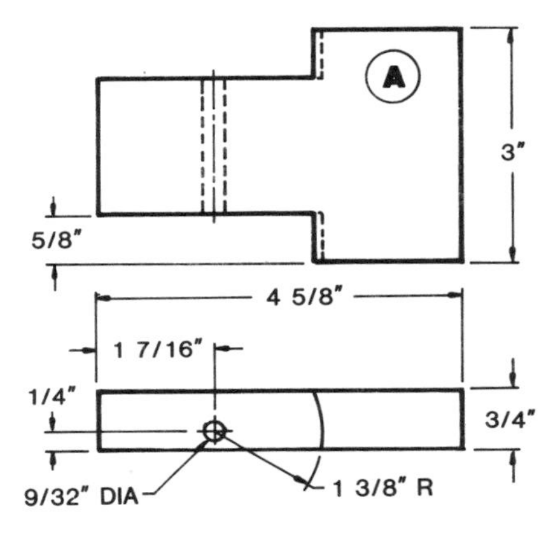

BASE DETAIL

3"
5/16"
1 1/2"
3 1/2"
H
1 3/8" R
5/8"
5/8"
1/2"

CAB BACK DETAIL

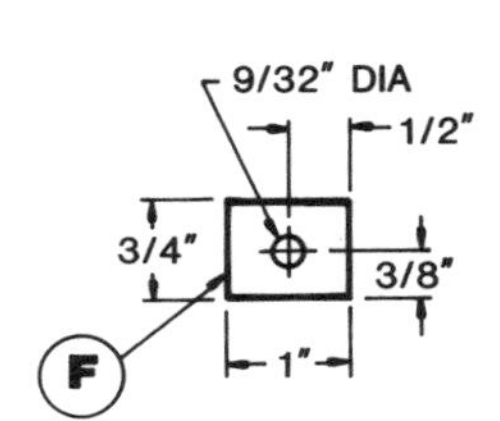

BLOCK DETAIL

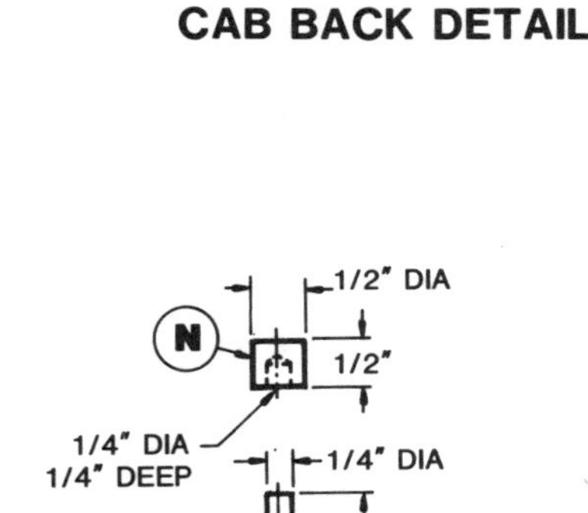

STACK & CAP DETAIL

Glue the yoke to the base and back. Glue the seat back (**R**) and seat (**Q**) to the yoke.

Drill a 1/4" dia hole in the center of the steering wheel (**K**). Glue the wheel to the steering column (**S**). Put a small amount of glue into the hole in the yoke and insert the end of the steering column.

Glue the door (**E**) to a post (**I**) on a flat surface covered with wax paper. Allow to dry and then glue to the bed and back. Glue the roof (**C**) to the back and posts.

Draw lines on the front of the hood (**J**) for the chamfers. Sand to the lines using several light passes. Lay out the center for the stack and drill the 1/4" dia hole 1/2" deep. Glue the hood to the base and back.

Drill a 1/4" dia hole 1/4" deep into the center of one end of the stack cap (**N**). Glue the cap to the stack (**M**). Put a small amount of glue into the hole in the hood and add the stack.

Form the radius in the front of the blade (**P**). Drill a 1/4" dia hole 1/2" deep as shown in the blade detail drawing. For the blade pin (**G**) get a dowel that is a snug fit in the yoke hole. With this snug fit the blade will stay in the up position if desired. Drill a 1/4" dia hole in the center of the blade wheel (**L**). Glue the blade wheel to the shaft.

Lay out the four 2 1/2" dia wheels (**O**) on a piece of 3/4" stock using a compass. Cut the wheels out using a circle cutter chucked in a drill press. Sand to edges and round over the corners. Glue one wheel to each of the axles (**D**).

Sand the finished road grader body with fine grit sandpaper. Remove the dust with a tack cloth, apply a child-safe finish and allow to dry. Do not put finish on the blade shaft or axles.

Slide the blade shaft through the hole in the top of the yoke. Put a small amount of glue into the blade hole and push the blade onto the end of the shaft. Put the axles through the axle holes and glue the other wheel to the end of the axle.

The road grader can now join the fleet of the other pieces of work equipment.

TOY

Sports Car

Sports cars are popular vehicles for the young adults and this wood toy vehicle will be a favorite for that youngster who receives this toy. Our toy is of pine, maple dowels and commercially purchased toy wheels.

Lay out the body (**A**) on a piece of 1 1/2" stock as shown in the body detail drawing. First cut the slot for the windshield. Tilt the blade to 15 degrees on a table saw and lower the blade to cut 1/4" deep. Run a scrap piece of wood through the saw to check the angle, width and depth of cut. When satisfied with the trial cuts, cut the body. Place the body on its side on a drill press table and clamp a piece of scrap wood next to the passenger compartment. With a 1 1/2" Forstner bit, drill the hole taking 3/4" from the body and the rest from the scrap piece. Drill the two front bumper peg holes and the two rear holes 1/4" dia 3/8" deep. Drill the radiator cap hole 1/4" dia 3/16" deep. Cut the angle at the front and the chamfer at the back. Locate the steering column hole in the dirvers compartment and drill the 3/16" dia hole 7/16" deep on a 30 degree angle.

The two sides (**B**) are laid out on 5/16" stock using the side detail drawing. With a band saw cut away from the line and

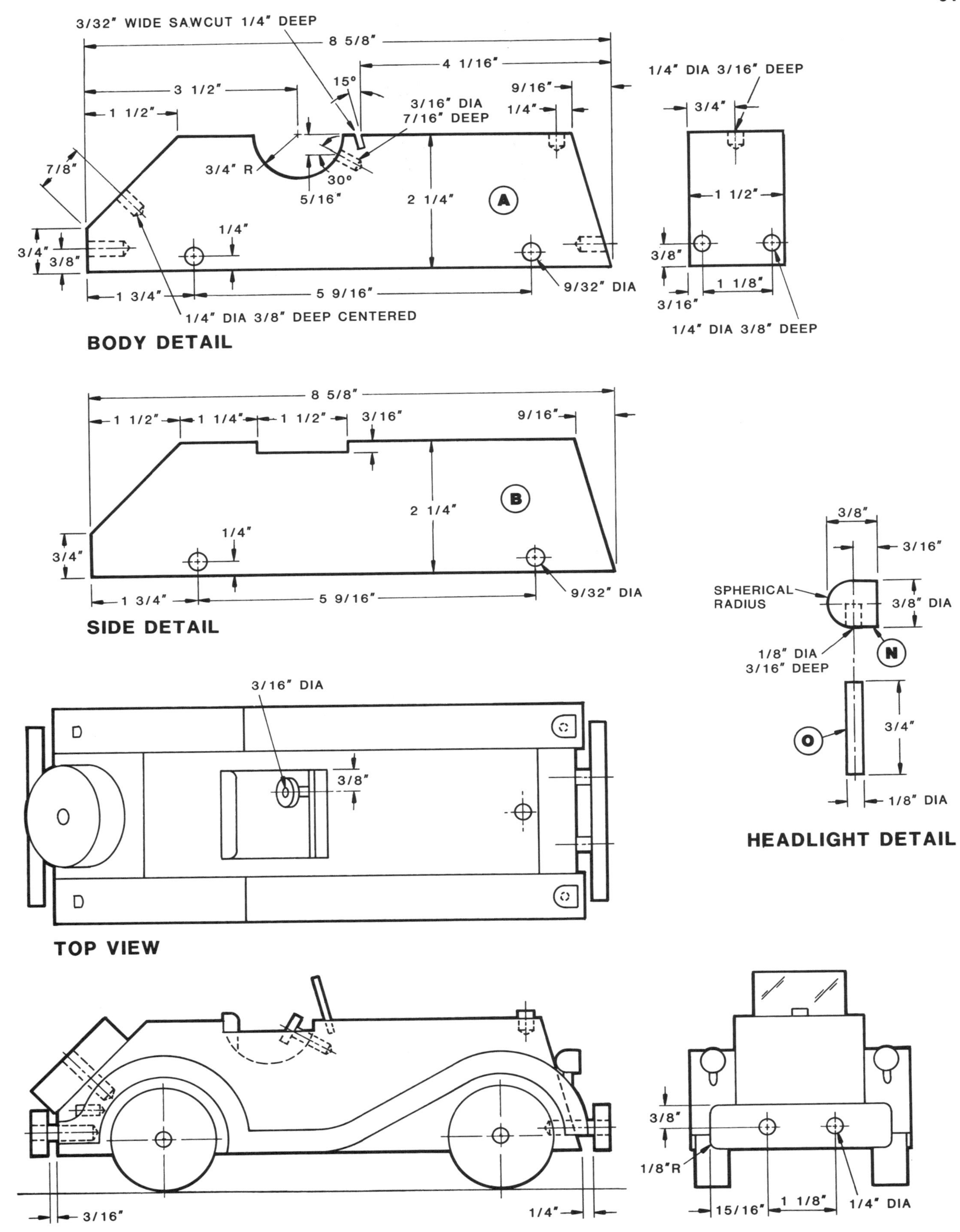

3/32" WIDE SAWCUT 1/4" DEEP
8 5/8"
4 1/16"
3 1/2"
15°
9/16"
1 1/2"
3/16" DIA
7/16" DEEP
1/4"
7/8"
3/4" R
30°
5/16"
2 1/4"
A
1/4"
3/4"
3/8"
1 3/4"
5 9/16"
9/32" DIA
1/4" DIA 3/8" DEEP CENTERED
BODY DETAIL
1/4" DIA 3/16" DEEP
3/4"
1 1/2"
3/8"
1 1/8"
3/16"
1/4" DIA 3/8" DEEP
8 5/8"
1 1/2"
1 1/4"
1 1/2"
3/16"
9/16"
2 1/4"
B
1/4"
3/4"
1 3/4"
5 9/16"
9/32" DIA
SIDE DETAIL
3/8"
3/16"
SPHERICAL RADIUS
3/8" DIA
1/8" DIA
3/16" DEEP
N
3/4"
O
1/8" DIA
HEADLIGHT DETAIL
3/16" DIA
3/8"
D
D
TOP VIEW
3/16"
1/4"
SIDE VIEW
3/8"
1/8"R
15/16"
1 1/8"
1/4" DIA
FRONT VIEW

then sand to the line. Glue a side to each side of the body. Clamp and allow to dry. When dry, sand the edges on a disk sander to eliminate any differences between the three piece assembly. Lay out the spare wheel peg hole on the back sloping face and drill 1/4" dia 3/8" deep.

The fenders are next. Begin by laying out a 1/2 inch grid pattern on a piece of card stock. Mark the point on each grid line where the outline crosses the grid line. Join the straight lines with the aid of a straightedge and freehand the curved lines. Cut out the full size pattern. Lay out the two fenders (**C**) on 3/4" stock using the fender pattern. Mark the headlight and taillight hole locations on each fender. Drill the 1/8" dia hole 1/4" deep for the headlight peg and the 1/4" dia hole 3/16" deep for the taillight in each fender. Make the cuts with a band saw and cut away from the lines. Sand the fenders with a drum sander chucked into a drill press chuck.

LIST OF MATERIALS

FINISHED DIMENSIONS IN INCHES

A	BODY	1 1/2 x 2 1/4 x 8 5/8
B	SIDE (2)	5/16 x 2 1/4 x 8 5/8
C	FENDER (2)	3/4 x 1 3/4 x 8 7/8
D	AXLE (2)	1/4 DIA x 3 1/2
E	RADIATOR CAP	1/4 DIA x 3/8
F	BUMPER (2)	1/4 x 3/4 x 3
G	BUMPER PEG (4)	1/4 DIA x 1
H	SEAT BACK	1/4 x 9/16 x 1 1/2
I	STEERING WHEEL	1/2 DIA x 1/8
J	STEERING COLUMN	3/16 DIA x 3/4
K	WHEEL PEG	1/4 DIA x 3/4
L	WHEEL (5)	COMMERICAL
M	WINDSHIELD (CLEAR PLASTIC)	3/32 x 1 x 1 1/2
N	HEADLIGHT (2)	3/8 DIA x 3/8
O	HEADLIGHT PEG (2)	1/8 DIA x 3/4
P	TAILLIGHT (2)	3/16 DIA x 3/8

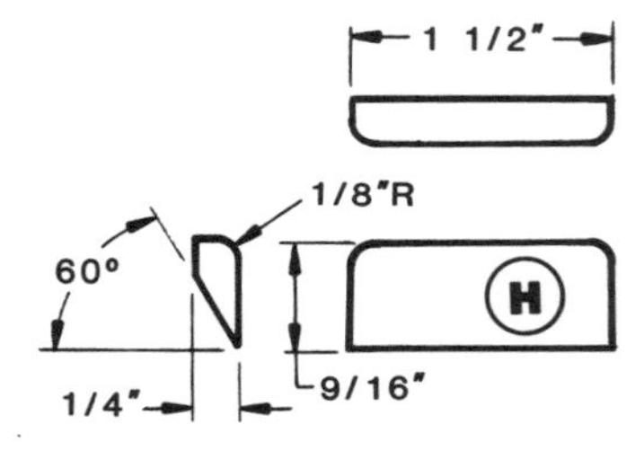

SEAT BACK DETAIL

Chuck a section of 3/8" dia dowel in a drill press and form the spherical radius with a file, followed by a sanding block. Drill th 1/8" dia hole and cut the headlight (N) to length. Make a second headlight the same way and cut tow headlight pegs (O) to length from 1/8" dia dowel. Glue the headlight and pegs together.

Cut the seat back (**H**) to size. Round over the top and side edges with a 1/8" router bit. Glue the seat back to the body.

Drill a 3/16" dia hole 3/8" deep in the end of a length of 1/2" dia dowel. Cut the

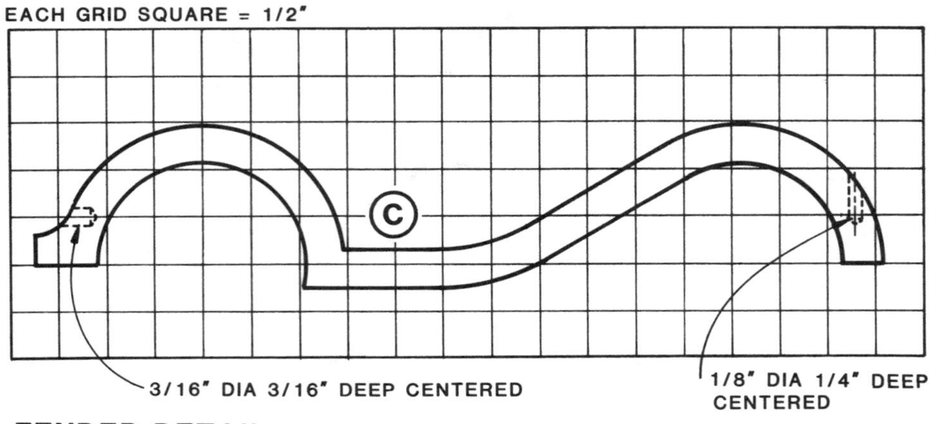

FENDER DETAIL

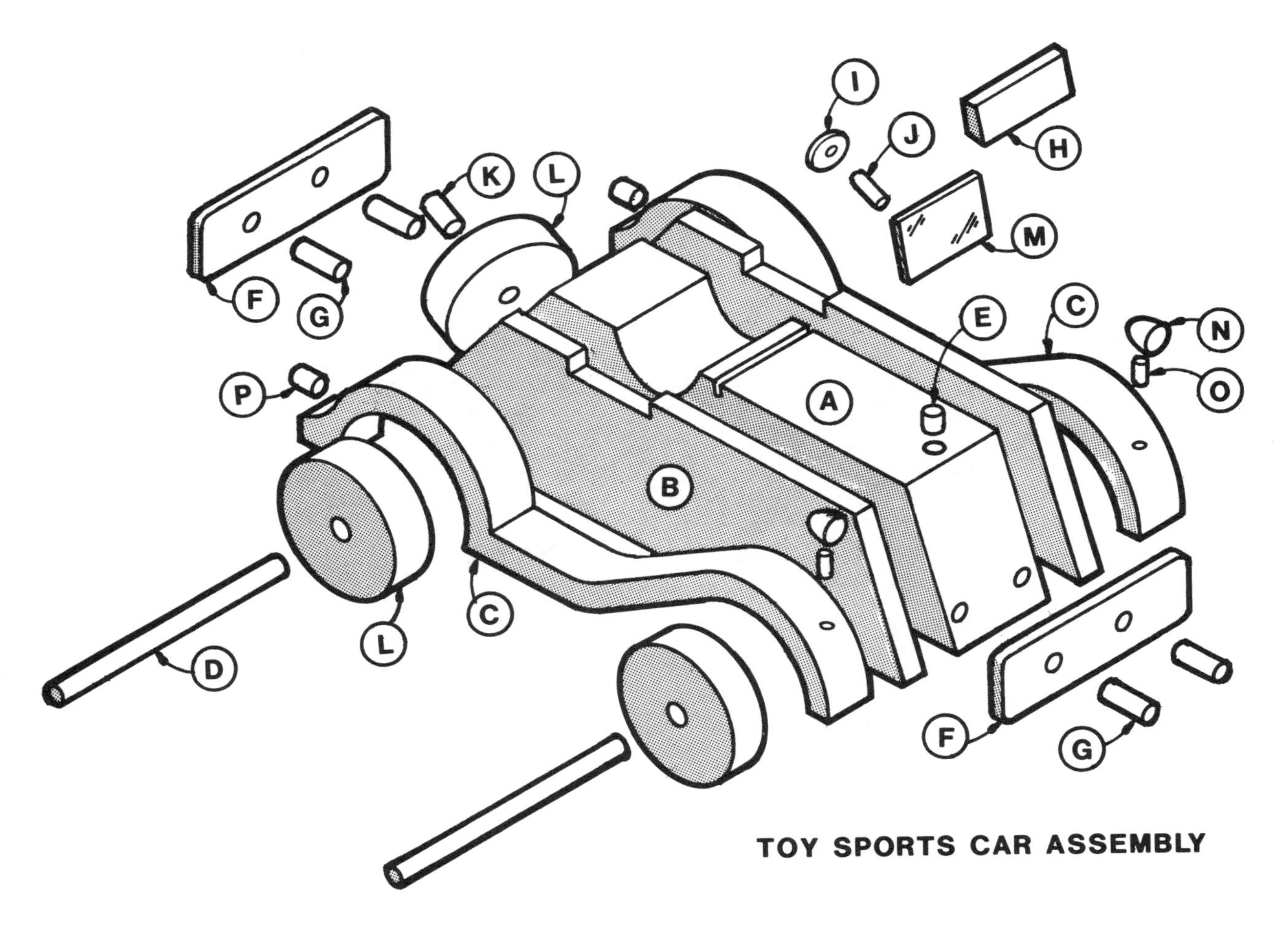

TOY SPORTS CAR ASSEMBLY

steering wheel (**I**) 1/8" thick from this dowel. Cut the steering column (**J**) 3/4" long from a 3/16" dia dowel. Glue the steering wheel to the end of the steering column.

From a 3/32" thick piece of clear plastic cut the windshield (**M**) to size.

Cut the two bumpers (**F**) to size from 1/4" stock. Lay out the center of the two holes in each bumper and drill with a 1/4" dia bit. Sand the 1/8" radius on the four corners. Cut the four bumper pegs (**G**) 1" long from 1/4" dia dowel. Glue the pegs into the holes in the bumper and when dry glue bumper pegs into the holes in the body.

The five wheels (**L**) could be cut from 1/2" stock with a circle cutter in a drill press. Sand the cut surface smooth and round over the edges. We used 1 3/4" dia commercial wheels with a 1/4" dia hole for this toy. Cut two axles (**D**), a wheel peg (**K**) and a radiator cap (**E**) to length from 1/4" dia dowel. Cut two taillights (**P**) from 3/16" dia dowel. The axles protrude about 1/16" outside the wheel face. Round over both ends about 1/16". Glue one wheel onto each axle and one wheel onto the wheel peg. The wheel peg is flush with the wheel face. Glue the taillights and headlights into the holes in the fenders.

Allow the glue to dry overnight and then sand to remove all sharp edges. Remove the dust with a tack cloth. Apply a child-safe finish and allow to dry. Glue the steering wheel column assembly into the hole in the driver's compartment. Apply a small amount of glue into the headlight peg holes in the fenders and slide in the headlight assemblies. Glue the wheel peg into the hole in the back of the body. Slide the axle into the holes in the body and glue the other wheels to the axles. Leave about 1/16" protruding beyond the wheel face.

Your sports car is now ready to display on the shelf or as a gift for that special youngster.

SMALL DIESEL

Freight Train

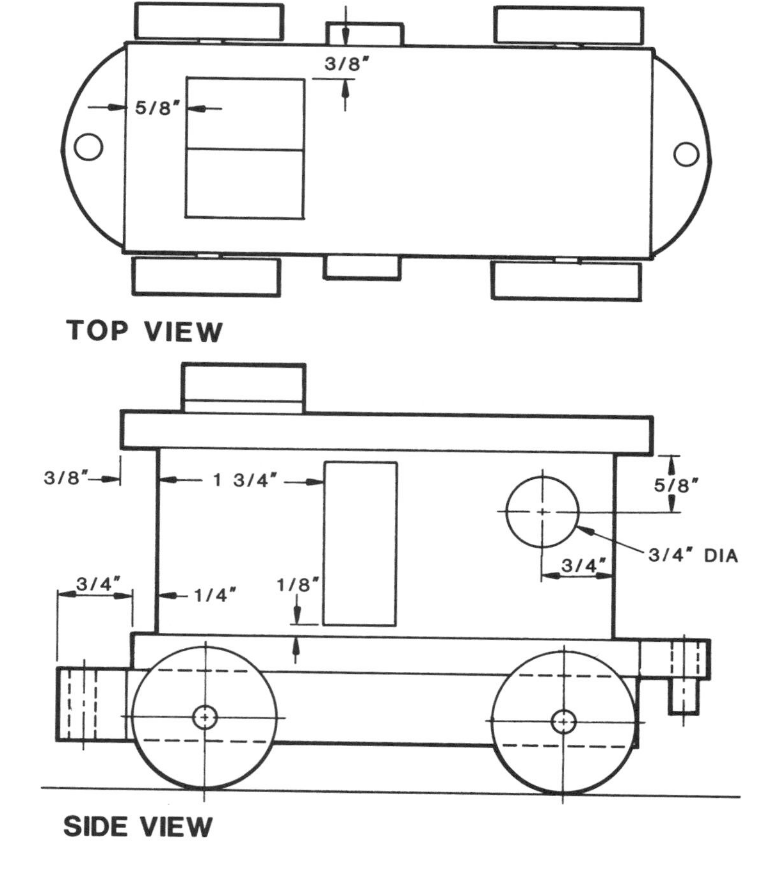

Over the years small trains have always been a favorite of children. With the popularity of the real life diesels that most children these days see, it's only natural to build a diesel wood toy. This train is the same size as the small steam freight train found else where in this book. Hook the cars up to either engine for a longer train. Build more than one car for a real long train.

To make enough upper bases and bases for the locomotive, coal car and the caboose, rip an 18" long piece of 3/4" pine stock to 2 1/4" wide. Rip another 18" long piece of 3/8" stock to 2 1/4" wide.

THE DIESEL LOCOMOTIVE

Cut a piece from the 3/8" stock just ripped 6" long for the upper base (**A**) for the diesel. Lay out the center of the end radius 1 1/4" back from one end and 1 1/8"

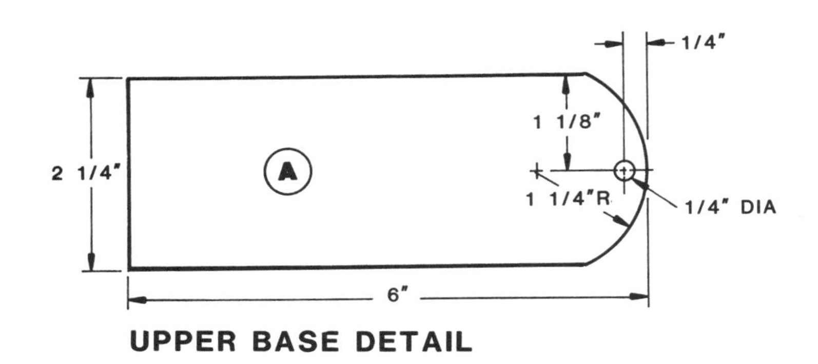

UPPER BASE DETAIL

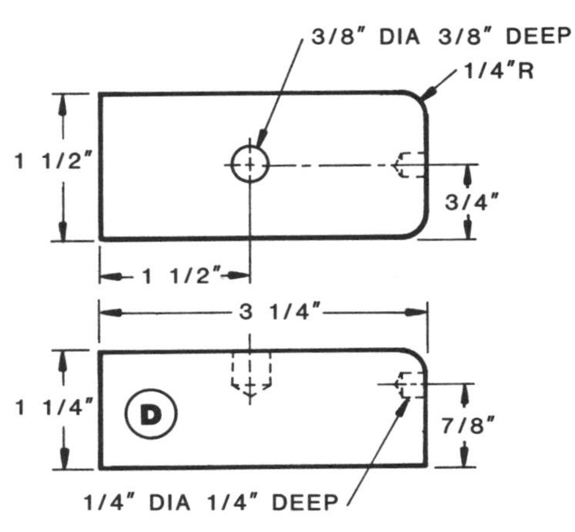

DIESEL HOOD DETAIL

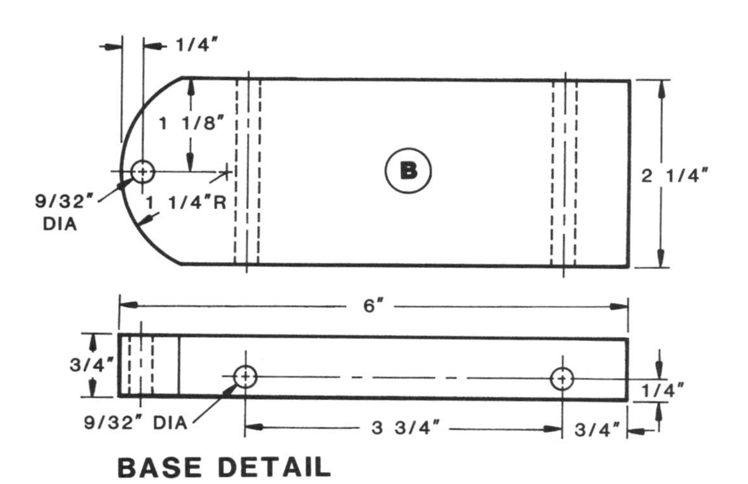

BASE DETAIL

from the side. With a compass mark the 1 1/4" radius. Cut the radius away from the line and sand to the line. Mark the pin hole 1/4" from the radius edge and 1 1/8" from the side. Drill the pin hole with a 1/4" dia bit.

Cut a piece from the 3/4" stock ripped earlier 6" long for the base (**B**) for the diesel. Lay out the 1 1/4" radius. Cut the radius away from the line and sand to the line. Lay out the axle holes 1/4" up from the bottom. One hole is 3/4" from the

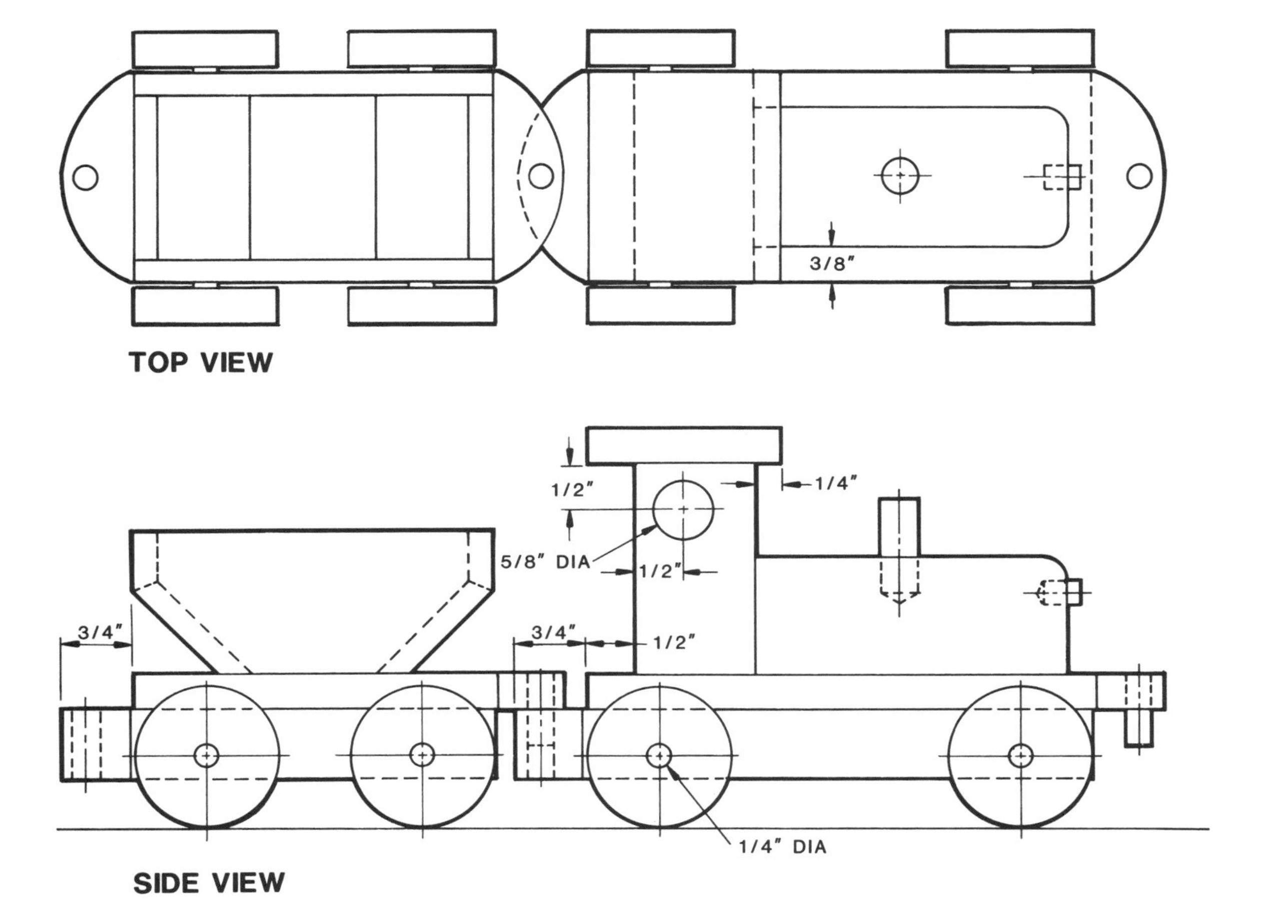

straight edge and the other is 3 3/4" from the first hole. Mark the pin clearance hole 1 1/8" from the side and 1/4" from the radius edge. Drill the three holes with a 9/32" dia bit. Glue the upper base to the base with the straight back 3/4" in from the radius of the base.

Cut three diesel cab (**C**) pieces from 3/4" thick stock and glue together to form the 2 1/4" wide cab. When the glue dries drill the 5/8" dia hole for the engineer's window. Glue the cab to the upper base.

Cut the diesel hood (**D**) 1 1/4" by 1 1/2" by 3 1/4" long. Mark the stack hole 3/4" from the side and 1 1/2" from the back edge and the headlight hole 3/4" from the side and 7/8" from the bottom edge. Drill the 3/8" dia stack hole 3/8" deep and the headlight hole 1/4" dia by 1/4" deep. With a 1/4" radius router bit round over the two front side edges and the top edge. Glue the hood to the cab and upper base.

Next cut the diesel roof (**E**) from 3/8" stock. Glue the roof to the cab.

Take a length of 3/8" dia dowel and cut the stack (**F**) to a length of 1". Cut the headlight (**G**) to length from 1/4" dia dowel. Glue the stack and headlight into the holes in the hood.

LIST OF MATERIALS

FINISHED DIMENSIONS IN INCHES

A	UPPER BASE (2)	3/8 x 2 1/4 x 6
B	BASE (2)	3/4 x 2 1/4 x 6
C	DIESEL CAB (3)	3/4 x 1 1/4 x 2 1/4
D	DIESEL HOOD	1 1/4 x 1 1/2 x 3 1/4
E	DIESEL ROOF	3/8 x 2 1/4 x 2
F	STACK	3/8 DIA x 1
G	HEADLIGHT	1/4 DIA x 3/8
H	COAL CAR UPPER BASE	3/8 x 2 1/4 x 4 1/2
I	COAL CAR BASE	3/4 x 2 1/4 x 4 1/2
J	COAL CAR SIDE (2)	1/4 x 1 1/2 x 3 3/4
K	COAL CAR END (2)	1/4 x 5/8 x 1 3/4
L	COAL CAR PANEL (2)	1/4 x 1 1/2 x 1 3/4
M	CABOOSE SIDE (3)	3/4 x 2 x 4 3/4
N	CABOOSE ROOF	3/8 x 2 1/4 x 5 1/2
O	ROOF	1/2 x 1 1/2 x 1 1/4
P	DOOR (2)	1/4 x 3/4 x 1 3/4
Q	PIN (3)	1/4 DIA x 3/4
R	WHEEL (12)	3/8 x 1 1/2 DIA
S	AXLE (6)	1/4 DIA x 3 1/8

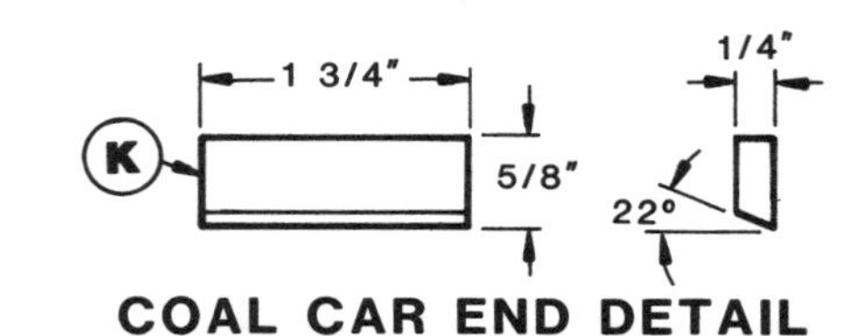

COAL CAR END DETAIL

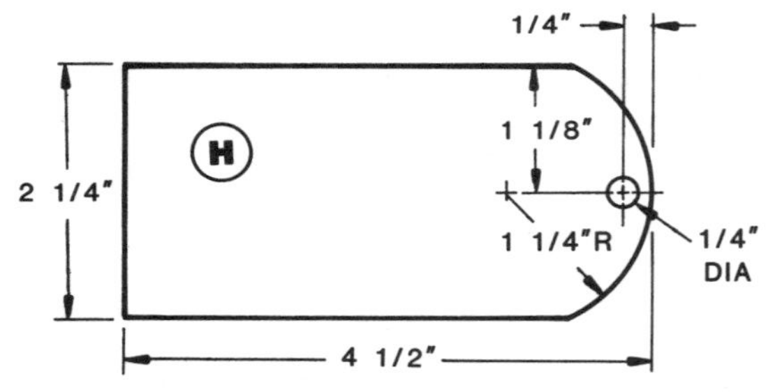

COAL CAR UPPER BASE DETAIL

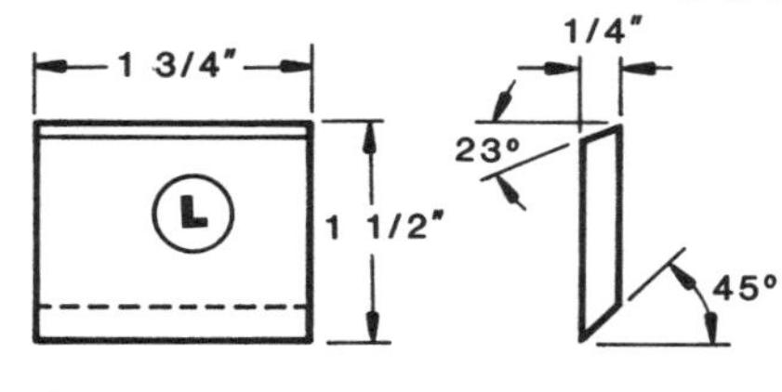

COAL CAR PANEL DETAIL

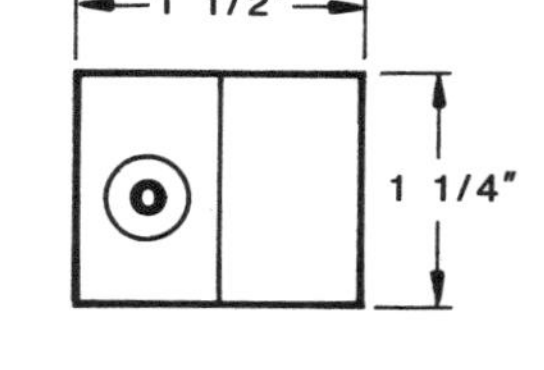

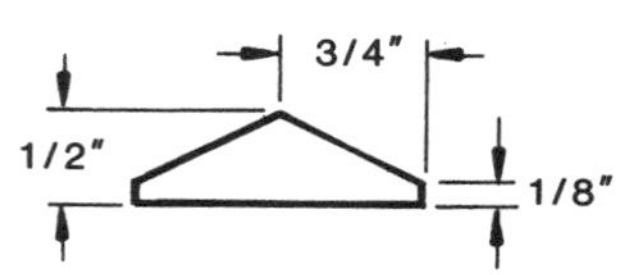

CABOOSE ROOF DETAIL

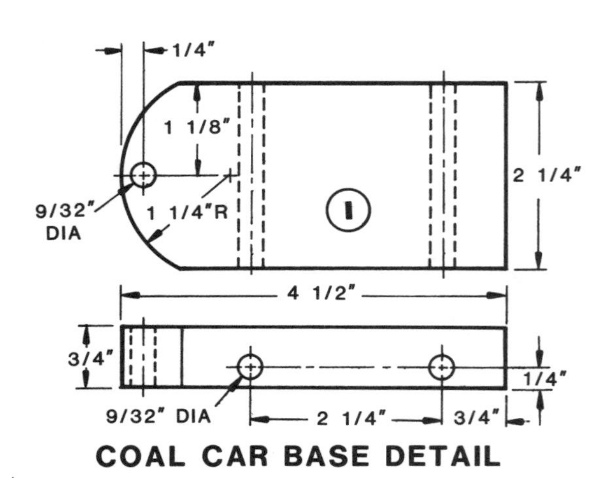

COAL CAR BASE DETAIL

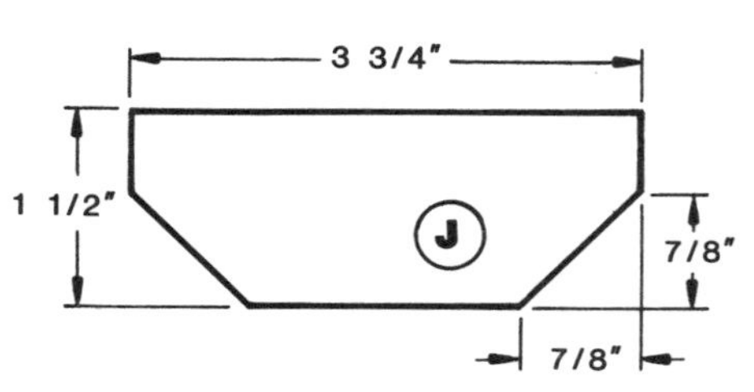

COAL CAR SIDE DETAIL

Make four wheels (**R**) for the diesel from 3/8" stock. Sand the cut surface of the wheels and round over the edges. Cut the two axles (**S**) for the diesel to length from 1/4" dia dowel. Glue one wheel to each axle. Cut the pin (**Q**) to length from 1/4" dia dowel. Glue the pin into the hole in the upper base.

Set the diesel aside to allow the glue to dry and start work on the coal car.

THE COAL CAR

Cut a piece from the 3/8" ripped stock 4 1/2" long for the coal car upper base (**H**). Lay out the center of the end radius 1 1/4" back from one end and 1 1/8" from the side. With a compass mark the 1 1/4" radius. Cut the radius away from the line and sand to the line. Mark the pin hole 1/4" from the radius edge and then 1 1/8" from the side. Drill the pin hole with a 1/4" dia bit.

Cut a piece from the 3/4" ripped stock 4 1/2" long for the coal car base (**I**). Lay out the 1 1/4" radius. Cut the radius away from the line and sand to the line. Lay out the axle holes 1/4" up from the bottom. One hole is 3/4" from the straight edge and the other is 3 3/4" from the first hole. Mark the pin clearance hole 1 1/8" from the side and 1/4" from the radius edge. Drill the three holes with a 9/32" dia bit. Glue the upper base to the base 3/4" in from the radius of the base.

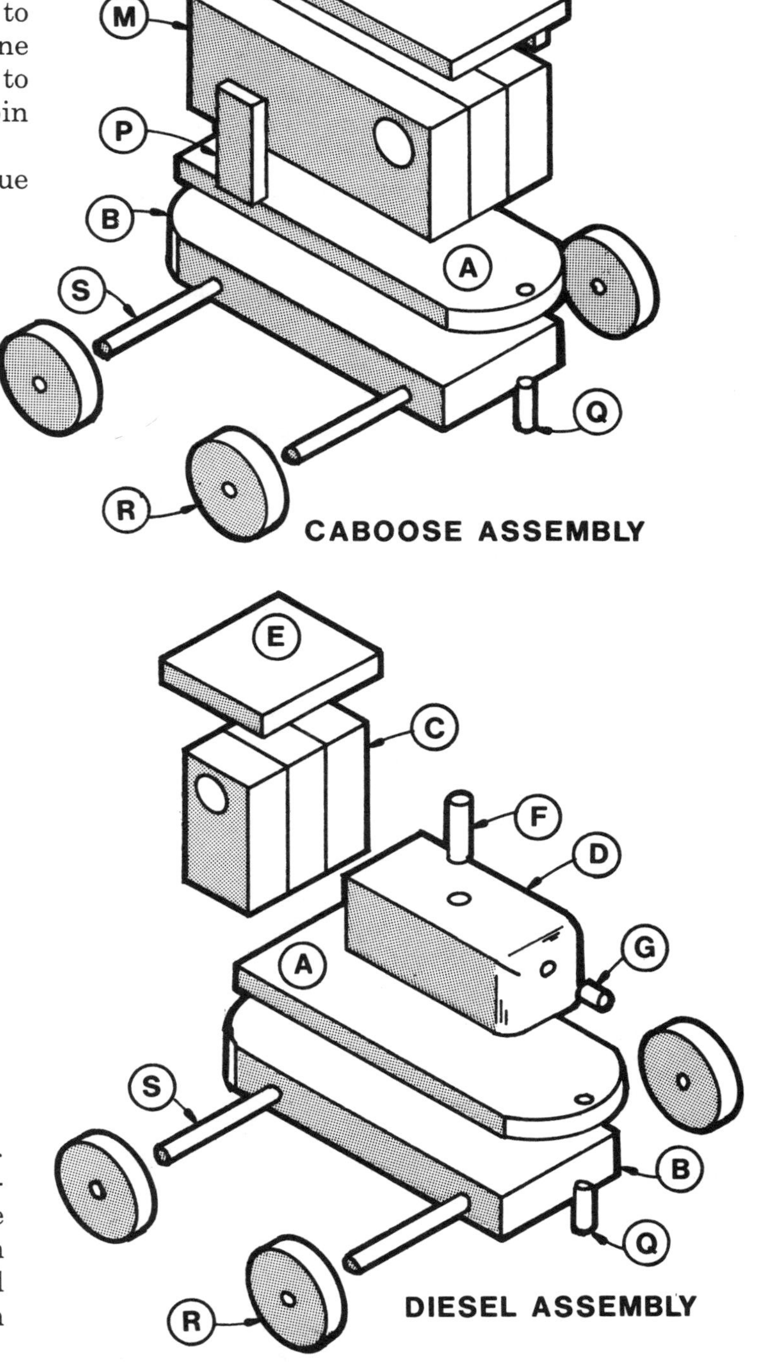

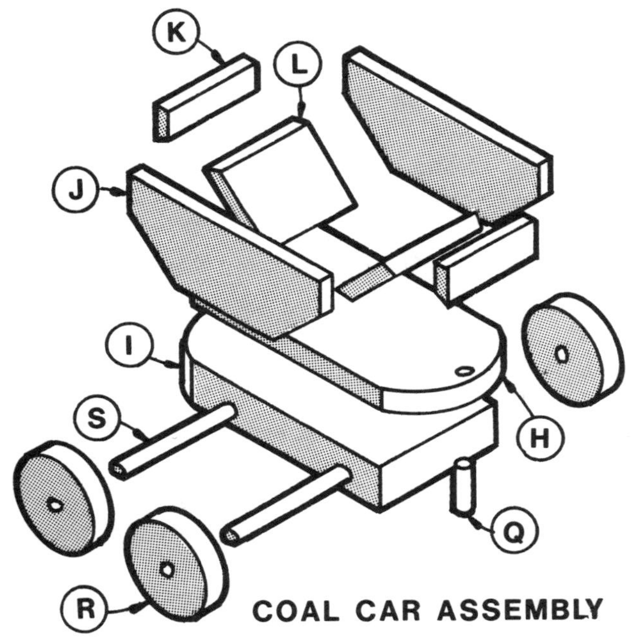

Lay out two coal car sides (**J**), two ends (**K**) and two panels (**L**) on 1/4" stock. Cut away from the line and then sand to the line. Make sure all the ends and panels are the same width so the body will not have any gaps. Lay one side, good side down, and edge glue one end and one panel to the side. Glue the other end and panel to the other end of the side. Glue the other side to the top of the ends and panels. Place a weight on the side and allow to dry. When dry, glue the body to the upper base. Keep the coal car body end in line with the straight end of the upper base.

Make four wheels (**R**) for the coal car from 3/8" stock. Sand the cut surface of the wheels and radius the edges. Cut the two axles (**S**) for the coal car to length from 1/4" dia dowel. Glue one wheel to each axle. Cut the pin (**Q**) to length from 1/4" dia dowel. Glue the pin into the hole in the upper base as shown on the drawings.

Set the coal car aside to allow the glue to dry and start work on the caboose.

THE CABOOSE

This piece of rolling stock is known as a side door caboose and was very common on the early railroads. The car is the same length as the diesel locomotive.

From the 3/8" stock already ripped to width for the upper base, cut the caboose upper base 6" long. Lay out the center of the end radius 1 1/4" back from one end and 1 1/8" from the side. With a compass mark the 1 1/4" radius. Cut the radius away from the line and sand to the line. Mark the pin hole 1/4" from the radius edge and 1 1/8" from the side. Drill the pin hole with a 1/4" dia bit.

Cut a piece from the 3/4" ripped stock 6" long for the caboose base. Lay out the center of the end radius 1 1/4" back from one end and 1 1/8" from the side. With a compass mark the 1 1/4" radius. Cut the radius away from the line and sand to the line. Lay out the axle holes 1/4" up from the bottom. One hole is 3/4" from the straight edge and the other is 3 3/4" from the first hole. Mark the pin clearance hole 1 1/8" from the side and 1/4" from the radius edge. Drill the three holes with a 9/32" dia bit. Sand the two pieces and remove the sawdust with a tack cloth. Glue the upper base to the base with the straight back 3/4" in from the radius of the base.

Lay out three caboose sides (**M**) on 3/4" stock and glue together to form the 2 1/4" wide body. Allow the glue to dry and then drill the 3/4" dia window. Glue the body 1/4" from the straight edge of the upper base.

Cut the caboose roof (**N**) from 3/8" stock. Sand the cut edges and glue to the top of the body with 3/8" overhang at the rear. Lay out the roof (**O**) on 1/2" stock. Draw the two 40 degree chamfers on the roof end. Cut away from the line and then sand to the line of the edges and the chamfer. Glue to the top of the caboose roof 3/8" from the side and 5/8" from the back edge of the caboose roof.

The two doors (**P**) are cut from 1/4" stock. Sand the cut edges and glue to the body side 1 3/4" from the back edge of the body and 1/8" up from the bottom edge.

Make four wheels (**R**) for the caboose from 3/8" stock. Sand the cut surface of the wheels and radius the edges. Cut the two axles (**S**) for the caboose to length from 1/4" dia dowel. Glue one wheel to each axle. Cut the pin (**Q**) to length from 1/4" dia dowel. Glue the pin into the hole in the upper base as shown on the drawings.

FINAL ASSEMBLY

Round over all exposed edges with sandpaper and remove the dust with a tack cloth. Apply a child-safe finish and allow to dry.

Slip the axles into the holes in the base and glue the other wheel to the axles. Leave a small space between the base and the wheel.

The train is now ready to earn some revenue hauling imaginary coal from that mine to the big city. Build several coal cars for a longer train.

WORK EQUIPMENT

Front End Loader

The front end loader will be a favorite wooden toy since it has more moving parts. The scoop will remain in any position, if the pivot hole is a snug fit for the dowel.

Cut the base (**A**) 2 1/2" wide by 6 1/2" long from 3/4" stock. Lay out the two axle hole centers as shown on the side view drawing. Drill the two 9/32" dia holes. Cut the block (**B**) 1 1/4" by 1 5/8" by 2" long. Lay out the angle at the front of the block and the center of the pivot hole. Cut and sand to shape and drill the 3/8" dia hole. Glue the block to the base flush with the front edge of the base and 5/8" from the side.

Cut the dashboard (**D**) 1 1/2" wide by 1 5/8" long from 1/2" stock. Lay out the angle and the center of the steering column hole as shown in the dashboard detail drawing. Cut out with a band saw and then sand the edges. Drill the 1/4" dia hole. Cut a piece of 3/4" dia dowel 1/4" long and drill a 1/4" dia hole in the center for the steering wheel (**Q**). The steering column (**P**) is cut to length from 1/4" dia dowel. Glue the steering wheel to the column. Put a small amount of glue into the hole in the dashboard and insert the end of the steering column.

Cut the back (**E**) 1 1/2" wide by 2 1/4" long from 1/2" stock. Cut the seat base (**X**) 5/8" by 5/8" by 1 1/2" long. Cut the seat (**V**) 1/2" wide by 1 1/2" and the seat back (**W**) 1" wide by 1 1/2" long from 1/4" stock. Glue the seat base, seat back and the seat to the back.

Cut the two doors (**N**) from 1/2" stock 1 1/4" wide by 1 1/2" long. Cut four posts (**M**) 1/2" wide by 3 1/2" long from 1/2" stock. On a flat surface covered with wax paper glue a post on each side of each door. When dry, glue the two door post assemblies to the bed and the dashboard.

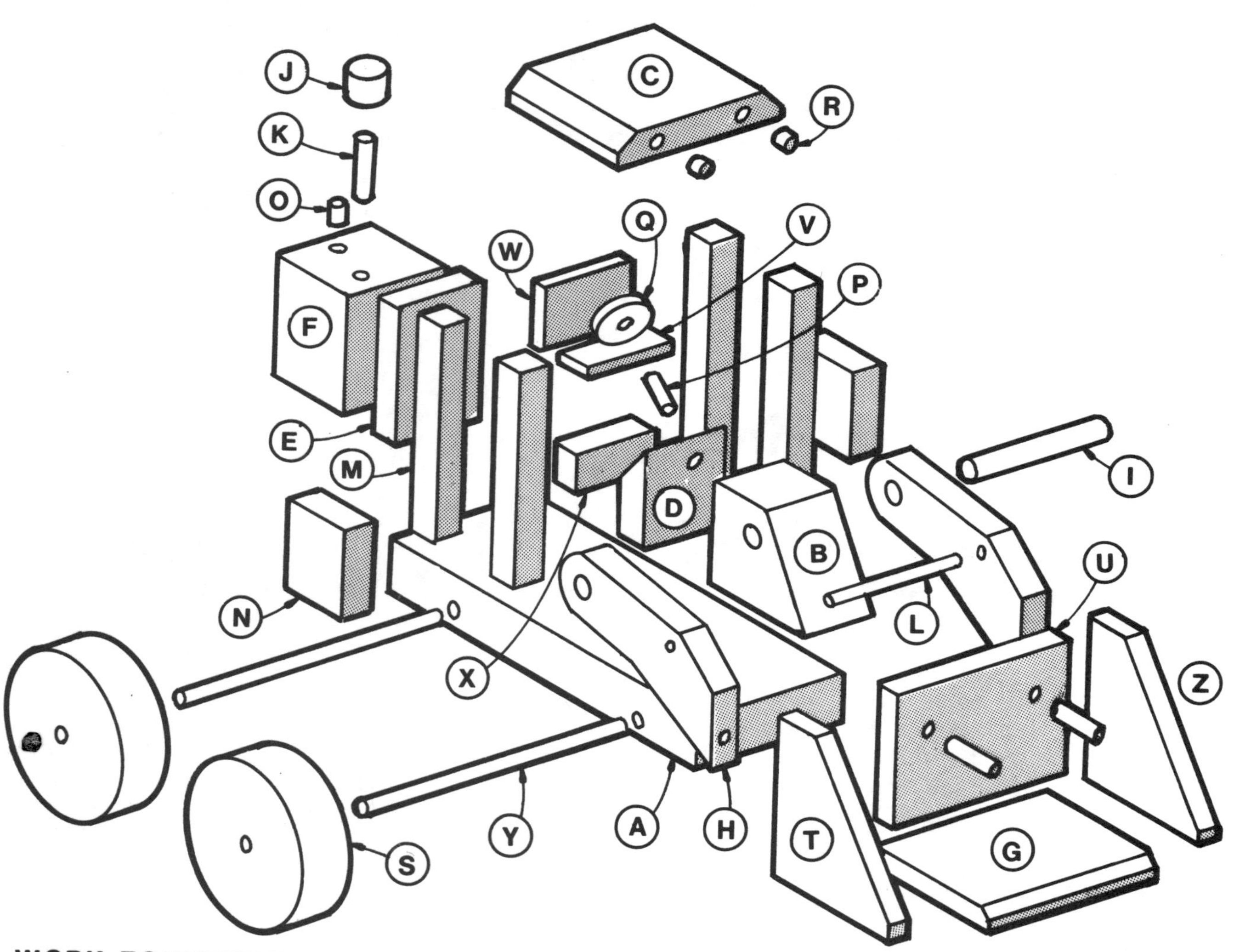

WORK EQUIPMENT FRONT END LOADER ASSEMBLY

LIST OF MATERIALS

FINISHED DIMENSIONS IN INCHES

A	BASE	3/4 x 2 1/2 x 6 1/2
B	BLOCK	1 1/4 x 1 5/8 x 2
C	ROOF	1/2 x 2 7/8 x 2 3/8
D	DASHBOARD	1/2 x 1 1/2 x 1 5/8
E	BACK	1/2 x 1 1/2 x 2 1/4
F	HOOD	1 3/4 x 1 15/16 x 2
G	SCOOP BOTTOM	3/8 x 2 1/2 x 3
H	SCOOP ARM (2)	1/2 x 1 3/4 x 3 5/8
I	PIVOT SHAFT	3/8 DIA x 2 3/8
J	EXHAUST CAP	1/2 DIA x 1/2
K	STACK	1/4 DIA x 1 3/8
L	DOWEL	1/4 DIA x 2 3/8
M	POST (4)	1/2 x 1/2 x 3 1/2
N	DOOR (2)	1/2 x 1 1/4 x 1 1/2
O	RADIATOR CAP	1/4 DIA x 5/8
P	STEERING COLUMN	1/4 DIA x 1
Q	STEERING WHEEL	3/4 DIA x 1/4
R	HEADLIGHT (2)	1/4 DIA x 1/2
S	WHEEL (4)	3/4 x 2 1/2 DIA
T	SCOOP SIDE (2)	3/8 x 2 1/2 x 2 1/2
U	SCOOP BACK	3/8 x 2 1/8 x 3
V	SEAT	1/4 x 1/2 x 1 1/2
W	SEAT BACK	1/4 x 1 x 1 1/2
X	SEAT BASE	5/8 x 5/8 x 1 1/2
Y	AXLE (2)	1/4 DIA x 4 1/8
Z	DOWEL (2)	1/4 DIA x 1

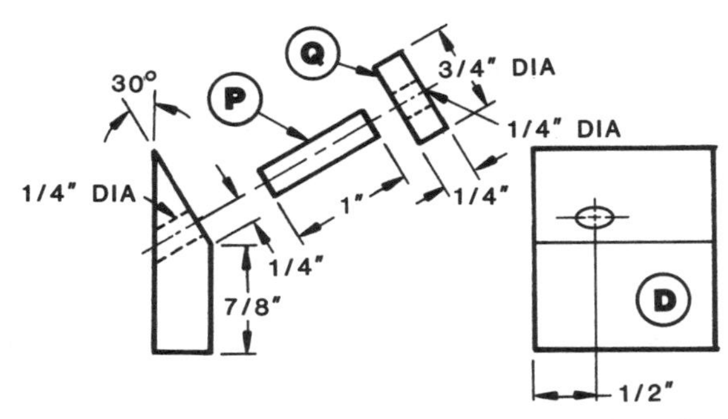

DASHBOARD AND STEERING WHEEL DETAILS

Glue the back to the base and rear side posts.

Cut the roof (**C**) 2 7/8" wide by 2 3/8" long from 1/2" stock. Sand a 3/16" by 45 degree chamfer to the back and a 5/16" by 45 degree chamfer to the sides. Locate and drill the two 1/4" dia headlight holes 3/8" deep. Glue the roof to the back and the posts. Cut two headlights (**R**) to length from 1/4" dia dowel and glue into the holes in the roof.

Cut the hood (**F**) 1 3/4" by 1 15/16" by 2" long. Draw lines on the front of the hood for the chamfers. Sand to the lines using several light passes. Lay out the centers for the stack and radiator cap and drill the two 1/4" dia holes 1/2" deep. Glue the hood to the base and back.

Cut the exhaust cap (**J**) 1/2" long from 1/2" dia dowel. Drill a 1/4" dia hole 1/4" deep into the center of one end of the cap. Cut the stack (**K**) 1 3/8" long from 1/4" dia dowel. Glue the cap to the stack. Put a small amount of glue into the hole in the hood and add the stack. Cut the radiator cap (**O**) 5/8" long from 1/4" dia dowel. Glue the radiator cap into the hole in the hood.

Lay out the two scoop arms (**H**) on 1/2" stock using the scoop arm detail drawing. Cut away from the line and sand to the lines. Drill the 1/4" dia and 3/8" dia holes. Cut the two scoop sides (**T**) 2 1/2" wide by 2 1/2" long on 3/8" stock. Cut out the scoop bottom (**G**) 2 1/2" wide by 3" long from 3/8" stock. Sand the chamfer on the scoop bottom to match the angle of the sides. Cut and sand the cut edges. Cut the scoop back (**U**) 2 1/8" wide by 3" long from 3/8" stock. Glue the scoop back to the scoop bottom and the scoop sides to the bottom and the back. Allow to dry and then lay out the centers of the two 1/4" dia dowel holes. Drill the two holes. Glue the scoop arms to the scoop bucket. When dry drill the two 1/4" dia holes 1" deep and glue the two dowels (**Z**) into the holes. Cut the dowel (**L**) 2 3/8" long from 1/4" dia dowel. Glue dowel into the holes in the scoop arms. Cut the pivot shaft (**I**) 2 3/8" long from 3/8" dia dowel.

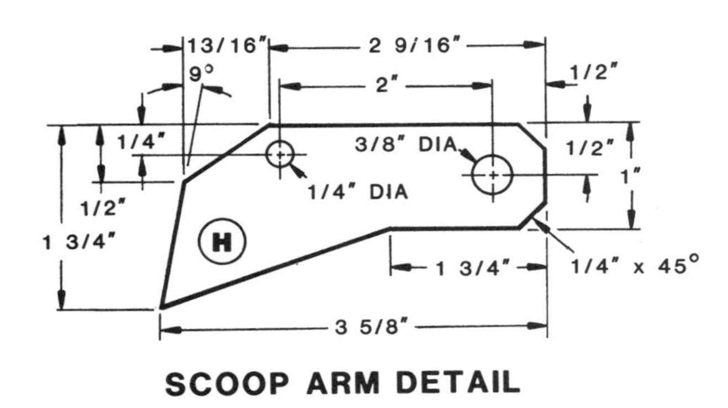

SCOOP ARM DETAIL

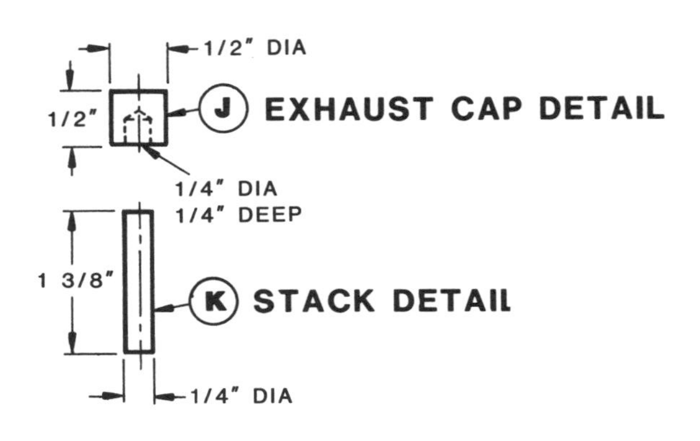

Lay out the four 2 1/2" dia wheels (S) on a piece of 3/4" stock using a compass. Cut the wheels out using a circle cutter chucked in a drill press. Sand to edges and round over the corners. Cut two axles (Y) to length from 1/4" dia dowel. Glue one wheel to each of the axles.

Sand the finished front end loader, body, scoop assembly and wheels with fine grit sandpaper. Remove the dust with a tack cloth, apply a child-safe finish and allow to dry. Do not put finish on the pivot shaft or axles. Put the axles through the axle holes and glue the other wheel to the end of the axle.

The front end loader can now join the fleet of work equipment to help clear the road.

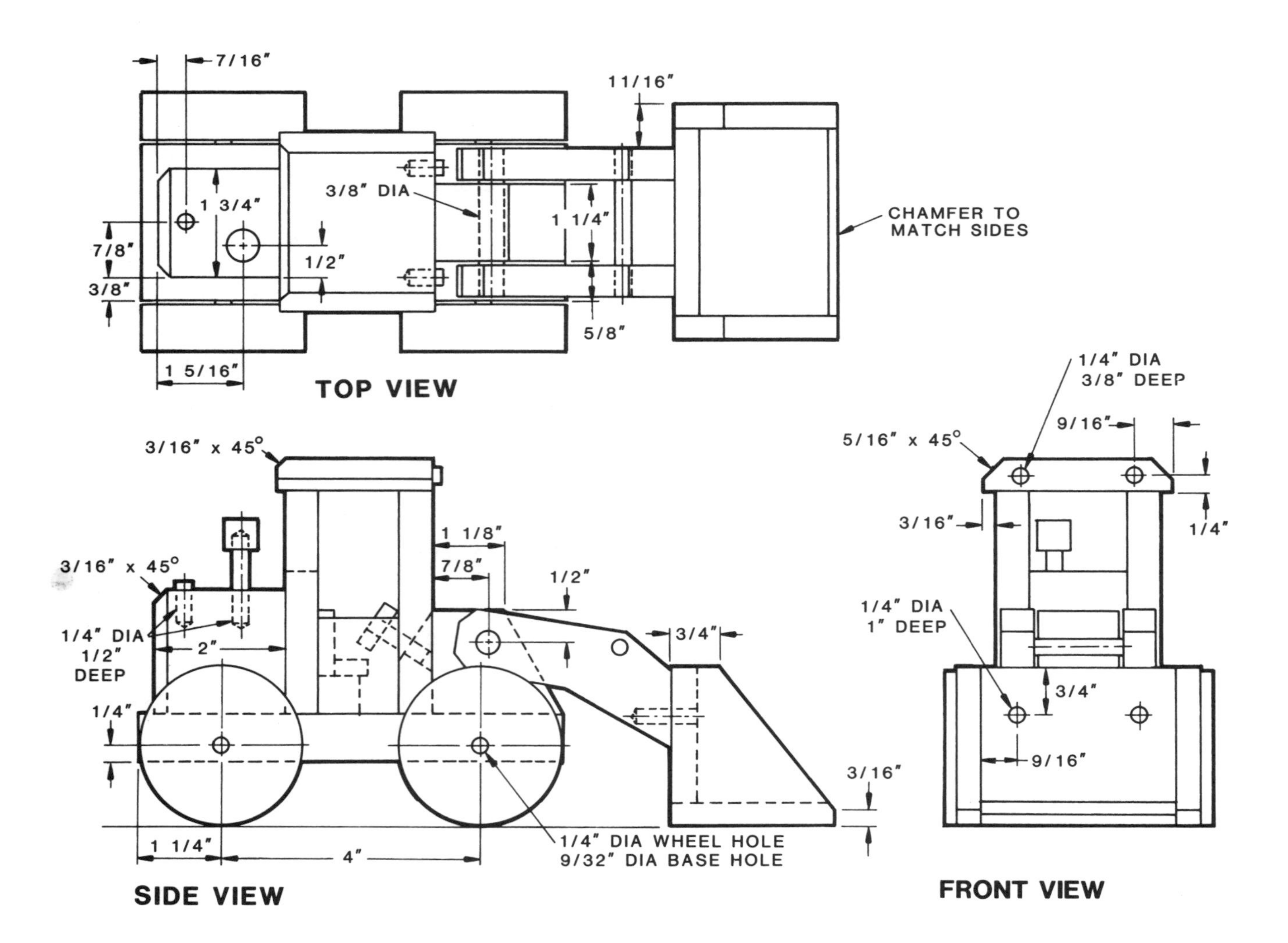

Airliner

Airplanes are a favorite of any child and this twin prop airliner will be a good wood toy.

Cut all the parts to finished size as shown in the list of materials. Lay out the fuselage (**F**) and locate the center of the holes using the dimensions on the side view drawing. With a band saw cut out the fuselage. Cut the notches for the wing and the elevator. Sand all the fresh cut surfaces. Drill the six holes with a 1/2" bit and the strut hole with a 1/4" bit 1" deep.

Lay out the two 1" and two 1 1/2" radius on the wing (**J**). Cut away from the lines and then sand to the lines. Draw a 1/2" radius on the four corners of the elevator (**G**). Cut and sand to the lines. Drill the 7/32" dia hole in each of the supports (**B**) and cut the angle at the back of the support.

Lay out the two engines (**E**) using the engine detail drawing. Drill the 7/32" dia hole 3/4" deep in each block. Cut and sand the edges.

Glue the wing and the elevator to the fuselage. Allow to dry, then glue the wheel supports to the underside of the wing 2 3/8" from the end and 1/4" back from the front edge. Glue the engine to the top of the wing, above the supports.

Cut two wheels (**C**) with a 1 1/8" dia hole saw, from 1/2" stock. Sand the cut surface and round over the edges.

Draw the propeller (**D**) on a 3/8 inch grid square to make a full size pattern. Transfer the outline and the hole center onto a piece of 1/4" stock using carbon paper between the pattern and the wood. Cut the part out using a scroll saw. Drill the shaft hole with a 1/4" bit. Turn two propeller pegs (**H**) down to a diameter of 7/32" for a length of 1 3/16" from a piece of 3/8" dowel. Cut to make the heads 3/16" wide.

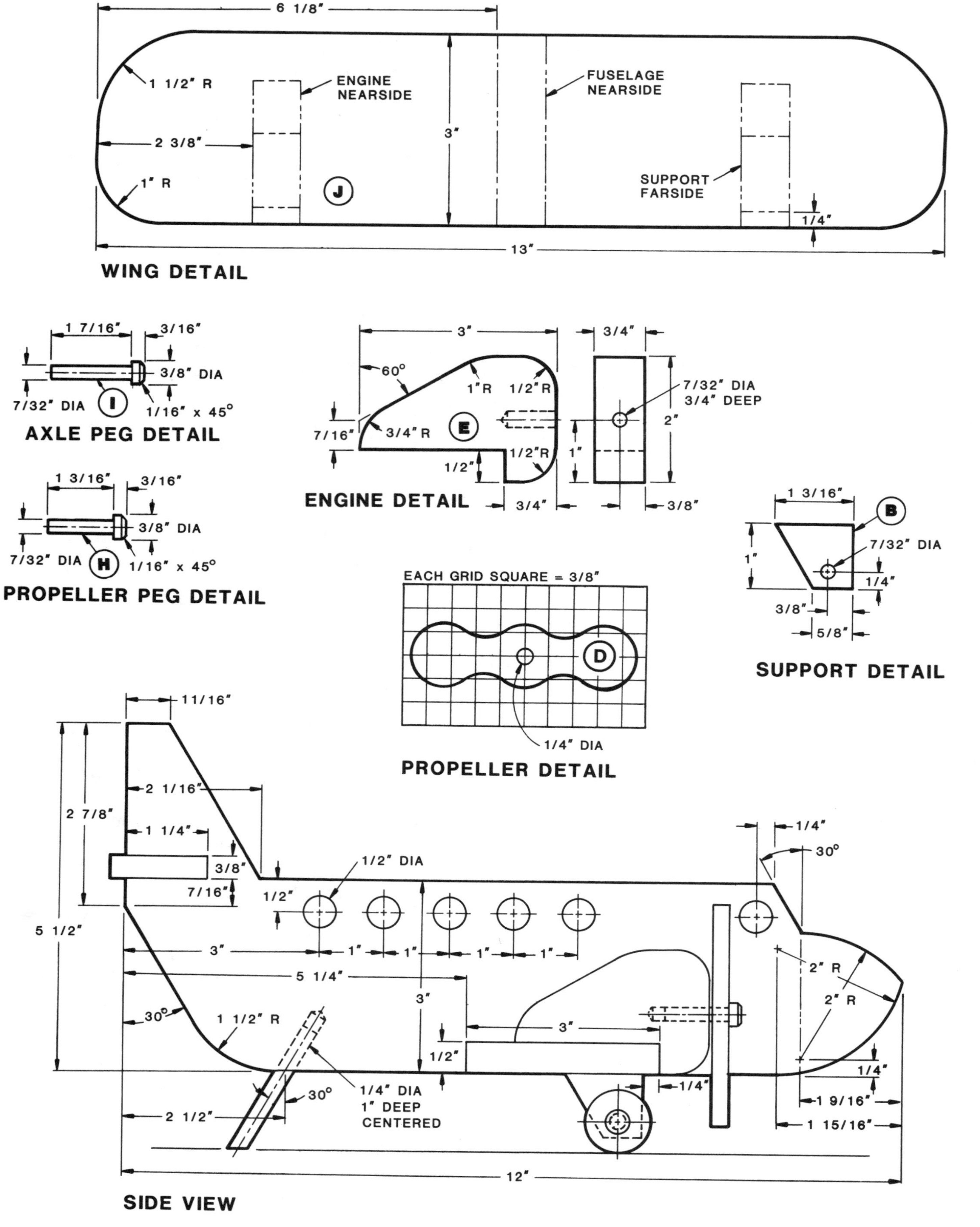
6 1/8"
1 1/2" R
ENGINE NEARSIDE
FUSELAGE NEARSIDE
2 3/8"
3"
1" R
J
SUPPORT FARSIDE
1/4"
13"
WING DETAIL
1 7/16"
3/16"
3/8" DIA
7/32" DIA
I
1/16" x 45°
AXLE PEG DETAIL
3"
3/4"
60°
1" R
1/2" R
7/32" DIA
3/4" DEEP
7/16"
3/4" R
E
2"
1/2" R
1"
1/2"
ENGINE DETAIL
3/4"
3/8"
1 3/16"
3/16"
3/8" DIA
7/32" DIA
H
1/16" x 45°
PROPELLER PEG DETAIL
EACH GRID SQUARE = 3/8"
D
1/4" DIA
PROPELLER DETAIL
1 3/16"
B
7/32" DIA
1"
1/4"
3/8"
5/8"
SUPPORT DETAIL
11/16"
2 7/8"
2 1/16"
1 1/4"
3/8"
7/16"
1/2" DIA
1/2"
1/4"
30°
5 1/2"
3"
1"
1"
1"
1"
5 1/4"
2" R
2" R
3"
30°
1 1/2" R
3"
1/2"
1/4"
1/4"
1/4" DIA
1" DEEP
CENTERED
30°
2 1/2"
1 9/16"
1 15/16"
12"
SIDE VIEW

LIST OF MATERIALS

FINISHED DIMENSIONS IN INCHES

A	STRUT	1/4 DIA x 2 1/4
B	SUPPORT (2)	3/4 x 1 x 1 3/16
C	WHEEL (2)	1/2 x 1 DIA
D	PROPELLER (2)	1/4 x 1 x 3 1/2
E	ENGINE (2)	3/4 x 2 x 3
F	FUSELAGE	3/4 x 5 1/2 x 12
G	ELEVATOR	3/8 x 1 1/2 x 4
H	PROPELLER PEG (2)	3/8 DIA x 1 3/8
I	AXLE PEG (2)	3/8 DIA x 1 5/8
J	WING	1/2 x 3 x 13

Turn the two axle pegs (**I**) diameter down to 7/32" for a length of 1 7/16". Slip one wheel on each axle peg and temporarily slip the pegs into the support holes. Insert the strut (**A**) into the hole in the fuselage. Place the plane on a flat surface and mark the end of the tail support. Remove the tail support and sand the end. Put a small amount of glue into the hole and slip the tail support into the hole. Place on a flat surface and adjust the tail support. Remove the wheels and axle pegs.

Sand all surfaces with sandpaper and wipe with a tack cloth to remove all the dust left from sanding. Apply a good grade of child-safe finish. Allow to dry, then slip one wheel on each axle peg and apply a small amount of glue into the hole in the support. Insert the axle peg into the hole and leave a small gap so the wheel will turn. Put some glue into the hole in engine. Slip the propeller onto the propeller peg and the peg into the hole. Leave a small gap so the propeller will turn freely.

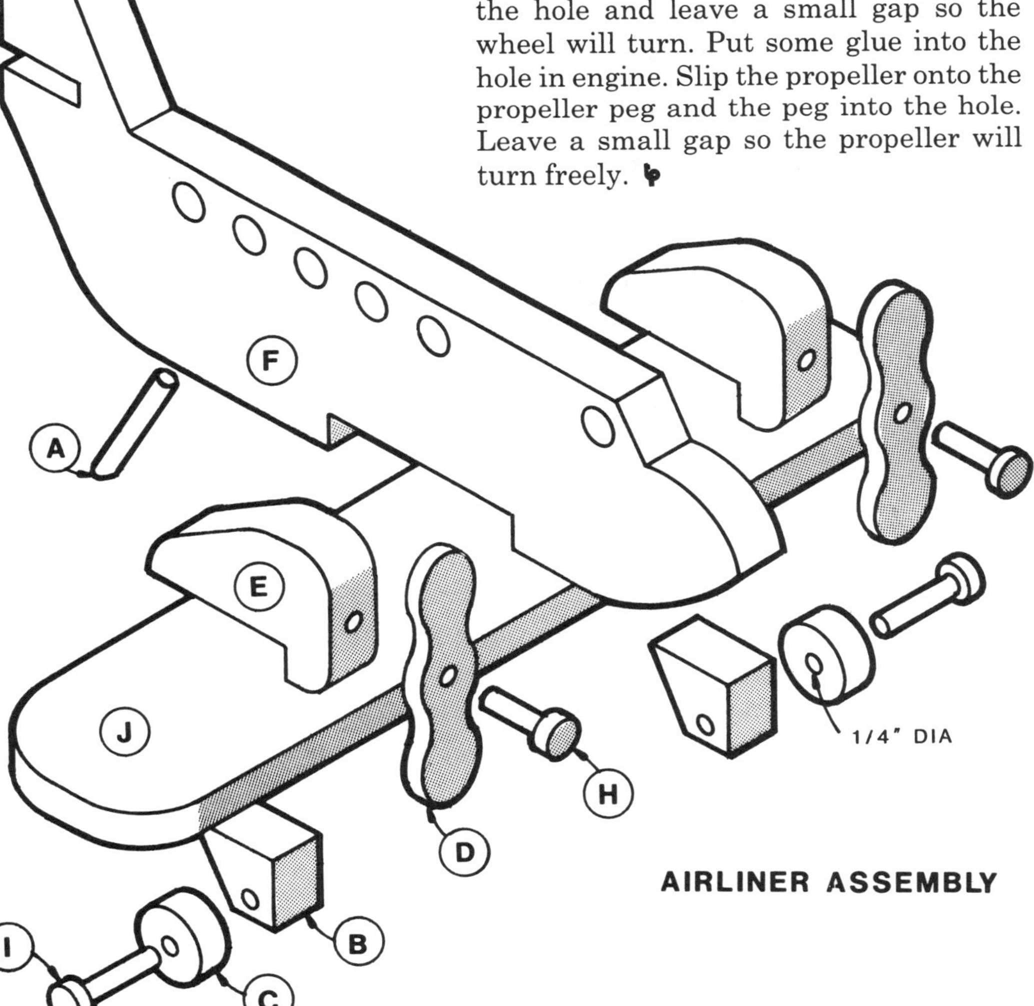

AIRLINER ASSEMBLY

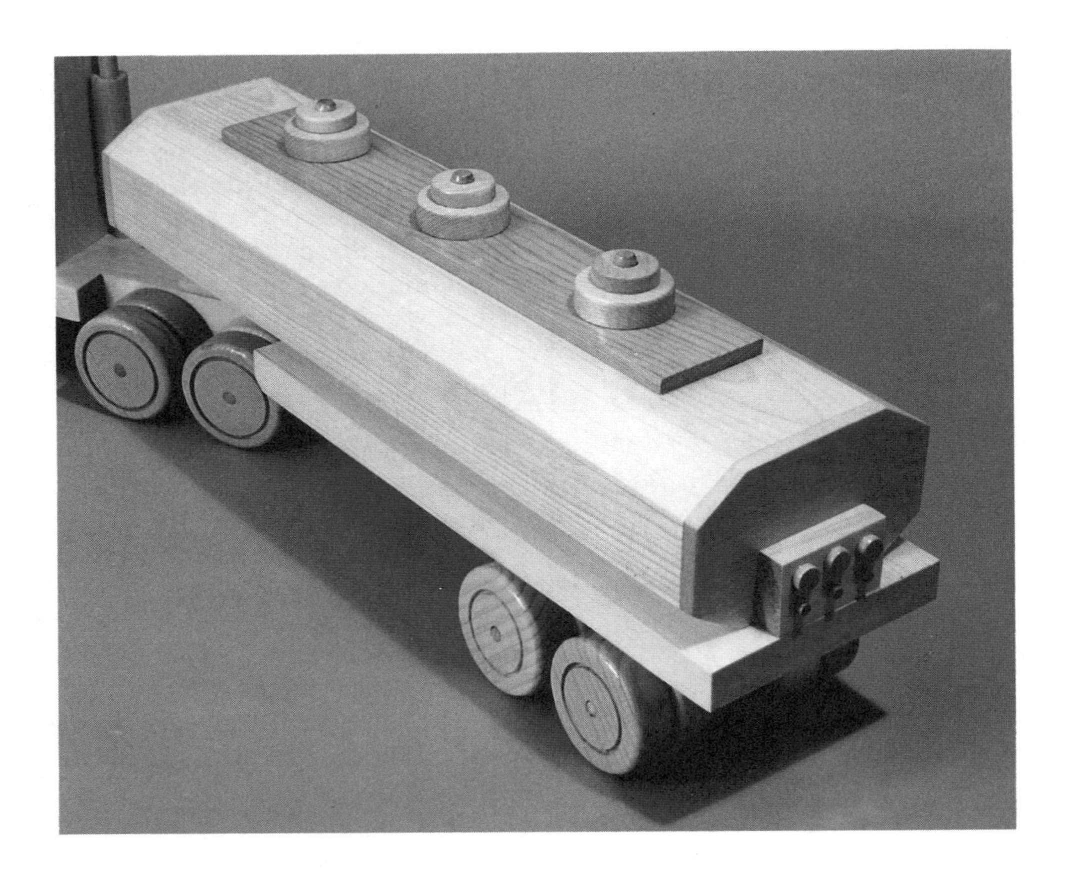

HEAVY HAULERS

Tank Trailer

The heavy haulers long hood tractor or the cab-over tractor can pull this heavy haulers tank trailer.

Cut the base (**A**) 4 1/2" wide by 12" long from a piece of 3/4" stock. Next cut a piece of 1 1/4" thick stock 1 7/8" wide by 3 1/2" long for the axle block (**B**). Locate and drill the two 9/32" dia axle holes. Glue the axle block to the underside of the base 2" from the back and 1 5/8" from the side.

Cut two pieces of 3/4" stock to 4 1/2" wide by 16" long for the tank bottom (**I**) and tank top (**H**). Then saw the two 5/8" by 1 1/8" chamfers on both pieces. Mark the hole center on the bottom 3/4" from the front and 2 1/4" from the side. Drill the 3/8" dia hole in the bottom for the hitch pin. Glue the tank sides to the tank top and tank bottom.

Cut two pieces of 3/4" stock to 1 1/4" wide by 16" long for the tank sides (**R**). Cut the two tank ends (**J**) from 1/4" stock and lay out the four chamfered corners on each piece. Cut away from the line and then sand to the line. Glue the tank ends to the tank assembly.

The valve block (**C**) is cut from 1/2" stock. Lay out the holes using the dimensions in the valve block detail drawing. Drill the three 3/16" dia and three 7/16" dia holes. Cut the three gauges (**E**) from 7/16" dia dowel and the three valves (**F**) from 3/16" dia dowel. Glue the gauges and valves into the holes in the valve block. Glue gauge block to the base flush with the back and 1 1/4" from the side. Glue the tank assembly to the base and the valve block.

Cut the dome base (**D**) 2" wide by 12" long from 1/4" stock. Lay out the three holes and drill 3/8" dia. Cut three domes (**N**) 1 1/2" dia from 1/2" stock. Drill a 3/8" hole in the center of each disk. Make three dome tops (**M**) and drill the 3/8" hole in the center. Cut three caps (**Q**) from 3/8" dia dowel. Glue the pieces together with the caps flush with the underside of the dome base. When dry glue to the top of the tank 2 1/4" from the back edge of the tank and 1/8" from the top chamfered edge.

Lay out the eight 2 1/4" dia wheels on a piece of 3/4" stock using a compass. Cut the tire outline for the four outside wheels (**O**) with a 1 1/2" dia hole saw. Make the saw cut about 1/16" deep. The four inner wheels (**P**) do not have the tire outline since it would not show. Cut the wheels out with a 2 3/8" dia hole saw. Sand the cut surface and round over the edges of the wheels.

BACK VIEW

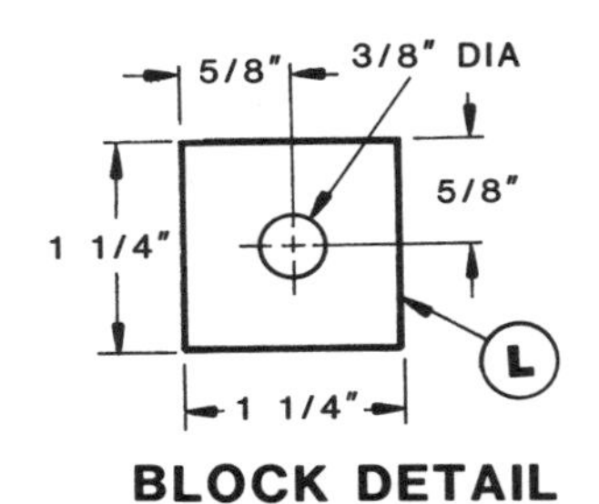

BLOCK DETAIL

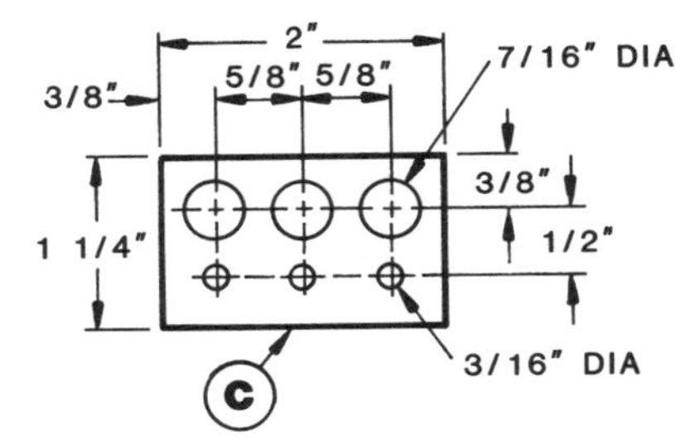

VALVE BLOCK DETAIL

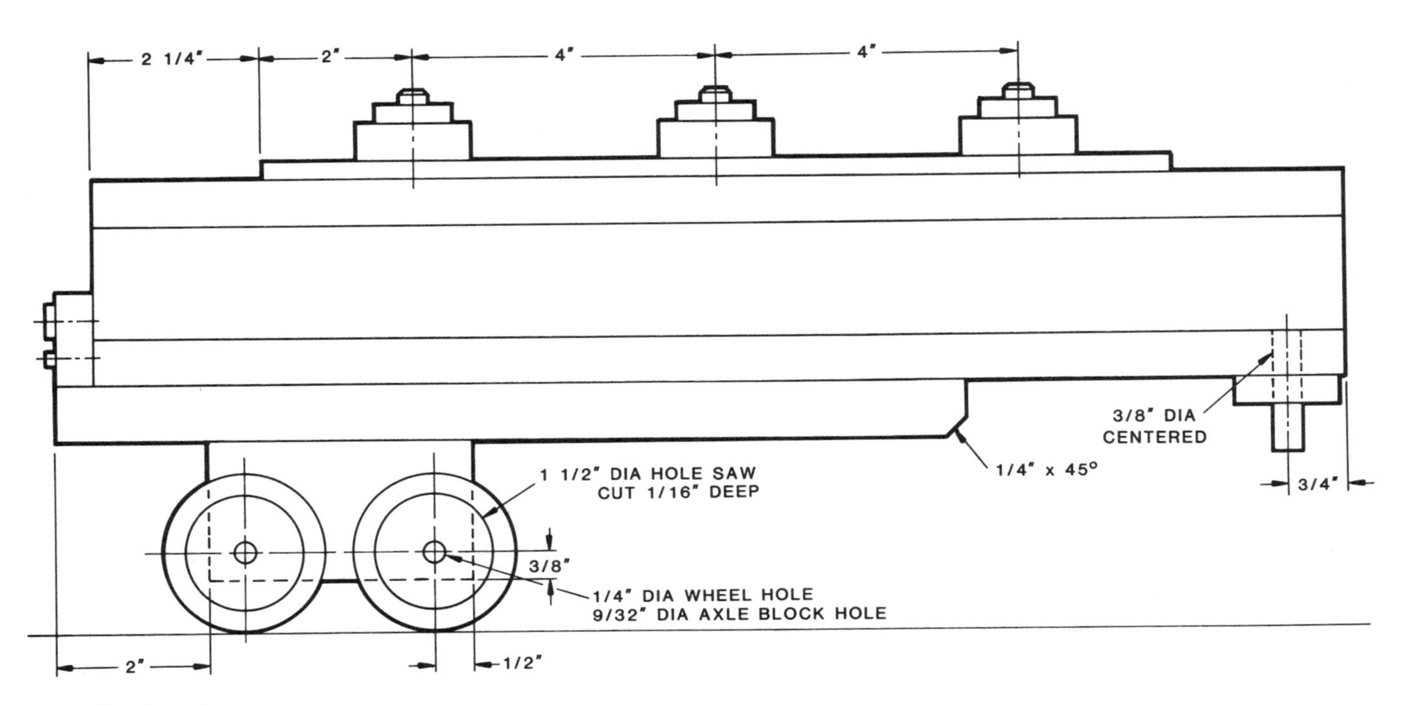

SIDE VIEW

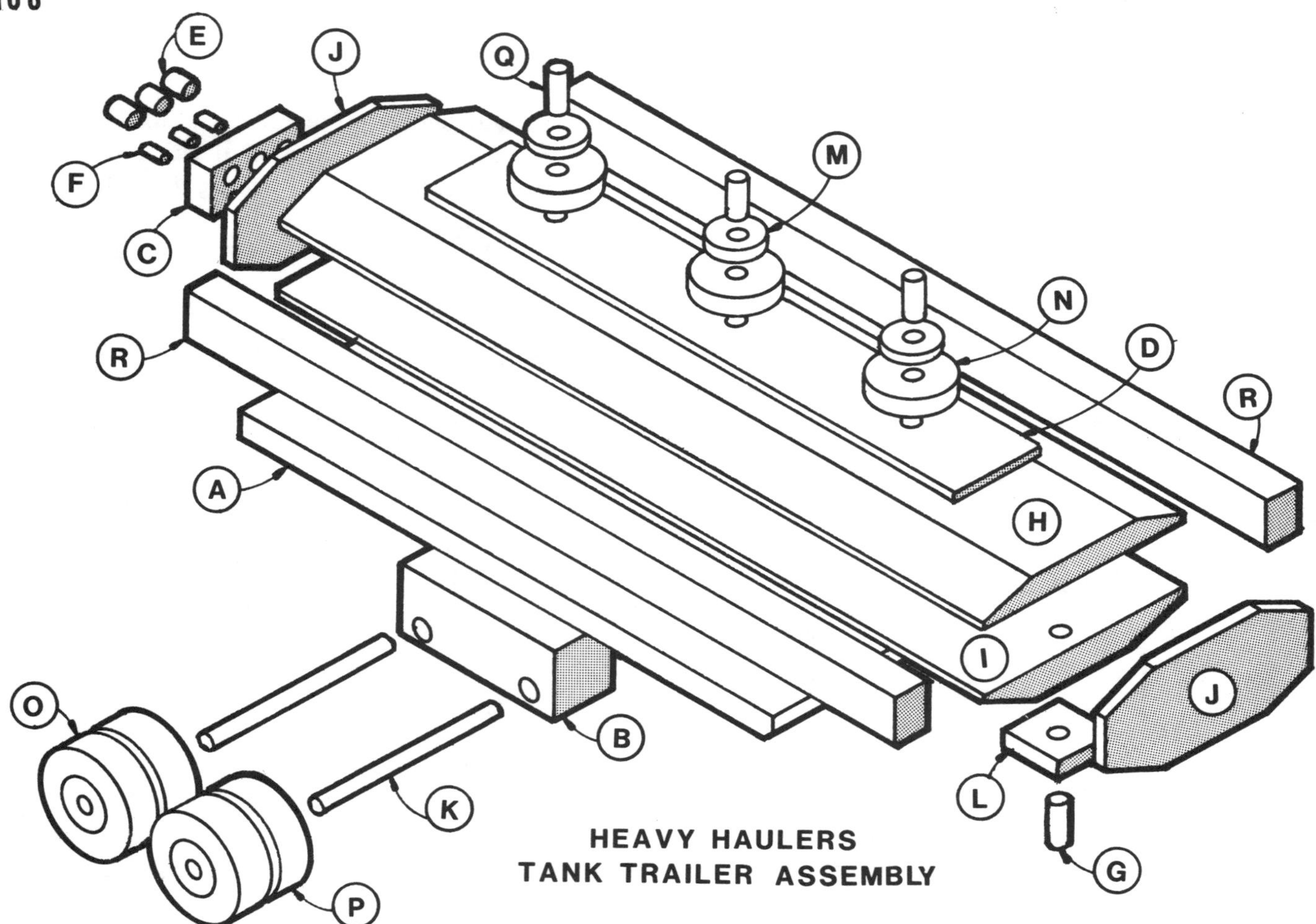

Cut two axles (**K**) 4 1/2" long from 1/4" dia dowel. Glue one inner wheel and one outer wheel to each axle. The tire outline face is flush with the end of the dowel.

Make the block (**L**) from 3/8" stock and drill the 3/8" dia hole in the center. Chamfer the end of a piece of 3/8" dia dowel by rotating it at an angle against a belt sander. Cut to a length of 1 1/2" for the hitch pin (**G**). Glue the dowel into the hole in the bottom of the tank with the chamfered end out. Then glue the block to the bottom of the tank.

Sand the pieces with fine grit sandpaper. Remove the sanding dust with a tack cloth, apply a child-safe finish and allow to dry.

Slide the axle assemblies through the axle holes and glue the inner and outer wheels to the dowel. Keep about a 1/16" gap between the inner wheel and the axle block and the inner and outer wheels.

Add the tank trailer to your fleet of heavy haulers.

LIST OF MATERIALS

FINISHED DIMENSIONS IN INCHES

A	BASE	3/4 x 4 1/2 x 12
B	AXLE BLOCK	1 1/4 x 1 7/8 x 3 1/2
C	VALVE BLOCK	1/2 x 1 1/4 x 2
D	DOME BASE	1/4 x 2 x12
E	GAUGE (3)	7/16 DIA x 1/2
F	VALVE (3)	3/16 DIA x 1/2
G	PIN	3/8 DIA x 1 1/2
H	TANK TOP	3/4 x 4 1/2 x 16
I	TANK BOTTOM	3/4 x 4 1/2 x 16
J	TANK END (2)	1/4 x 2 3/4 x 4 1/2
K	AXLE (2)	1/4 DIA x 4 1/2
L	BLOCK	3/8 x 1 1/4 x1 1/4
M	DOME TOP (3)	1/4 x 1 DIA
N	DOME (3)	1/2 x 1 1/2 DIA
O	WHEEL (4)	3/4 x 2 1/4 DIA
P	WHEEL (4)	3/4 x 2 1/4 DIA
Q	CAP (3)	3/8 DIA x 1 1/8
R	TANK SIDE (2)	3/4 x 1 1/4 x 16

BIG RIGS

Moving Van

The big rigs moving van is a good proportioned small toy. The cab with the house on the back makes it a long hauling moving van. Fuel tanks, exhaust stacks and cab top running lights can be added for more detail.

TRACTOR

Cut the base (**A**) from 1/2" stock to 2" wide by 5" long. Lay out the two long notches and cut with a band saw. The front notch (shown in the tractor assembly drawing) will be cut when the front wheel wells are cut. Locate and drill the two 9/32" dia axle holes.

The cab (**B**) is cut from 1 1/2" stock 2" wide by 2" long. The windshield is cut 1" up from the bottom and back 15 degrees. Locate and drill the two 1/4" dia by 1/8" deep headlight holes.

Glue the cab to the base 1/8" back from the front. When dry use a 1 3/8" Forstner bit to drill the front wheel well 9/16" deep in both sides of the cab base assembly. Drill the 9/32" dia hole.

Lay out the house (**C**) on 1" stock using the dimensions in house detail drawing. Cut away from the line and then sand to the line.

The cab back (**H**) is cut from 1/2" stock 2 1/4" wide by 2 3/8" long. Glue the cab back to the base and cab. Then glue the house to the base and the cab back.

Cut the 3/4" wide by 3/4" long trailer hitch plate (**E**) from 1/2" stock. Drill the 9/32" dia hole in the center of the block. Glue to the hitch 1/4" from the back and 1/16" from the side of the base notch.

Cut two headlights (**F**) 1/4" long from 1/4" dia dowel. Glue the headlights into the holes in the cab.

Cut out six wheels (**J**) with a 1 3/8" dia hole saw, from 1/2" stock. Sand the cut surfaces smooth and round over the edges. Cut the three tractor axles (**K**) to length from 1/4" dia dowel. Glue one wheel to each axle.

TRAILER

Cut two van blocks (**N**) from 3/4" stock to 3 1/2" wide by 10" long. Lay out the front notch using the dimensions on the side view drawing. Cut away from the line and then sand to the line. Glue the blocks together and clamp until dry.

Lay out the two van sides (**I**) from 3/8" stock. Lay out the front notch using the dimensions on the side view drawing. The rear notch is for clearing the rear wheels. Cut with a band saw and sand all cut edges. Sand the 1/2" chamfer at the front of each side. Glue the sides to the van block.

LIST OF MATERIALS

FINISHED DIMENSIONS IN INCHES

A	BASE	1/2 x 2 x 5
B	CAB	1 1/2 x 2 x 2
C	HOUSE	1 x 2 x 2
D	TRAILER WHEEL (4)	7/8 DIA x 3/8
E	HITCH	1/2 x 3/4 x 3/4
F	HEADLIGHT (2)	1/4 DIA x 1/4
G	HITCH PIN	1/4 DIA x 3/4
H	CAB BACK	1/2 x 2 1/4 x 2 3/8
I	VAN SIDE (2)	3/8 x 3 1/2 x 10
J	WHEEL (6)	1 1/4 DIA x 1/2
K	TRACTOR AXLE (3)	1/4 DIA x 2
L	TRAILER AXLE (2)	1/4 DIA x 2 3/8
M	AXLE BLOCK	3/8 x 1 1/2 x 1 5/8
N	VAN (2)	3/4 x 3 1/2 x 10

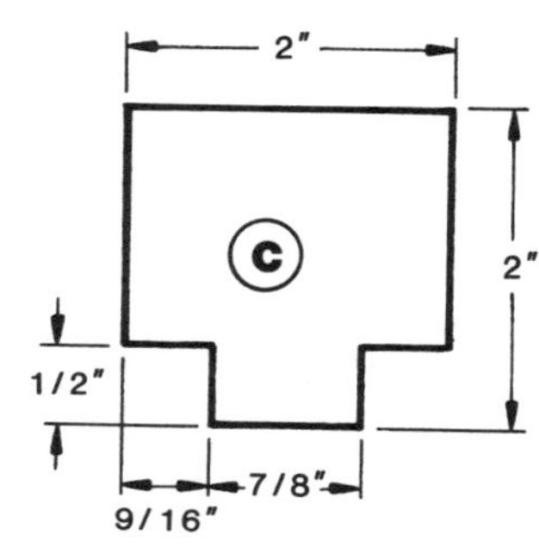

HOUSE DETAIL

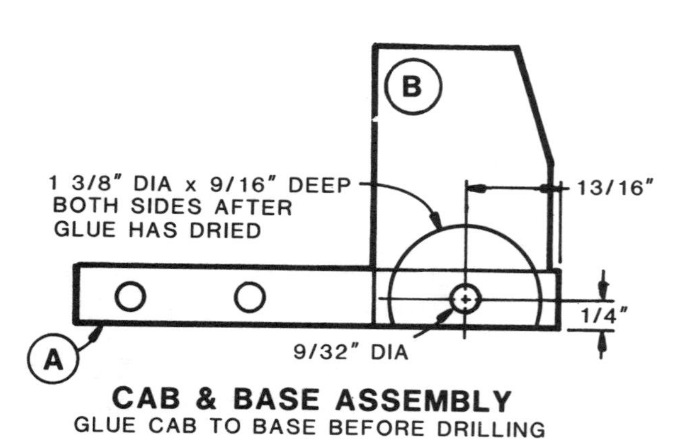

CAB & BASE ASSEMBLY
GLUE CAB TO BASE BEFORE DRILLING

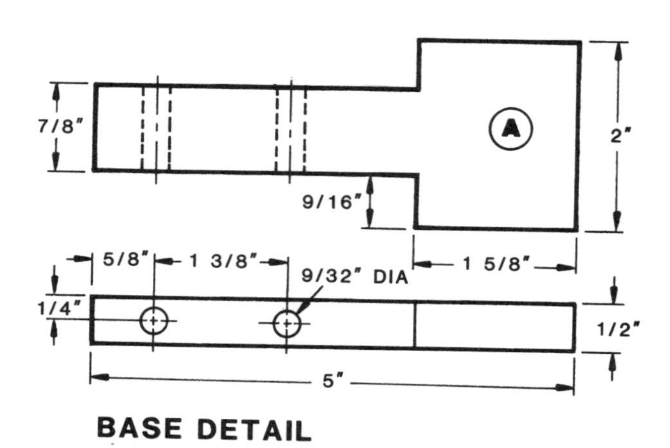

BASE DETAIL

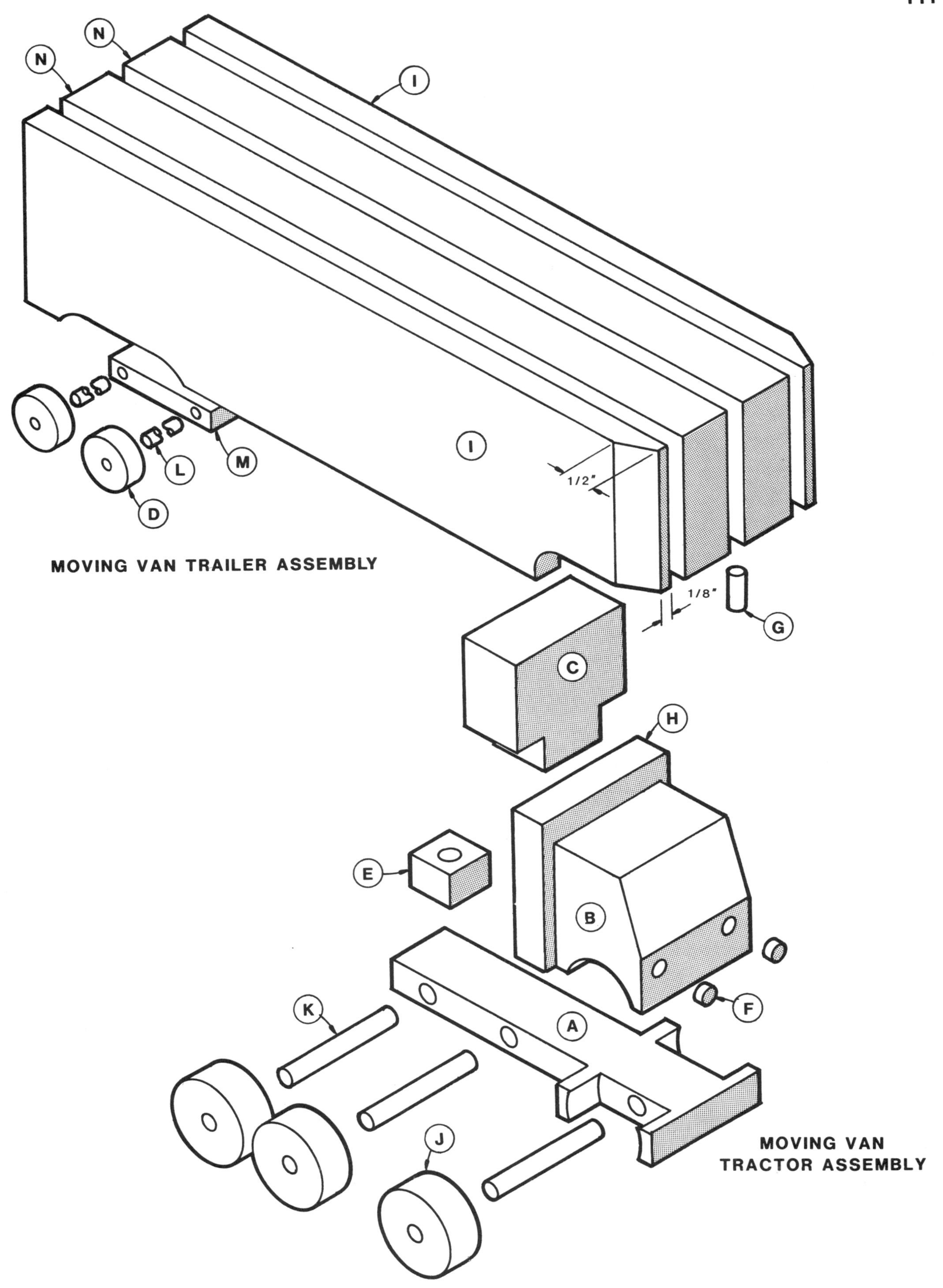
N
N
I
I
1/2"
L
M
D
MOVING VAN TRAILER ASSEMBLY
1/8"
G
C
H
E
B
F
K
A
J
MOVING VAN
TRACTOR ASSEMBLY

The axle block (**M**) is cut from 3/8" stock 1 1/2" wide by 1 5/8" long. Lay out and drill the two 9/32" dia axle holes. Glue the axle block to the underside of the van. The rear axle hole is 1" from the back edge of the van. Lay out and drill the 1/4" dia hitch pin hole 3/8" deep 1/2" back from the front edge and 1 1/8" from the side.

Cut the hitch pin (**G**) to length from 1/4" dia dowel. Sand a slight chamfer on one end. Glue the hitch pin into the hole in the van body with the chamfer end up.

Cut out four wheels (**D**) with a 1" dia hole saw, from 3/8" stock. Sand the cut surfaces smooth and round over the edges. Cut the two trailer axles (**L**) to length from 1/4" dia dowel. Glue one wheel to each axle.

FINAL ASSEMBLY

Sand the pieces with medium grit sandpaper followed with fine grit sandpaper. Remove the dust with a tack cloth and apply two coats of a child-safe finish. After the finish dries, slide the axle wheel assemblies through the axle holes and glue the other wheels to the end of each axle. Leave about a 1/16" gap between the wheel and base.

Put the hitch pin into the tractor hole and the big rigs moving van is ready to roll with that make believe load of family furniture.

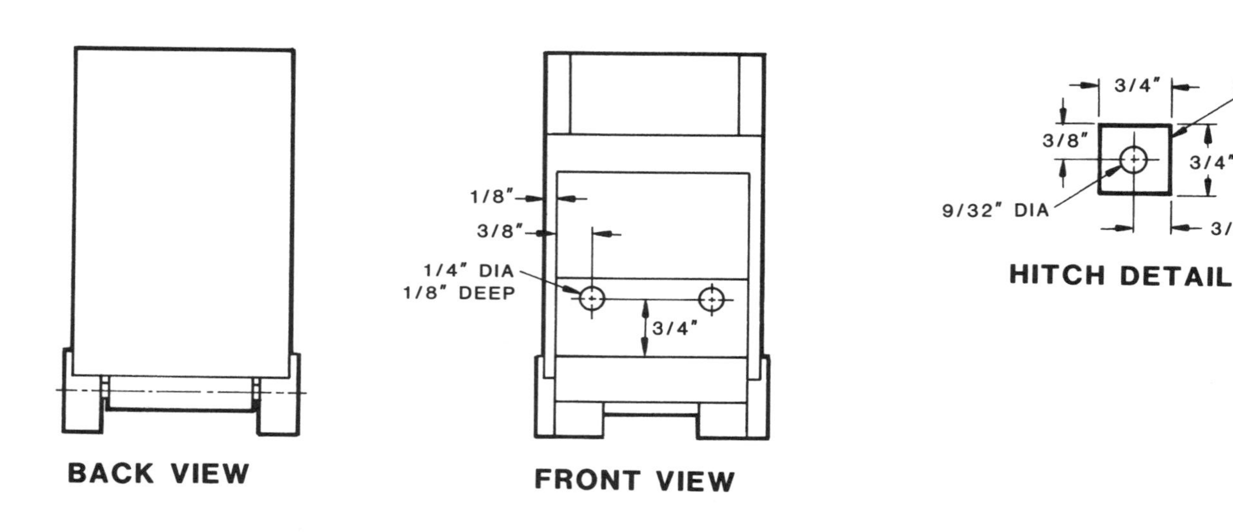

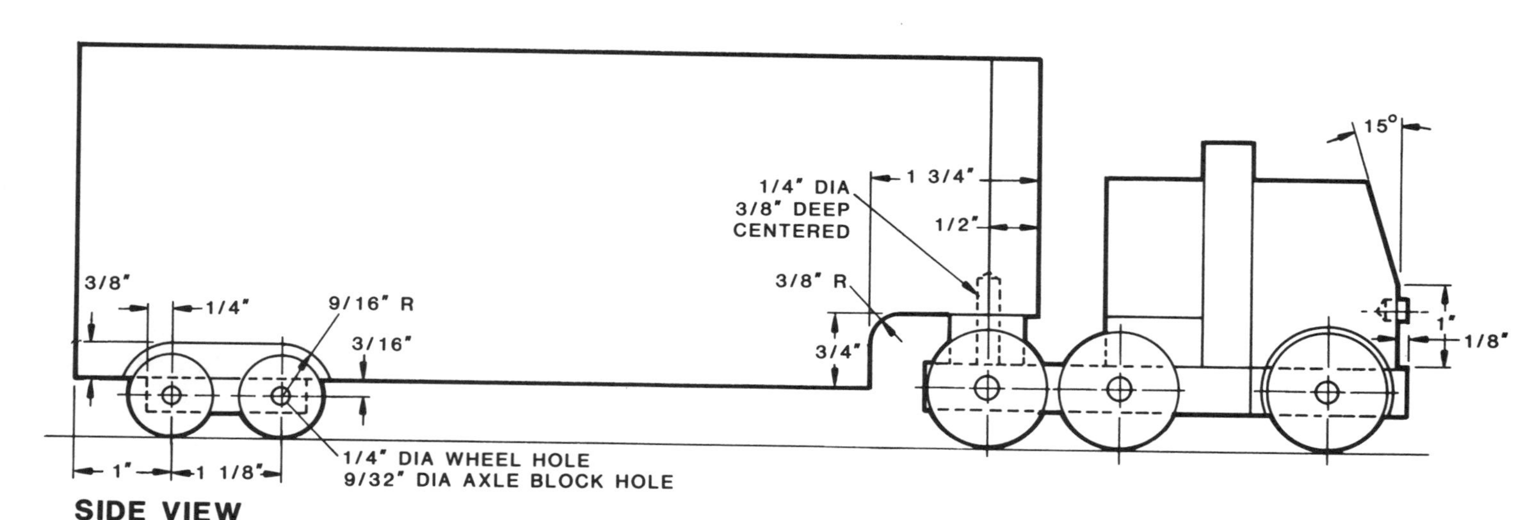

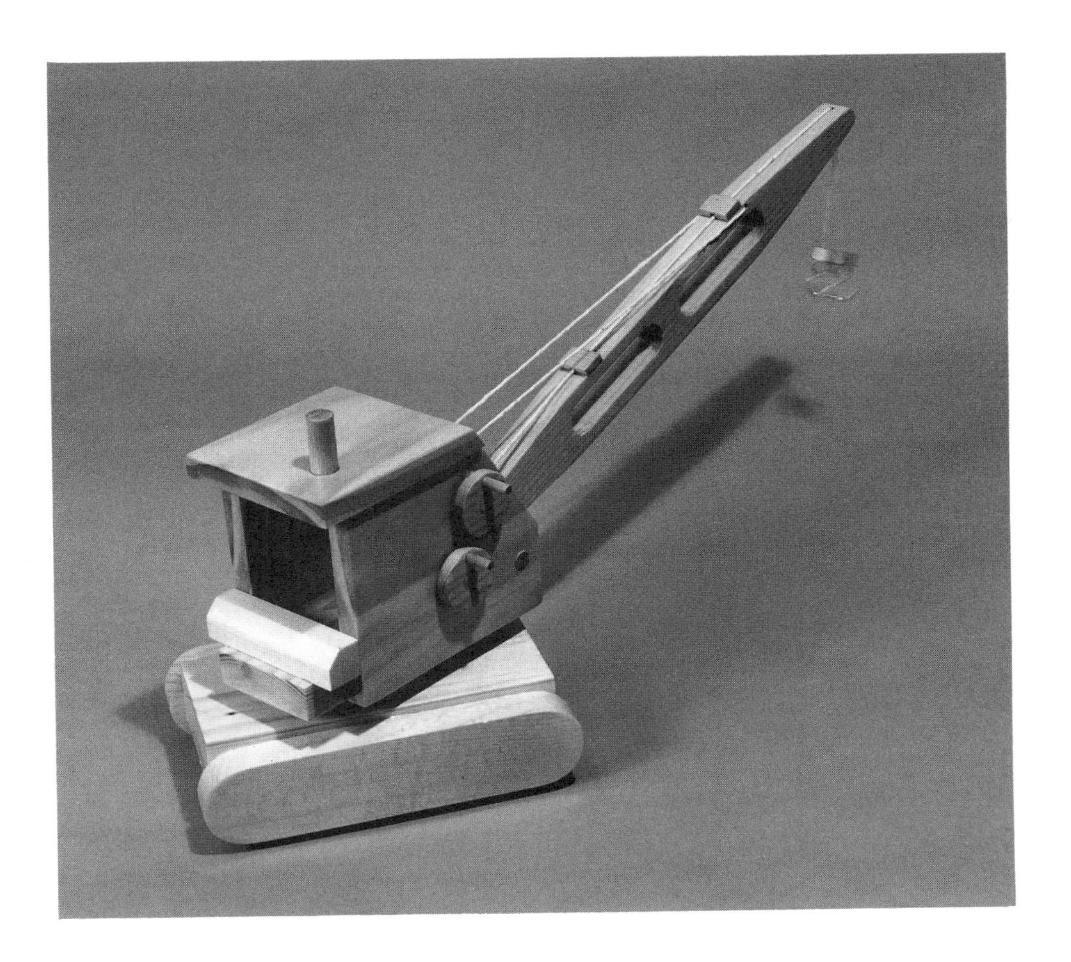

WORK EQUIPMENT
Crane

Large cranes make interesting wood toys. That youngster will enjoy this toy for many years with its many moving parts. The cab rotates, the boom goes up and down and the hook goes up and down on a cable. The wheels, hidden behind the track make it easy to roll on any surface.

Cut all the pieces as indicated in the list of materials. After cutting the pieces to size take the two bases (**A**) and lay out the axle hole center as shown on the side view drawing. Drill the 9/32" dia holes.

Lay out the center of the pivot hole in the deck (**B**) and drill the 25/64" dia hole. Cut and sand the chamfer on the two base ends (**F**). Glue the base ends to the deck flush with the ends. Glue the bases to the deck and the base ends 15/16" from the side.

Shape the radius on both ends of the tracks (**H**). Drill a 1/4" dia hole in the center of each wheel (**D**) and round over the edges. Glue one wheel to each axle (**C**) and when dry slip the axle through the hole in the bases and glue the other wheel to the axle. Glue the track to the base ends and the deck 1/8" below the top of the deck with an equal overhang at the front and rear.

Drill a 3/8" dia hole in the center of the keeper (**E**) and a 25/64" dia hole in the center of the spacer (**I**). Glue the keeper to the end of the dowel (**G**).

That completes the track assembly; now we will begin the cab. Lay out the center of the pivot hole in the cab base (**J**) and drill the 3/8" dia hole. Lay out the chamfer and the holes on the two cab sides (**K**) as shown in the cab side detail drawing. Cut the chamfer and sand the edge. Drill the three 3/8" dia holes in each side and the four 3/16" dia holes in one of the sides. Sand the chamfer to the front of the cab roof (**L**) and locate the hole for the stack. Drill the 1/2" dia hole. Lay out the chamfer and the center of the hole for the two blocks (**Q**) as shown in the block detail drawing. Cut the chamfer and sand

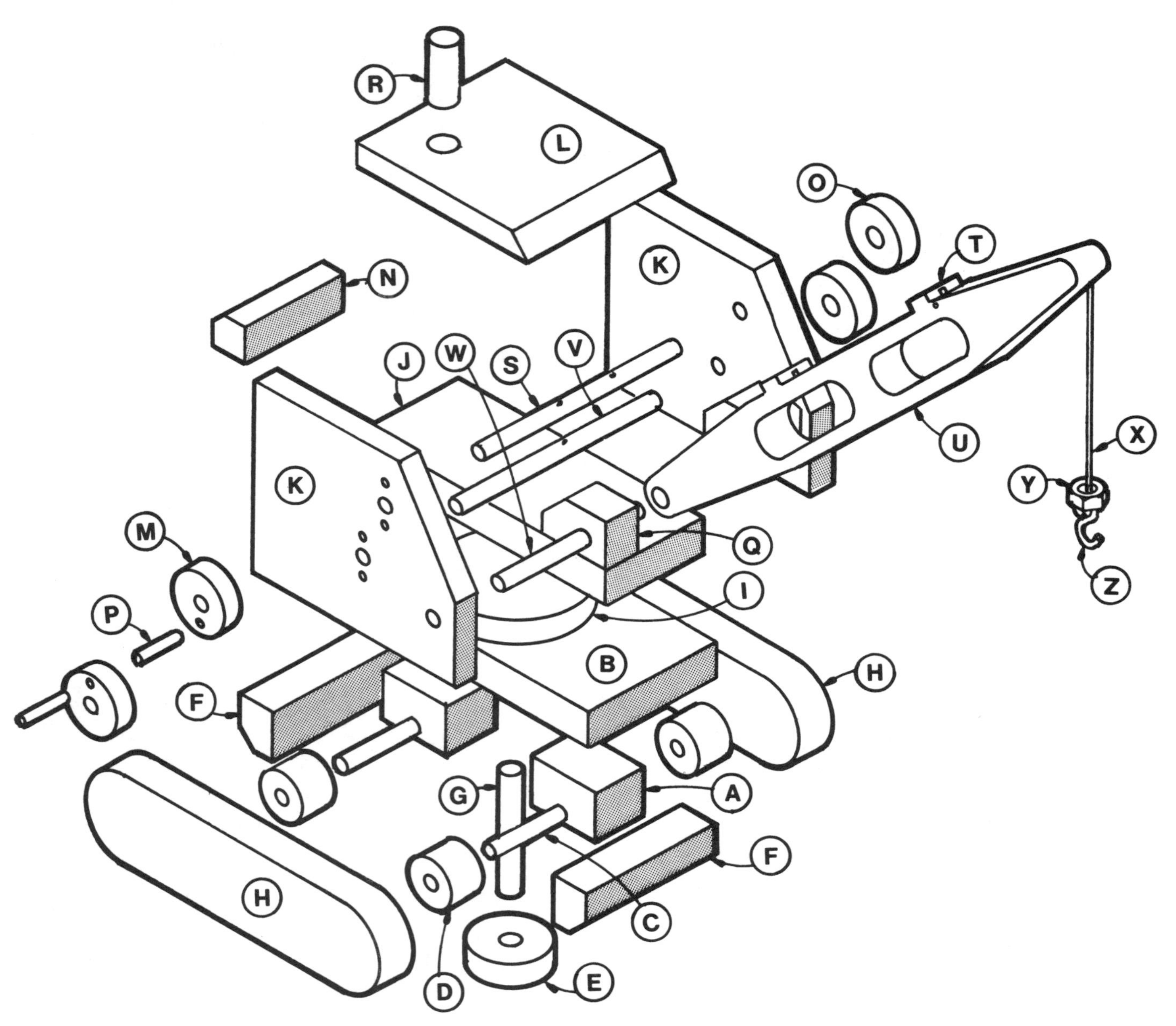

WORK EQUIPMENT CRANE ASSEMBLY

LIST OF MATERIALS

FINISHED DIMENSIONS IN INCHES

A	BASE (2)	1 1/8 x 1 1/16 x 1 1/2
B	DECK	3/4 x 3 x 6 1/2
C	AXLE (2)	1/4 DIA x 2 3/4
D	WHEEL (4)	3/4 x 1 DIA
E	KEEPER	1/2 x 1 1/2 DIA
F	BASE END (2)	3/4 x 1 1/16 x 3
G	DOWEL	3/8 DIA x 2 9/16
H	TRACK (2)	3/4 x 1 3/4 x 7
I	SPACER	1/2 x 2 3/4 DIA
J	CAB BASE	3/4 x 2 1/4 x 5 3/4
K	CAB SIDE (2)	1/2 x 4 x 4 3/4
L	CAB ROOF	1/2 x 3 1/2 x 3 15/16
M	CRANK WHEEL (2)	3/8 x 1 1/4 DIA
N	TOOL BOX	3/4 x 3/4 x 3 1/4
O	SHAFT KEEPER (2)	3/8 x 1 1/4 DIA
P	CRANK HANDLE (2)	3/16 DIA x 1
Q	BLOCK (2)	3/4 x 1 x 1 1/2
R	STACK	1/2 DIA x 1 1/2
S	BOOM SHAFT	3/8 DIA x 4 9/16
T	RETAINER (2)	3/16 x 1/2 x 3/4
U	BOOM	3/4 x 1 3/8 x 14
V	CABLE SHAFT	3/8 DIA x 4 9/16
W	DOWEL	3/8 DIA x 3 1/4
X	CABLE	STRING
Y	WEIGHT	3/8 STEEL NUT
Z	S-HOOK	1 INCH LONG

the edge. Drill the 3/8" dia holes in each block. Glue the blocks to the cab base and the cab sides to the blocks and the base. Clamp the sides and then glue the roof to the sides. Glue the stack (**R**) into the hole in the roof. Cut and sand the chamfer to the back of the tool box (**N**) and glue to the base and the cab sides.

Drill a 3/8" dia hole in the center of the two crank wheels (**M**) and the 3/16" dia hole 7/16" from the center. Glue the crank handle (**P**) into the hole with 3/16" of the dowel sticking out the back of the crank wheel. Drill a 3/8" dia hole in the center of the two shaft keepers (**O**). Lay out the

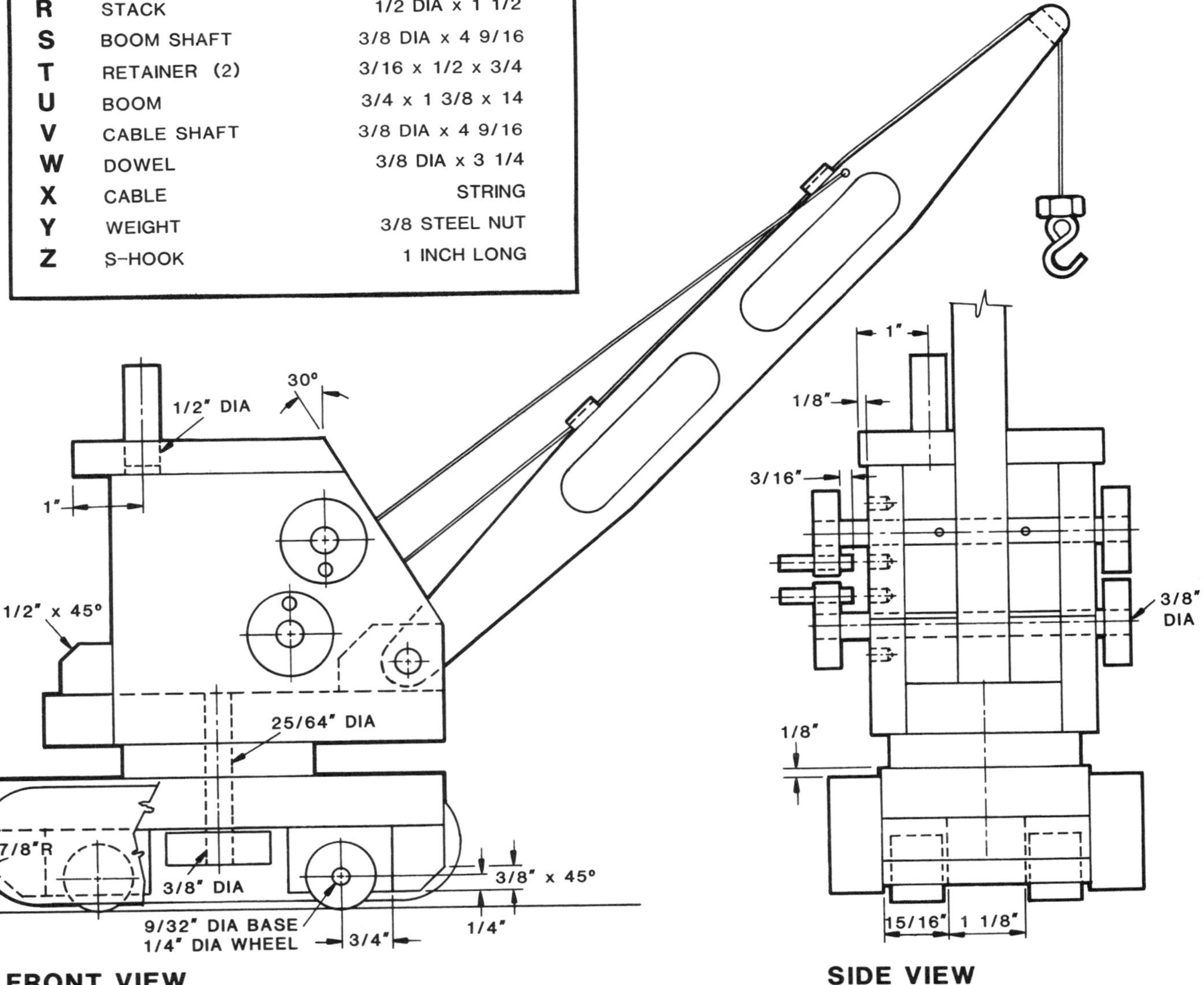

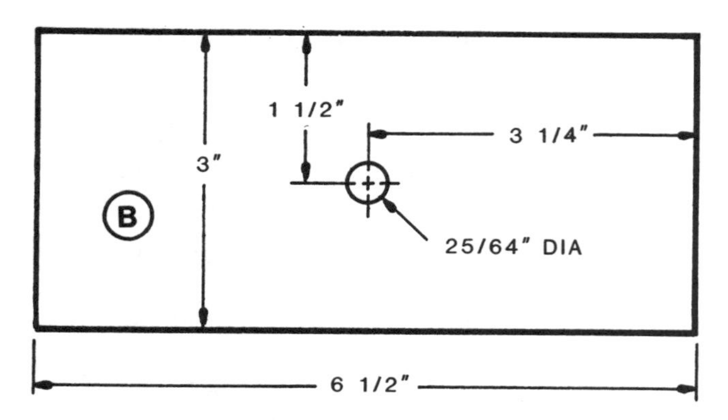

DECK DETAIL

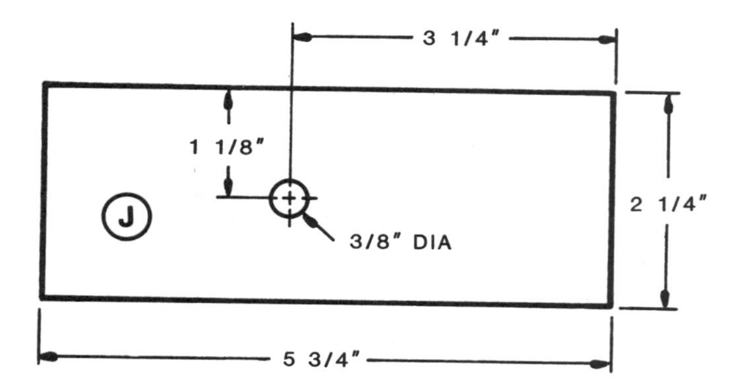

CAB BASE DETAIL

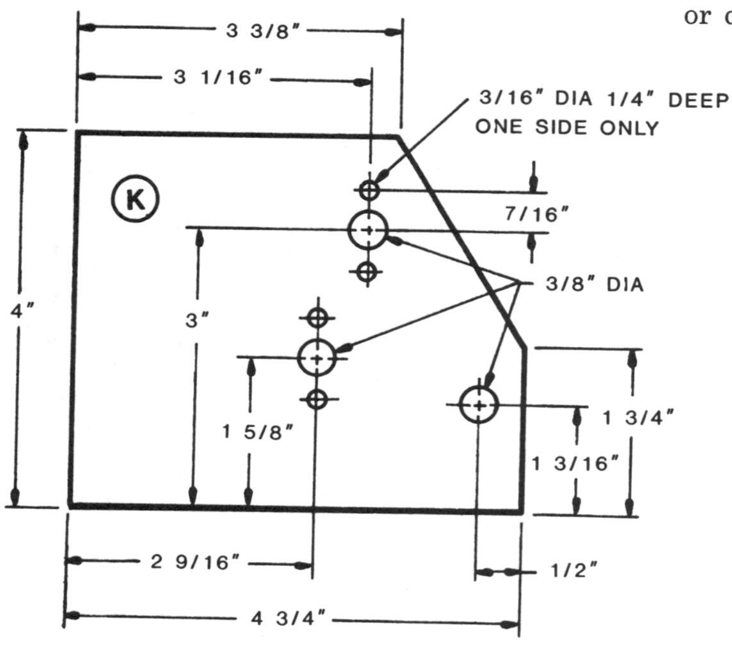

CAB SIDE DETAIL

center for the two holes in the boom shaft (S) and the hole in the cable shaft (V). Drill the three 1/8" dia holes. Glue one crank wheel to the boom shaft and the other to the cable shaft. Slip the shafts through the holes in the cab sides and temporarily slip the keepers on the shaft.

Lay out the tapers, hole centers and the slots on the boom (U) as shown in the boom detail drawing. Drill the 3/8" dia and the 1/8" dia hole. Drill four 3/4" dia holes for the slots. Turn the boom on its side and drill the 1/8" dia hole. Insert a scroll saw blade into one of the slot holes and cut to the other hole. Cut the other sloted hole. Cut the tapers and sand the edges and sand a radius at both ends. Notch the two retainers (T) and glue to the top of the boom. Slip the boom between the two blocks and slide the dowel (W) into the holes. Check the movement of the boom. When these parts work well together, remove the loose pieces.

Sand the finished crane body, track assembly, boom assembly and crank wheel assemblies with fine grit sandpaper. Remove the dust with a tack cloth and apply a child-safe finish and allow to dry. Do not put finish on the pivot shaft or dowel. Put the crank shafts through

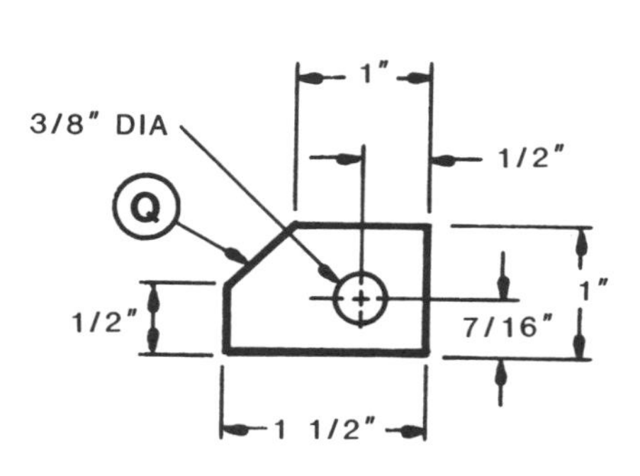

BLOCK DETAIL

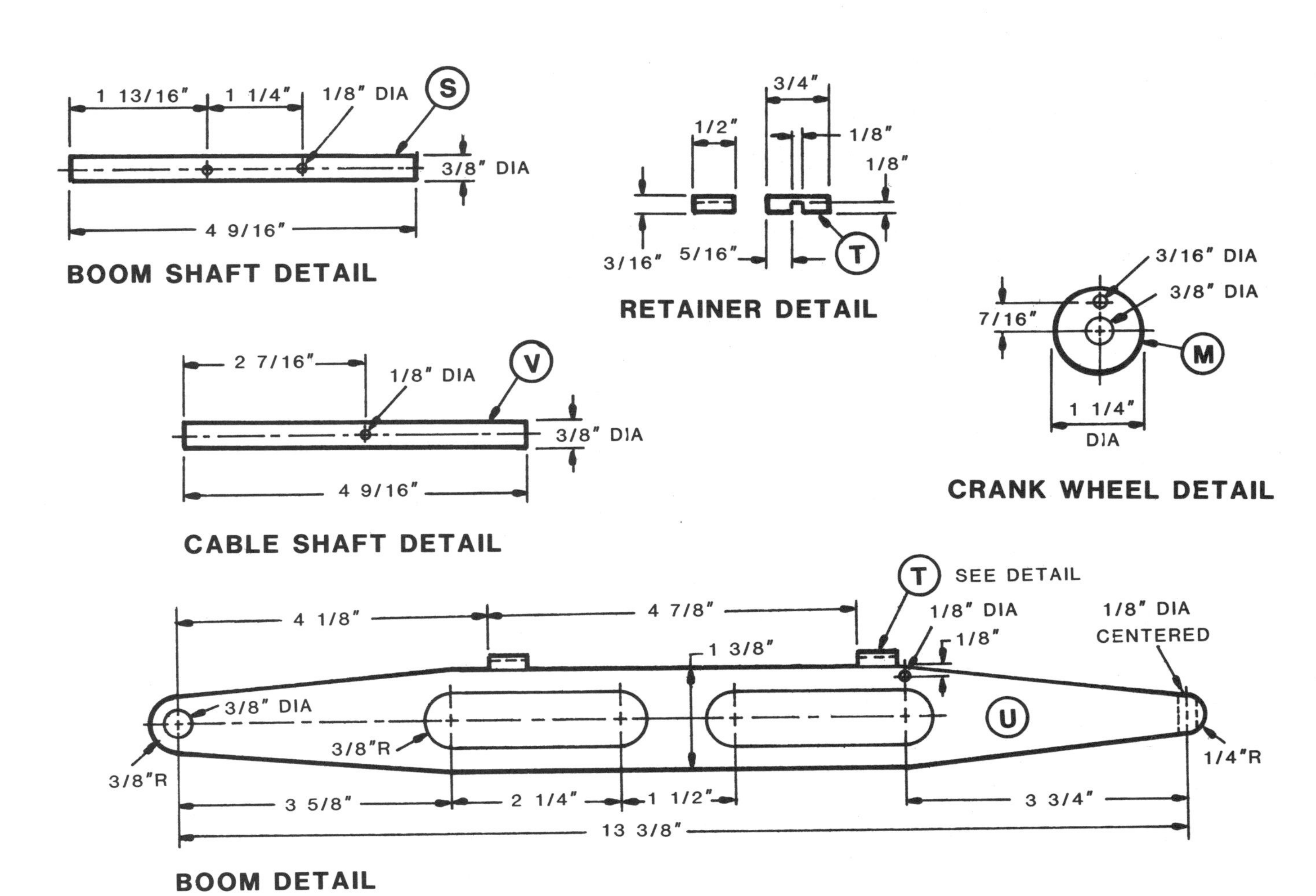

the crank holes and glue the shaft keepers to the end of the shafts.

Thread one end of the cable (X) into one hole in the boom shaft and tie a knot in the end. Rotate the handle until six coils of cable are on the shaft. Thread the other end into the hole in the top of the boom and down to the other side of the boom shaft. Coil six coils around the shaft in the opposite direction of the other and then thread the end into the hole and tie a knot in the end. Cut the cable near the knot. Crank the handle and test the boom movement.

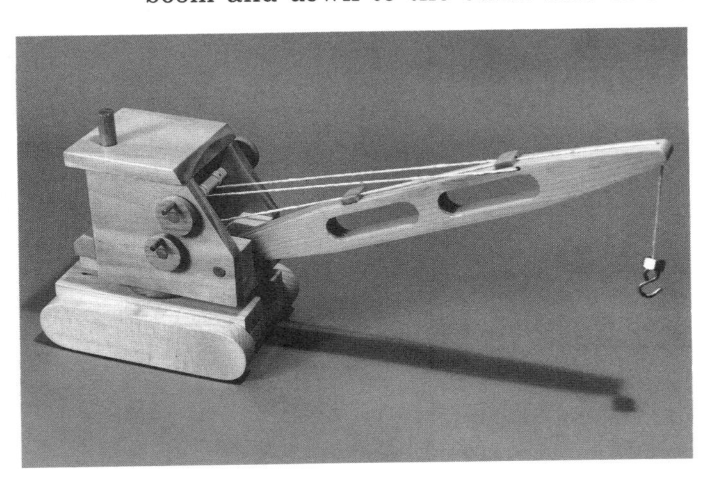

Next, thread one end of the cable into the hole in the cable shaft and tie a knot in the end. Rotate the handle to get about ten coils on the shaft. Then thread the other end of the cable through the retainer slots in the top of the boom. Slip the cable through the hole in the end of the boom and through the weight (Y). Close one end of the s-hook (Z) and tie the end of the cable to this end of the hook. Crank the handle to test the cable movement.

This crane can now join the fleet of work equipment and heavy haulers tractor and trailers that appear elsewhere in this book.

Inches to Metric Conversion Chart

Inches Fraction	Inches Decimal	Millimeters	Centimeters	Inches Fraction	Inches Decimal	Millimeters	Centimeters
1/16	0.063	1.588	0.159	2 9/16	2.563	65.088	6.509
1/8	0.125	3.175	0.318	2 5/8	2.625	66.675	6.668
3/16	0.188	4.763	0.476	2 11/16	2.688	68.263	6.826
1/4	0.250	6.350	0.635	2 3/4	2.750	69.850	6.985
5/16	0.313	7.938	0.794	2 13/16	2.813	71.438	7.144
3/8	0.375	9.525	0.953	2 7/8	2.875	73.025	7.303
7/16	0.438	11.113	1.111	2 15/16	2.938	74.613	7.461
1/2	0.500	12.700	1.270	3	3.000	76.200	7.620
9/16	0.563	14.288	1.429	3 1/16	3.063	77.788	7.779
5/8	0.625	15.875	1.588	3 1/8	3.125	79.375	7.938
11/16	0.688	17.463	1.746	3 3/16	3.188	80.963	8.096
3/4	0.750	19.050	1.905	3 1/4	3.250	82.550	8.255
13/16	0.813	20.638	2.064	3 5/16	3.313	84.138	8.414
7/8	0.875	22.225	2.223	3 3/8	3.375	85.725	8.573
15/16	0.938	23.813	2.381	3 7/16	3.438	87.313	8.731
1	1.000	25.400	2.540	3 1/2	3.500	88.900	8.890
1 1/16	1.063	26.988	2.699	3 9/16	3.563	90.488	9.049
1 1/8	1.125	28.575	2.858	3 5/8	3.625	92.075	9.208
1 3/16	1.188	30.163	3.016	3 11/16	3.688	93.663	9.366
1 1/4	1.250	31.750	3.175	3 3/4	3.750	95.250	9.525
1 5/16	1.313	33.338	3.334	3 13/16	3.813	96.838	9.684
1 3/8	1.375	34.925	3.493	3 7/8	3.875	98.425	9.843
1 7/16	1.438	36.513	3.651	3 15/16	3.938	100.013	10.001
1 1/2	1.500	38.100	3.810	4	4.000	101.600	10.160
1 9/16	1.563	39.688	3.969	4 1/8	4.125	104.775	10.478
1 5/8	1.625	41.275	4.128	4 1/4	4.250	107.950	10.795
1 11/16	1.688	42.863	4.286	4 3/8	4.375	111.125	11.113
1 3/4	1.750	44.450	4.445	4 1/2	4.500	114.300	11.430
1 13/16	1.813	46.038	4.604	4 5/8	4.625	117.475	11.748
1 7/8	1.875	47.625	4.763	4 3/4	4.750	120.650	12.065
1 15/16	1.938	49.213	4.921	4 7/8	4.875	123.825	12.383
2	2.000	50.800	5.080	5	5.000	127.000	12.700
2 1/16	2.063	52.388	5.239	6	6.000	152.400	15.240
2 1/8	2.125	53.975	5.398	7	7.000	177.800	17.780
2 3/16	2.188	55.563	5.556	8	8.000	203.200	20.320
2 1/4	2.250	57.150	5.715	9	9.000	228.600	22.860
2 5/16	2.313	58.738	5.874	10	10.000	254.000	25.400
2 3/8	2.375	60.325	6.033	11	11.000	279.400	27.940
2 7/16	2.438	61.913	6.191	12	12.000	304.800	30.480
2 1/2	2.500	63.500	6.350	13	13.000	330.200	33.020

INDEX